SCOTTISH AVIATION
BULLDOG

TRAINER FOR THE WORLD

Tom Wenham

Published in the United Kingdom by Air-Britain Publishing

Air-Britain Publishing, Sales Department, Unit 1A, Munday Works
Industrial Estate, Morley Road, Tonbridge, Kent TN9 1RA

Membership Enquiries: Barry J. Collman, 1 Rose Cottages,
179 Penn Road, Hazlemere, Bucks HP15 7NE

Correspondence regarding this book to Tom Wenham
tjwenham@gotadsl.co.uk

ISBN 978-0-85130-520-2

Printed in the United Kingdom by Latimer Trend
Origination by Carolyn Gibson
Cover Origination by Lee Howard

Front Cover: Upper Photo – a Bulldog, XX547 of
London University Air Squadron (Robert Shaw)
Lower Photo: The Bulldog prototype, G-AXEH, at Shoreham
in 1969 (Masefield Archive at Brooklands Museum)

CONTENTS

This fine photo by Keith Wilson shows Bulldog G-BCUS in aerobatic pose. It is operated by Skysport UK at Kemble for advanced aerobatic and air race training.

FOREWORD

I was more than pleased when I heard that Tom Wenham was to write a history of the Scottish Aviation Bulldog. His previous work, False Dawn, charted the rise and fall of Beagle until the end of Beagle Pup production, but left fans of the Bulldog yearning for more. Now we have it!

I count myself fortunate to still be the custodian of my beloved Bulldog "Juliet-Whisky" after some 17 years. The maker's plate may state "Scottish Aviation" but it is a Beagle through and through, and if circumstances had been different, it would have been produced as one.

The Beagle Pup & Bulldog Club has supported me - and Juliet-Whisky - for more than 15 years, and it would be a much more difficult process to operate and preserve this wonderful aeroplane without that support.

We aim to continue providing engineering knowledge and support through associated organisations and experts, a social focus for our members with visits to places of interest and a potential to extend our horizons; to preserve the heritage of Beagle Aircraft via the maintenance, restoration and use of our aircraft, and to maintain connection with the history and the people of the Beagle Aircraft company.

As we move into our 35th year, we continue to face challenges from legislation, loss of airfields and not least the increasing age of our cherished aircraft. But with the continued support of our many knowledgeable members, our type-responsible organisation DeHavilland Support Ltd. and the excellent engineering partners that we choose, I am confident that we may continue to operate and even improve our charges whilst remaining true to our traditions and aims.

We are constantly affected by changing regulations, the reactions to aviation incidents and the varying political climate, but with the network of contacts the club enjoys, some of these impacts may be anticipated; and I must applaud the Club committee for their sterling work in keeping abreast of ever changing requirements and steering the club safely. It is often a difficult task, but with the ongoing engagement of the membership it is a satisfying endeavour to maintain the freshness and relevance that the members want.

The Club continues to enjoy association with like-minded clubs, such as the Vintage Aircraft Club, The International Auster Club, The Light Aircraft Association and The Miles Aircraft Collection, benefitting from invitations to relevant events and exchanges of information, and we look forward to further collaboration in the future.

We engage with our members via a quarterly newsletter by e-mail, an annual yearbook which is printed in large glossy format, and via the Club's Facebook page. There is also a Scottish Aviation Bulldog enthusiasts' page on Facebook that complements the Club communications. We continue to build a closer and stronger family that reacts to the needs of its members more readily and in more directed fashion by continued engagement both socially and formally, and to preserve the history and legacy of these wonderful aircraft by researching and informing about them.

Tom's much anticipated publication of this history of the Bulldog can only make our mission easier and more satisfying!

Mike Miles
Chairman -
Beagle Pup & Bulldog Club

Mike Miles is seen here beside his faithful Bulldog G-SIJW (formerly XX630). *(MM)*

INTRODUCTION

The Scottish Aviation Bulldog emerged from the ashes of the Beagle company following its abandonment by the Government of the day as the only Beagle design to survive and go into production. It did so only because Beagle had already entered into contracts to supply the Bulldog to the Air Forces of Sweden, Zambia and Kenya, of which the Swedish order was by far the largest, and the British Government found itself, albeit unwillingly, compelled to honour those contracts. Undoubtedly had it not been for the existence of those contracts the Bulldog project would have suffered the same fate as the other Beagle types and died in December, 1969.

Unlike many aircraft histories, the history of the Bulldog has to start well before the aircraft design was finalised and it went into production. The story of the Bulldog starts with the genesis of the type at Beagle's factory at Shoreham where the first prototype was built and went on to complete a certain amount of test flying including the hot weather trials and winter trials. It then moves on to the long and convoluted process whereby the Bulldog was separated from the defunct Beagle company and eventually ended up in the hands of Scottish Aviation and, finally, follows the production of 325 aircraft by Scottish Aviation, as detailed in the Production Histories section, and the service use of the aircraft. By the time production ceased in 1982 the Bulldog was in service with eleven military operators including the Royal Air Force where it was responsible for primary flying training at the Flying Training Schools and the University Air Squadrons (UAS). It went on to earn its place as a worthy successor to de Havilland's stalwarts, the Tiger Moth and the Chipmunk.

Throughout this book Beagle Aircraft Limited has been referred to as 'Beagle' and Scottish Aviation Limited has been abbreviated to 'SAL'. Following the formation of the new company, Scottish Aviation (Bulldog) Limited, specifically to manufacture the Bulldog, this company has been referred to as 'SABL'. Of the many companies in the Miles group the company that handled the negotiations for the Bulldog was Miles Aviation and Transport (R&D) Limited and has been referred to simply as 'Miles'.

The University Air Squadrons were the main RAF users of the Bulldog and this photo by Keith Wilson shows a four-ship formation from the Cambridge University Air Squadron - with their tail codes spelling out CUAS.

ACKNOWLEDGEMENTS

This book would not have been possible without the input and support of a large number of people. Foremost, I was fortunate to be able to benefit from the experience of Air-Britain's Malcolm Fillmore and Rod Simpson. As he did for my book on Beagle Aircraft and the co-authored book on Auster, Malcolm has once again produced the most comprehensive and up-to-date individual aircraft histories. Rod Simpson has been a skilful editor as well as shepherding me through the process of pulling all the various threads together. I am also most grateful to Nigel Dingley for his guidance through the publishing process and to Tony Jupp for proof reading the final manuscript. At Prestwick I was able to draw on the experiences of several employees of Scottish Aviation with first hand knowledge of the Bulldog, namely Ian Adams, the late John Chalmers and the late Len Houston who have provided detailed accounts of their work on the Bulldog and its intended successors. In Sweden, Sven Stridsberg of Svensk Flyghistorisk, and Fredric Lagerquist have provided much information on the 78 Bulldogs sold to Sweden. I am grateful to Mike Miles, Chairman of the Beagle Pup and Bulldog Club for agreeing to write the Foreword and to Jeremy Pratt for his description of operating the Bulldog. Juanita Franzi of Aero Illustrations has once again produced stunning colour side-view drawings and Keith Wilson has also contributed opening photographs. Paul Jackson has done an outstanding job in producing the most accurate three-view drawings ever published following meticulous measurement of real Bulldogs and the Bullfinch. Others who contributed are Steve Bond, Chris Gibson, Lee Howard, Michael Magnusson and David Wise. The sale of the Bulldog project by Beagle Aircraft's Receiver to Scottish Aviation is recorded in files held at the National Archive and I am grateful to the staff at Kew for their kind assistance. The story of the genesis of the Bulldog at Beagle Aircraft is contained in the company records held in the Masefield Collection at Brooklands Museum and, as ever, I am grateful to the staff at the Museum for permitting me access to this Collection. Many people have sent me photographs and they are recognised by the following initials in the photo captions. Fred Lagerquist (FL), Sven Stridsberg (SS), Ian Adams (IA), Steve Maric (SM), Andy Marden (AM), the Masefield Archive at Brooklands Museum (MA), David Cain (DC), George Jenks, Avro Heritage (GJ), Ian Gibson (IG), Keith Brooks (KB), the late Peter Berry (PB), the late Peter Heathcote (PH), Rod Simpson (RS), Robert Shaw (RSh), Lars Lundin (LL), Chris England (CE), 4Aviation (4A) and Vaclev Kudela (VK). I am also most grateful to Aviation Ancestry for use of the Scottish Aviation advertisements. Every endeavour has been made to identify ownership of copyright but if any inadvertent breaches are identified the author undertakes to remedy the situation in any future editions. Finally, any errors and omissions are entirely the responsibility of the author.

GLOSSARY OF ABBREVIATIONS

AAC	Army Air Corps
A&AEE	Aeroplane and Armaments Experimental Establishment
ABSF	AB Svenska Flygverkstaderna
AEF	Air Experience Flight
ARB	Air Registration Board
ASR	Air Staff Requirement
ATC	Air Traffic Control
BAe	British Aerospace
CCF	Combined Cadet Force
CFI	Chief Flying Instructor
CFS	Central Flying School
CG	Centre of Gravity
CofA	Certificate of Airworthiness
DOI	Design Office Instruction
DH	de Havilland
DHC	de Havilland Canada
FC	Försökscentralen
FI	Fatigue Index
FMV	Försvarets Materielwerk
HSA	Hawker Siddeley Aviation
IFR	Instrument Flight Rules
MBB	Messerschmitt-Bölkow-Blohm
MFI	Malmö Flygindustri
MinTech	Ministry of Technology
RAF	Royal Air Force
RAFVR	Royal Air Force Volunteer Reserve
RNEFTS	Royal Navy Elementary Flying Training School
SAF	Swedish Air Force
SAL	Scottish Aviation Limited
SAM	Surface to Air Missile
SABL	Scottish Aviation (Bulldog) Limited
SBAC	Society of British Aircraft Constructors
SFAB	Svensk Flygtjänst AB
STOL	Short Take-off and Landing
TFHS	Trafikflyghogskolan
UAS	University Air Squadron

CHAPTER ONE

BULLDOG GENESIS

It is not possible fully to appreciate how the Bulldog survived the collapse of Beagle and came to enter production with SAL at Prestwick without first understanding the historical background of both companies. The 1960s were a turbulent period in British aviation and the events of the closing months of the decade were to decide the fate of the Bulldog. The collapse of Handley Page, followed shortly after by the collapse of Beagle, were the direct cause of SAL's decision to take on the Bulldog, a course only made possible by their own rescue from the near collapse of its parent company, Cammell Laird. Another company, Miles Aircraft, was also to play a significant part in the story and the reasons for their interest in the Bulldog need to be examined. A brief description of the historical background to Beagle, Miles and SAL to the extent that they affect the Bulldog story is necessary to place in context the events of 1970. Beagle's rise and fall is charted in the author's 'False Dawn – The Beagle Aircraft Story' published by Air-Britain in 2015. The story of SAL is told admirably in Alan Robertson's 'Lion Winged and Rampant', self-published in 1986 and in Peter Berry's 'Prestwick Airport and Scottish Aviation' published by Tempus in 2005. The Miles history can be found in Peter Amos's excellent three-volume account published by Air-Britain.

BEAGLE ORIGINS

Beagle came into being in 1960 after Peter Masefield, the then Managing Director of Bristol Aircraft, convinced the directors of the Pressed Steel Company that Britain could once again become a major player in light aviation. Pressed Steel had already begun a process of diversification in an attempt to reduce its reliance on car bodies for the volatile automobile industry and they saw light aviation as offering a promising outlet for pressed steel components. The RAF's imminent requirement for a replacement for the Avro Anson communication aircraft provided further incentive. Once formed, the company had to put together the resources needed to produce aircraft and, rather than establishing new premises and personnel, Pressed Steel decided that the quickest way to get into production was to acquire an existing light aircraft manufacturing company. Following a survey of the British light aircraft industry it was deduced that there were only two companies with experience of volume manufacture and Pressed Steel quickly acquired both. Auster Aircraft and Miles Aircraft were absorbed into the new company, Beagle Aircraft Limited. Whilst the Auster factory at Rearsby, Leicestershire, continued producing their high-wing designs to keep the workforce employed until the range of new Beagle aircraft were ready for production, the former Miles factory at Shoreham, Sussex, began work on the prototype of the B206, the twin-engined communication aircraft which Beagle was certain would be ordered by the RAF in large numbers and thereafter sell well in both the military and civil markets worldwide. Beagle suffered the first of many setbacks when, after a prolonged battle with the RAF, who preferred de Havilland's Dove 8 to the B206, only 20 aircraft were ordered instead of the 100 or more that Beagle was anticipating. Producing such a paltry number would not begin to cover the massive development costs and as a project the B206 never recovered commercially and there were no further military sales and only sparse civil sales. When, in 1965, Pressed Steel became part of the British Motor Corporation the escalating losses at Beagle combined with a substantial downturn in the automobile industry led to the decision being taken to withdraw from aircraft manufacturing.

Rather than closing down the company Pressed Steel sought a buyer to try to recoup some small part of its investment but strenuous efforts at home and abroad to find a buyer prepared to take on a company with a poor record of profitability proved fruitless and closure seemed inevitable. At the eleventh hour the British Government stepped in to buy the company and Beagle became effectively a nationalised company in July, 1968. The launch of the Pup range in 1967 seemed at first to herald a new dawning for Beagle. Orders poured in and for the first time Beagle had more orders than it had aircraft to sell but the Pup's high build cost meant that several thousand aircraft would have to be sold before any profit would be made. To produce aircraft at a rate that would keep pace with orders and ensure the break-even point would be reached within a reasonable period meant that there would have to be investment in new buildings and equipment but, in the fragile economic climate of the time, the Government was reluctant to put up the money for a venture that looked increasingly unlikely ever to pay its way. Finally, in December, 1969, following yet another plea from the company for more money, the Government took the decision to withdraw its support and, in the absence of a buyer, the only recourse was to appoint a Receiver.

In the preceding twelve months Beagle had been working on the military version of the Pup and the first prototype had flown in May, 1969. In a situation reminiscent of the Anson replacement saga of ten years earlier Beagle were banking on the military Pup being selected to supersede the Chipmunk as the

The Beagle Pup prototype, G-AVDF was the design basis for the Bulldog and it is seen here as part of the Beagle exhibit at the Paris Air Show in 1967. *(RS)*

RAF's primary trainer. But whilst the Ministry of Defence was not yet ready to implement the replacement of the Chipmunk firm orders were received from Sweden, Kenya and Zambia for a total of 71 aircraft. With the appointment of the Receiver the Government found themselves with three binding contracts with international customers and were faced with the dilemma of fulfilling these orders.

When Miles Aircraft was approached by Pressed Steel in 1960 as a potential acquisition they could be described as a reluctant suitor. Initially Miles had been appointed as a sub-contractor to Beagle to build the prototype B206 but within a few weeks of starting work it had agreed to sell its aviation interests to Pressed Steel. Miles saw the prospect of ready finance supplied by the cash-rich Pressed Steel Company as a means of bringing its own designs into production, something its own meagre resources had prevented it from doing. But things did not go Miles' way and it found their designs were given low priority or ignored altogether and the relationship with Pressed Steel, and with Masefield in particular, deteriorated rapidly. The Miles brothers had expected to have complete control over aircraft design and production whereas

Masefield and his newly-formed team of designers and managers took the front seat. By 1963 both brothers had departed acrimoniously and returned to their own premises adjacent to the airfield at Shoreham to pursue other ventures. Seven years later George Miles would reappear when he became a major player in the negotiations with the Receiver over the future of Beagle and the Bulldog.

SCOTTISH AVIATION

Whilst both Beagle and Miles soon faded into the background of the Bulldog story, SAL took centre stage. Founded in 1935 the company had proved resilient in overcoming several episodes of hardship, imaginative in its concept of Scotland's place in modern aviation and commercially shrewd in its dealings in an industry notorious for its failure rate among less sharp-minded organisations. The company's founders, Douglas Douglas-Hamilton (Marquess of Douglas and Clydesdale, later the 14th Duke of Hamilton which was Scotland's premier peerage), and David Fowler McIntyre. Douglas-Hamilton and McIntyre had met when both served with No 602 (City of Glasgow) Squadron, Royal Auxiliary Air Force and, together, they came to prominence in 1933 when they became the first men to

fly over the summit of Mount Everest. They formed the Scottish College of Aviation to provide flying training before changing the name to Scottish Aviation when the company's role extended beyond training. Land was bought at Prestwick on Scotland's west coast close to Ayr and a grass airfield constructed. During the war the company was a Civilian Repair Organisation and large numbers of damaged Hurricanes and Spitfires passed through Prestwick. The airfield's location and benign weather made it the obvious choice for the European terminal for the Atlantic air bridge and the construction of a hard runway in 1942 made Prestwick the best equipped airport this side of the Atlantic. In common with other manufacturers Scottish Aviation suffered in the immediate aftermath of the war with the sudden decline in military work and had to resort to non-aviation work to survive. In 1946 Scottish Airlines was formed and provided schedule services on behalf of British European Airways until it was closed down in 1960. The company's first venture into manufacturing was the Pioneer light communications aircraft with them building 59 in total, followed, in 1955, by the Twin Pioneer of which 87 were built with the last leaving the production line in

1963. By the end of the 1950s the company was struggling financially but non-aviation work and a contract to service Royal Canadian Air Force aircraft saw it through. McIntyre was killed in a Twin Pioneer accident in 1957 and Douglas-Hamilton stepped back from running the company, handing over to T D M Robertson and H W Laughland, Chairman and Managing Director respectively who steered the company through the difficult years of the 1960s.

In 1966 SAL became part of Cammell Laird, the shipbuilding conglomerate, which was seeking to hedge against difficult times for the British shipbuilding industry by diversifying into other manufacturing sectors. In 1966 SAL was awarded an order by Handley Page to build 54 sets of wings for the Jetstream feeder-liner, but disaster struck in August, 1969 when Handley Page went into receivership owing SAL £2.2 million. This calamity occurred just as Cammell Laird was suffering its own financial meltdown which resulted in a major reorganisation of the group that involved separating the shipbuilding company from the rest of the group. Now unencumbered by the debts incurred by the shipbuilding arm the remainder of the companies in the group were free to continue trading as a new group (the Laird Group), and SAL found itself able to take the bold step of making an

Scottish Aviation manufactured the Prestwick Pioneer which was sold to the RAF and to Malaysia. This example, XK367, is seen at Seletar in Singapore. *(RS)*

offer to the Receiver to acquire the Jetstream project as a whole and production restarted at Prestwick. The failure of Handley Page was followed closely by the collapse of Beagle, resulting in an approach from the Receiver to take over production of the various Beagle types but it was clear that it was only the Bulldog that stood any chance of being a viable commercial proposition. SAL had already been looking for a suitable light aircraft design to build under licence and had got as far as negotiating with the Wing Aircraft Company to acquire the rights to their twin-engined Derringer but the Bulldog seemed to be a much better proposition.

Very few commercial records for SAL have survived so any figures

for the financial success or otherwise of the Bulldog can only be conjecture. Given the greatly enhanced sale prices negotiated from the outset by SAL and the healthy number of aircraft eventually built it is highly likely that the Bulldog turned out to be a commercial success. By the time the RAF decided to order the Bulldog in 1972 the price of each aircraft was almost double the figure agreed by Beagle for the Swedish order. Given the extremely low figure agreed by Beagle with the Swedish, Zambian and Kenyan Governments there can be little doubt that had they been in a position to see the Bulldog project through they would have lost heavily.

At the time the opportunity arose to purchase the Bulldog project, SAL was in the late stages of discussions with Wing Aircraft regarding building the Derringer light twin, a plan that was dropped once the Bulldog deal was signed. *(RS)*

CHAPTER TWO

BEAGLE AND THE BULLDOG

Following its formation, one of Beagle's first and most fundamental decisions was to concentrate its efforts on the B206 light twin instead of a smaller single-engine tourer/trainer. This was to prove a serious error and taking on a relatively complex aircraft with a new design team and workforce was to prove an expensive misjudgement. Peter Masefield and Pressed Steel were beguiled by the prospect of a substantial order for the replacement of the RAF's venerable Anson but were to be misled by civil servants advising them that the B206 was to be the preferred aircraft when the RAF much preferred de Havilland's Dove 8. Eventually, to placate those Ministers lobbying on behalf of Beagle, the company was given an order for just twenty B206 Bassets, a quantity so small that the whole B206 project was in jeopardy. The B206 never recovered from this poor start and proved unsaleable to other Air Forces and failed to make any impression in the civil market against American competition.

Miles brought with it to Beagle two current designs it had prepared for submission to the Transport Aircraft Requirements Committee, the M114 single-engine trainer/tourer (re-designated by Beagle as the M117) and the M115 twin-engine tourer (re-designated M218). Perversely, ignoring the comparatively simple single-engine design, Beagle chose to proceed with the M115 which, with the B206, gave it two twin-engine projects simultaneously. Had Beagle chosen instead to go ahead with the M117 it could well have gone on to be developed into other variants, including a military trainer, and the Pup and Bulldog, as we know them, might never have reached the drawing board. The growing antipathy between the Miles brothers and what was perceived as the Masefield camp meant that no Miles project would be given preference over other Beagle types

The Miles brothers had hoped their M114 design would be produced by Beagle - and if it had been it is probable the Pup and Bulldog would not have been produced as we know them. *(MA)*

when it came to the allocation of resources. The departure of the Miles brothers only three years after they had joined Beagle with much-heralded optimism for the future of British light aviation was only the first of many turbulent events that would follow and set Beagle on the road to failure. Masefield's refusal to countenance the B206 as a commercial failure meant that it would continue draining money from the company to the very end.

Having discarded the M117, lack of factory space and shortage of finance meant it would be five years before Beagle could consider producing a single-engine aircraft. As with the B206 and the Anson, that decision was led largely by the inevitability of a replacement being needed in the near future for the RAF's de Havilland Chipmunks. Beagle was encouraged by a 1968 survey that identified that 985 single-engine trainers were going to be needed by 54 Air Forces - figures that excluded any RAF requirement. With such a sizeable market to be tapped Beagle planned to build 350 military trainers between 1969 and 1973, a projection that was not that far away from the 325 Bulldogs eventually built by SAL.

THE PUP AND DERIVATIVES

In laying out their plans for the first indigenous single-engine Beagle aircraft it was decided to design an aircraft that would match the requirements of both civil and military customers. The design team set up in 1966, led by John Larroucau as Chief Designer and Alan Greenhalgh as Chief Project Engineer, initially decided there would be six variants of the B121, the type that would eventually be named the Pup. They were the B121C (a two-seat, 100hp, civil version), B121T (two-seat, 160hp, military version), B123 (the four-seat Pup Major), B242 (Pup Major Twin, with two 150hp engines, a derivative of the M218), the Bull Pup (a two-seat 210hp single) and the B143 (a six-seat retractable-gear single). Soon realising that six types were too ambitious the programme was reduced to just three, the B121C, B121T (with a 150hp engine instead of the 160hp) and the B123.

Like John Larroucau, Alan Greenhalgh was also at Avro where he worked his way up from apprentice to Assistant Chief of Projects responsible for a wide range of design studies. After Beagle he joined Link-Miles at Shoreham as Chief Engineer spending two years working on flight simulators before joining Vinten to work on aerial reconnaissance systems and camera pods.

With the training fleets of the Royal Air Force and College of Air Training foremost in its mind Beagle prioritised the B121T and a mock-up was constructed. Photographs of this mock-up show an aircraft that looked very little like the eventual Pup. With its sliding canopy it resembled more closely the lines of the eventual Bulldog. When the B121C mock-up appeared shortly after the B121T there were recognisable similarities to the final Pup design. At this point Beagle changed tack and sidelined the B121T and concentrated instead on the civil B121C and this was to be the version which became the first prototype, flying for the first time in April, 1967. A 150hp version of the B121C soon followed and both versions proved a success, especially with flying schools, and orders came thick and fast presenting Beagle with the new and unfamiliar problem of meeting demand.

Whilst the B121T and the B123 four-seater were still sidelined, Beagle took the development of the Pup a stage further in the Spring of 1968 when it decided to produce a more powerful version of the B121C, the Series 4, with a 200hp engine. With Beagle's customary ability to cause confusion over designations the Series 4 was given the same B123 designation as it had originally allocated to the four-seat Pup Major.

With the B123 as its core, Beagle attempted to pre-empt the likely specification of a training aircraft for the RAF and College of Air Training and produced their own 'Operational Requirement'. The most obvious requirement for a military training aircraft over and above a civil version would be a strengthening of the structure. Whilst a retractable undercarriage would be ideal this would necessitate the redesign of the inboard portion of the wings to accommodate the landing gear in the retracted position and the idea was soon abandoned as too complex and too heavy. The wing span would have to be increased to provide a larger

As Beagle's Chief Project Engineer, Alan Greenhalgh was responsible for both the Pup and Bulldog projects. *(MA)*

wing area and the leading edge modified to improve the spinning characteristics. To help with spin recovery larger spin strakes would be needed. The tailplane would have to be increased both in span and chord and a new fin, with a more upright leading edge, together with a larger rudder would be necessary. A new large ventral fin would, together with the larger area of the fin and rudder, increase the surface area that would be unshielded by the tailplane during a spin. The additional weight of these modifications would require larger main wheels and larger oleo diameter and enhanced brakes. Initially, unlike the B121T which sported a

Beagle's mockup of the B121T, their early design for a military trainer version of the Pup. *(MA)*

A model of Beagle's military Pup, probably the B123. *(PH)*

John Larroucau, seen here on the right in 1966 with Fred Mulley, Minister of Aviation, was Beagle's Chief Designer. *(MA)*

John Larroucau joined Beagle from Avro where he had been a section leader in the stress analysis group working primarliy on the Avro 748. A gifted and imaginative design engineer he was highly thought of at Beagle and, together with Alan Greenhalgh, was responsible for the design of the Pup range and eventually the Bulldog. Following Beagle's closure Larrroucau worked for a brief period with the British Aircraft Corporation on Concorde before joining Scottish Aviation to oversee the introduction of the Garrett-powered Jetstream II. Whilst at Prestwick Larroucau would have witnessed the successful production of the type he had instigated at the other end of the country at Shoreham.

sliding canopy, the B123 was to have doors, albeit jettisonable, but eventually the sliding canopy was reintroduced to facilitate escape. The shape of the canopy had to have the headroom to accommodate bone-dome helmets. In common with many other light aircraft the thrust line of the engine would be slightly offset to the right and downwards to improve handling.

Despite Beagle's laudable efforts to define a comprehensive specification for a military trainer the Ministry of Technology (MinTech), who by this time had become the agents for Beagle's owner, the British Government, was sceptical. Whilst acknowledging that many hundreds of aircraft might be required worldwide over the next seven years they felt most military needs could be met by the Pup-150 or even a civil version of the B123. Anxious to minimise the company's losses it took an ultra-cautious line, scared that introducing a military version might further impede the civil programme which was already delayed and leading to extended delivery times. The high cost of the changes would require the pre-ordering of a substantial number of aircraft to finance the development, otherwise additional funds would be needed or money would have to be diverted from the civil Pup programme which was thought to be far more important.

Whilst Mintech was cool towards the military B123, Beagle had, during its foreign sales trips, elicited the views of various Air Forces and received a largely positive response. A strategy was adopted of establishing a base specification which, by incorporating relatively minor changes, could satisfy each Air Force's individual needs. This was, in fact, how SAL went on to handle development of the Bulldog in due course.

BULLDOG FOR SWEDEN

The Swedish had first been introduced to the civil Pup when Eric Greenwood, Beagle's Sales Director, undertook a European tour in Autumn, 1967. Greenwood met with General Thunberg, the then Chief of the Air Staff, and Brigadier Ohlin to discuss the provision of 60 ab initio trainers. It was Greenwood and Ben Gunn, Beagle's Sales Manager responsible for Europe, who were responsible for the dealings with the Swedish authorities with Greenwood directing the strategy and Gunn doing the leg work. The Kunnliga Flygförvaltningen (KFF), the Royal Swedish Air Board, was sufficiently interested in the Pup for it to request a quotation for 78 Series 4 Pups, the 180hp version which was still part of Beagle's intended range at the time, with 50 intended for its Air Force and 28 for the Army. The Army's specification went further than the Air Force's as it required an aircraft capable of the utility role rather than simply a trainer and this would require a Short Takeoff and Landing (STOL) capability.

As the discussions between Beagle and the Swedish military developed, Beagle appointed Svensk Flygtjänst AB, (SFAB), known internationally as Swedair, to act as intermediary. From 1963 Beagle had been represented in Sweden by Swedenflyg AB which had handled sales mainly of the Beagle-Auster types but had gone out of business in 1967. Although a quotation was eventually submitted for 78 Series 4s no order was forthcoming but close contact was maintained and, in 1968, Gunn took the Pup-150 demonstrator, G-AVLN, to the headquarters of the Swedish Central Flying School at F5 Ljungbyhed in Sweden. This was on loan to Försvarets Materielwerk (FMV), the Government department that owned all military equipment in use by the Swedish armed forces and was responsible for aircraft purchases. Gunn left Shoreham for Malmö in November and his brief was to convert five Air Force pilots to fly the Pup before leaving the aircraft in Sweden for three weeks during which time the newly-qualified instructors would train student pilots. The Army also took the opportunity to fly the Pup and were so impressed they were prepared to amend its operational requirements to suit the Pup.

Whilst this was a useful exercise for both parties, the Swedish requirements, in its specification 125/09/01-69, had not changed and the Pup-150 still fell short of the need for a much stronger aircraft. Back at Shoreham, with Swedish input, Beagle first designed

Beagle Pup G-AVLN was flown to Sweden by Ben Gunn where it impressed the Air Force and Army top brass. However, it fell short of their specification, leading to Beagle developing the B123 and then the B125. *(SS)*

the upgraded version of the Pup, the B123, but this was soon abandoned to be replaced by the B125.

The proposed B123 had already diverged considerably from the B121 and when Beagle decided to incorporate the requirements put forward by the Swedish armed forces the result differed so extensively from the B123 that it was given a new designation, the B125, and named the Bulldog. Having already strengthened the B121 to produce the B123, to meet the Swedish requirements the B125 had to be stronger still. Whilst the wing geometry would be the same as the B121, the wing would be attached to a centre section integral with the fuselage, thereby adding 24 inches (610mm) to the overall wing span. The wing would be further strengthened by introducing an additional beam within the wing section, reducing the wing volume available for fuel by 2 gallons (9 litres) to 34 gallons (153 litres). Inevitably the changes would incur a gain in empty weight from the Pup-150's 1,200 lbs (545kg) to 1,431 lbs (649kg). The maximum weight for normal operations was set at 2,350 lbs (1,066kg) but for aerobatics and spinning there would be a limit of 2,150 lbs (975kg).

Beagle planned to complete all the drawing work for the B125 by the end of February, 1969 and the first flight of the prototype was to follow at the end of May. Air Registration Board (ARB) certification was to be achieved

A 200hp Lycoming engine was installed in the Pup prototype, G-AVDF, to get some indication of the likely performance and handling, although this yielded little useful data as the Bulldog was a very different aircraft. *(MA)*

by February, 1970 and the first production aircraft would be ready by May. Despite the major changes there was still considerable commonality with the basic Pup airframe and jigs so Beagle retrieved an early-stage Pup airframe from the production line and work on the prototype B125 Bulldog got under way.

To assess the extent that the more powerful engine would affect handling, the Pup Series 1 prototype, G-AVDF, was fitted with a 200hp Lycoming and testing began on 1 April, 1969. The findings could only be of limited use as the substantial changes in shape, structure and weight of the Bulldog would affect any test results considerably. For six weeks G-AVDF carried out handling and performance trials ceasing on 12 May, one week before the first flight of the Bulldog. This was probably to enable the 200hp engine to be removed and installed in the Bulldog.

Beagle's Chief Test Pilot, Pee Wee Judge, and Flight Test Observer

David Cummings, had carried out the majority of test flying of the Pup over the past two years. On 19 May, 1969 they made the first flight of the Bulldog, G-AXEH, at Shoreham with Charles Masefield flying the Pup-150 prototype, G-AVLN, as chase plane. In a flight lasting 55 minutes the aircraft was subjected to a comprehensive programme of manoeuvres including stalls and speed tests up to 150 knots. Judge was so satisfied with the way the aircraft handled that he performed some basic aerobatics (with the Pup-150 following in formation to get photographs). It cannot be said of many aircraft that the pilot was sufficiently confident of its performance that he performed aerobatics on its maiden flight. On landing Judge's summation was that handling was good with pleasant control harmony but the increased wing span was causing some lateral damping and loss of aileron crispness compared with the Pup.

Subsequent test flights revealed slightly different spin characteristics

John Judge, known throughout the aviation industry as Pee Wee, joined the RAF straight from school in 1941 and flew Hurricanes in North Africa before returning to Britain in time to fly Spitfires on fighter sweeps and bomber escort missions following D-Day. As the Allies made their way across Europe he flew Typhoons on train-busting sorties. After the war Judge was sent to India to ferry Spitfires before transferring to test-flying duties. He left the RAF in 1946 and joined No 615 (County of Surrey) Squadron, Royal Auxiliary Air Force, based at RAF Biggin Hill

where he resumed his partnership with the Spitfire before eventually moving on to the Meteor 8. For employment he ferried Tempests and Furies to Pakistan before joining Vickers-Supermarine to test-fly the Attacker, Swift and Scimitar. Made redundant by Vickers-Supermarine, Judge worked for a short time for Rolls-Royce on the Tyne development programme and then joined F G Miles Limited at Shoreham. Judge became a Beagle employee when Miles was acquired by Pressed Steel to become part of the Beagle group and he remained with Beagle until its

demise. Judge lost his life whilst flying a Wallis autogyro at the Farnborough air show in 1970.

Pee Wee Judge and David Cummings in good spirits during the hot weather trials in Athens in August, 1969. *(MA)*

The prototype, G-AXEH en route to the Paris Air Show in 1969. It was the last opportunity for Beagle to display it before their collapse. (MA)

On its return from Paris Beagle gave G-AXEH a red and white colour scheme not seen before on any Beagle prototypes. (CE)

compared to the Pup. Whereas the Pup was prepared to spin from 5 knots above the stall the Bulldog only entered a spin once the aircraft had stalled. Once in the spin the Bulldog's attitude was steeper than the Pup's and the rotation was slower. Provided the correct procedure was followed, recovery from the spin was straightforward and immediate. Although the oil system of the Lycoming installed in the prototype only tolerated inverted flight for up to ten seconds the engines of production aircraft would be fitted with two oil pumps to give unlimited inverted capability.

On 10 June, 1969 the B125 received its full Transport Category Certificate of Airworthiness (CofA) which included full aerobatics and unlimited spinning. A few days after receiving the C of A the Bulldog was demonstrated at the Paris Air Show at Le Bourget. This would be the only opportunity Beagle had to show off the Bulldog at an international air show and during the show the contract for the 58 aircraft for the Royal Swedish

Air Force (SAF) was signed.

Determined to keep the Bulldog programme on track despite the worsening financial situation, Beagle sent the prototype on 28 August, 1969 for its tropical trials. Pee Wee Judge and David Cummings left for Nicosia with a B206S as support aircraft, meeting up with the ARB's representative on arrival. Nicosia was ideal as it had one of the highest ambient temperatures in Europe and was a good airfield with cooperative authorities. In 38 flights totalling 51 hours over two weeks the tests included climb performance, engine and system cooling, and measured takeoffs and landings. Tropical trials were followed by high-altitude trials in Switzerland. Again, ARB representatives joined Judge and Cummings at Samedan on 3 October for three days of trials.

The Bulldog was the first Beagle type with a canopy and, before it could enter service, jettisoning tests were required to confirm that the canopy could be operated satisfactorily under emergency conditions and that the

canopy would depart cleanly. As Beagle was encountering such tests for the first time, arrangements were made in early January with the A&AEE at Boscombe Down for the use of its wind tunnel but, following the appointment of Beagle's Receiver on 2 December, 1969, the tests were cancelled. It eventually became SAL's responsibility to carry out these tests and to overcome the considerable problems that the jettisoning of the canopy raised.

In February, 1970, shortly after the Receiver's appointment, the Bulldog underwent a brief preliminary assessment at the A&AEE at Boscombe Down. The glowing report that followed that assessment fully justified Beagle's endeavours to produce an up-to-date basic military trainer and it only remained for the Air Ministry to follow the lead given by the Swedish armed forces by ordering the type in large numbers. Given that the orders would be forthcoming all Beagle had to do was build the aircraft at a cost that would ensure a profit.

The cockpit layout of G-AXEH. (DC)

The first prototype Bulldog under construction in the Shoreham experimental hangar in 1969. (MA)

CHAPTER THREE

THE SWEDISH ORDER

By now there was some degree of urgency as both the Royal Swedish Air Force (later the Swedish Air Force, now referred to as the SAF) and the Swedish Army needed to replace outdated aircraft which had been in service for a long time. The Air Force intended to take its North American Sk16A Harvard IIbs used for liaison out of service in the early 1970s and the Saab 91 Safir trainer (designated Sk 50) which had been in service since 1952, was due to be reassigned to take its place. The Army was seeking to replace its Piper Fpl 51 Super Cubs but their need was not quite so urgent as the Cubs were not due to be taken out of service until between 1972 and 1975. Despite their slightly differing requirements and timing the Air Force and the Army were collaborating to find a type that would suit the requirements of both.

BULLDOG COMPETITORS

The FMV had looked at a long list of aircraft that might be suitable as the Safir replacement including a more up-to-date version of the

Super Cub, the Piper PA-28 Cherokee, Cessna's 172 and 177, the Zlin Trener, the Fuji FA200, the SIAI-Marchetti SF260 and S205, the Socata Horizon, the Bölkow Monsun and the SIAT Flamingo. This long list of possibles was shortened to just four aircraft. In December, 1967 the Army tested a Reims-Cessna FR172 Rocket, the civilian version of the USAF's T-41 Mescalero. Saab had taken on the Swedish agency for Cessna in 1967, probably with the sale/lease of the Rocket to the Army and Air Force in mind, and it arranged for the first FR172, F-BOQN (c/n FR172-001), to be made available for trials at Norrkoping/Kungsangen which was the base for Saab's Cessna sales. Intent on winning the military order, in 1968 Saab had acquired Malmö Flygindustri (MFI), based at Malmö Bulltofta airport, and the development of the MFI-15 was well underway but, realistically, there was no chance of it being ready to enter service before 1972. A Fuji FA-200 (JA3336) was also brought to Sweden in November,

1968 to be tested. Gunn happened to be at Malmö when the Fuji arrived and did not see the type as any threat to the Pup. Indeed, he commented back to Shoreham that the Fuji team seemed embarrassed at the comparison and they soon fled the scene.

All the types considered, with the exception of Saab's MFI-15, were rejected as being too expensive or lacking the required performance. The MFI-15, while no more suitable than any of the other types considered, had to be given serious consideration as it would be built in Sweden. The Air Force had experience of operating the MFI-9B as it had ten on lease in 1966-67 for use as an economical primary trainer but it was too small and the unfavourable impression it created was to do no favours for Saab's endavours to promote the MFI-15. The MFI-9 did achieve limited success in the civil field when Bölkow built it under licence as the Bö208. The prototype MFI-15 had flown for the first time at Bulltofta on 11 July, 1969, seven weeks after the first flight of the Bulldog prototype, but there was still a great deal of development work to be done and production was still at least a year away (if not two). In its present form it failed to meet the Air Force's specification, which the RSAB had intentionally written around the Bulldog, and it was generally disliked, not least because of its high-wing configuration. Forecasts suggested it was likely to be between £1,000 and £2,000 more expensive than the Bulldog.

Beagle's design for the B125 was based on the FMV's requirements for an aircraft capable of full aerobatics to limits of +6g/-3g whilst carrying two occupants in full kit. An engine of 200hp would be essential but as a British engine was not available in Rolls-Royce's Continental range it would have to be the American Lycoming IO-

The Swedish Air Force was looking to replace the Safir which was reassigned as a liaison aircraft. (SS)

The Swedish Army needed to replace its Piper PA-18 Super Cubs between 1972 and 1975. (SS)

Cessna 172 F-BOQN was the Reims FR172 demonstrator taken to Sweden for evaluation by the Swedish Air Force and Army. *(RS)*

Fuji FA200, JA3336 was assessed by the Swedish military - but failed to impress. *(SS)*

360-AIC. The Lycoming would drive a Hartzell constant-speed propeller meaning that aerobatics would be more straightforward and students would learn the use of constant-speed controls. The fuselage was to be strengthened at the rear and the lower and forward upper sections of the fuselage were to be modified and a new centre and rear upper fuselage shape designed to accommodate a sliding canopy.

FMV had been monitoring closely the development work on the Bulldog and the decision to place an order was taken on 29 May, 1969 followed two weeks later, on 12 June, by the signing of the order by the Supreme Commander of the Swedish Armed Forces, Torsten Rapp, at the Paris International Air Show. The order (ref. 09-10-91700), was for 58 aircraft for the SAF at £10,565 each, a total of £612,770. Spare engines and other spares brought the total value of the contract to £640,614. The contract included an option for a further 45 aircraft for the Swedish Army, the option to be taken up by June 1971. Both within Beagle and in the aviation press, this substantial order was seen as historic and the event which could transform all Beagle's disappointments up to this point into success, bringing about the long-awaited profit and a return on the public investment.

The news that an order had been placed for a British aircraft was met with alarm in Sweden. The press claimed that the MFI-15 had not been given a fair chance and the whole procurement process had been mishandled. On 20 July the Ombudsman for Justice was notified that there had been possible misconduct in the deal. This allegation arose because of the appointment by Beagle of Svensk Flygtjanst AB, (SFAB), as its agent. SFAB was controlled by a former Chief of the Air Force (CFV), Bengt Nordenskiold, and his son, Claes-Henrik Nordenskiold, who had recently been appointed the Chief of the Air Staff. Between June and September 1968, the period when much of the selection process was taking place, Claes-Henrik Nordenskiold was acting Chief of the Air Force. Father and son had been major shareholders in SFAB since 1946 and had acted for British manufacturers throughout the 1950s and 1960s handling deals that included Spitfires, Mosquitos, Vampires, Venoms and Hunters. But times had changed and the sort of relationship that had existed between SFAB, the Swedish procurement authorities and the aircraft manufacturers was no longer permissible. Initially SFAB had agreed a deal with Beagle to act as its Swedish agent early in 1969 and took delivery of the first Pup for the Swedish market in May and there was nothing untoward about dealing with the civil market in this way. But when it came to a serving officer acting on behalf of a manufacturer seeking to win a military contract it was considered to be highly dubious. Eventually the Secretary of State at the Defence Department, Anders Thunborg, called in Claes-Henrik Nordenskiold, and told him to resign which he duly did in January, 1970, quoting "dissatisfaction with the organisation of the defence and certain trends in Sweden".

In August the Defence Staff held a press conference to clarify the choice of the Bulldog emphasising the superiority of the Bulldog over the MFI-15. The Bulldog was a better aircraft on skis; it had better artillery support capability; delivery times were better with the Bulldog being ready in about a year whilst the MFI-15 would not be available until the end of 1971, the cost of the Bulldog would be approximately 1.5 million Krone less for the same number of aircraft and the warranty commitments for the Bulldog were superior to those for the MFI-15. Bearing in mind that at this time neither type had been trialled and that the capabilities of the Bulldog were being extrapolated from those of the Pup-150 the FMV was going out on a limb so far as the flying characteristics of the Bulldog were concerned.

THE SWEDISH CONTRACT

The FMV made it a point of principle that it would not submit to Government or industrial pressure to buy a Swedish product when a superior product was available elsewhere but in placing an order for a foreign-built aircraft it had attracted the ire of Swedish politicians, press and public and provoked a strong reaction from Saab, the indigenous aircraft manufacturer. To placate these critics the contract contained provision for not less than 15% of the total labour content to be carried out at Malmo by AB Svenska Flygverkstaderna (Swedish Airworks) (ABSF), a subsidiary of

The prototype MFI-15, SE-XCB was the Bulldog's main competitor for the Swedish order. *(RS)*

Svensk Flygjänst, using materials of Swedish origin as far as possible. The first five aircraft were to be delivered to Malmö in various states of finish to be completed by ABSF. The remaining 53 aircraft were to be delivered to Malmö unpainted, with only the minimum number of instruments necessary for flight, untrimmed and unfurnished and with only sufficient electrical installation for safe flight.

The contract provided for a 'deposit' of 33%, amounting to £210,000, to be paid and this helped to reduce Beagle's burgeoning bank overdraft. Delivery of the first aircraft was to be by 31 August, 1970 and the last by 31 July, 1971, a total of 58 aircraft in 11 months or just over five aircraft per month. Building 58 aircraft from scratch in 11 months, albeit only with the aircraft partially-completed, was a considerable task. If further orders were to be received from other customers, or the option for the Army aircraft was confirmed sooner rather than later, the undertaking would become even harder.

Saab attempted to have the order cancelled. By now the first MFI-15 prototype (SE-301 c/n 15001 later SE-XCB) had flown and was being demonstrated. To get over the delay in delivery Saab offered to lease aircraft during the transition period, and this would probably have been the Reims Rocket, but the FMV did not change its mind.

The placing of the order by the FMV did not mean the end of dialogue with Beagle whilst development work continued and at the beginning of December, the FMV amended the contract to include revisions to the radio fit, shoulder harnesses and special seats, furnishings and trim, instrument panel, rear windows, special control knobs, and coaming. It was also agreed that the contract sum would be amended to include a contribution towards the cost of the mockup.

BEAGLE'S COLLAPSE

When, on 2 December, 1969, Barclays Bank appointed a Receiver the future of Beagle looked bleak and the Bulldog project was in jeopardy. In the final meetings leading up to the Government's decision to withdraw financial support Beagle's directors had pleaded with MinTech for more time for the measures they had introduced to reduce Pup production costs and to improve the rate of Pup production to one aircraft per day to become effective. They also needed time to decide whether to persevere with the Series 3 B206 or to abandon all hope of the type ever selling in any worthwhile numbers, time to allow the discussions with Ling-Temco-Vought to crystallise into a firm deal for the American conglomerate to buy Beagle, and, above all, time to bring the Bulldog into production. The Swedish order, coupled with the early favourable

response to the type, especially from the RAF which was displaying positive signs that the type would be selected to replace the Chipmunk, was proof that, given the time, Beagle would be able to turn the corner and the future would be bright. The Government's action, when Beagle had an order book for 352 aircraft, 293 of which were for export, as well as orders for sub-contract work worth more than £500,000, might on the surface be said to be precipitate and ill-judged but the volume of orders was not the whole story. There were problems, seemingly insurmountable, due to Beagle's inability to build aircraft for less than they could sell them for. Whether, given the time, Beagle would have overcome these problems can only be conjecture and, in any case, the situation was now what it was and it was up to the Receiver to decide on the fate of the company and indeed of the Bulldog.

The Receiver, Kenneth Cork, of W.H. Cork Gully & Co, decided to keep the company in business in the short term to give himself time to assess the options. With the sanction of MinTech, test flying of the Bulldog continued as did demonstrating of the aircraft to potential customers. Ski and weapons trials had already been arranged for January and it was agreed that these would go ahead and a delegation of five Swedish pilots arrived at Shoreham on 8 December to familiarise themselves with the Bulldog ahead of these trials. There was a crisis when, just days before the prototype was due to leave for the winter trials, the ARB withdrew approval for the trials on the grounds that as Beagle would be unable to provide adequate support for the aircraft in service there was no point in pursuing the issue of a CofA. John Larroucau took the matter up with the ARB and the ban was lifted.

Whilst the Receiver was assessing the company's position during December, work on the Bulldog continued, but at a slower pace. The point was reached when some jigs and tools were needed but there was not the money to buy them. The purchase of the bought-out items for the first ten aircraft, which would have cost £81,500, was put on hold. The Swedish took a dim view of this reluctance to provide the money to keep the project on programme seeing it as a lack of commitment on the British Government's part to fulfilling the order.

BULLDOG SKI TRIALS

It was agreed with the FMV that it would hire the prototype from 15 January to 31 March, 1970 at a rate of £10 per day plus £8 per flying hour, with engineering support paid for on top. On 17 January Pee Wee Judge flew G-AXEH to Sweden, with ground engineer Jim Waddington as crew, both now being technically employed by the Receiver. The aircraft routed via Calais, Ostend, Rotterdam, and Hamburg, where they overnighted, before continuing via Malmö and Visby, arriving in Stockholm (Bromma). On arrival in Sweden G-AXEH was assigned to the Försökscentralen (FC), the FMV's Test and Evaluation Centre, and given its code FC.71 (call sign Victor 71) and the aircraft remained at Bromma for two days during which it was fitted with skis under the supervision of the Finnish ski manufacturer. The fuselage side brackets fitted at Shoreham were rejected as too flimsy, so these were removed and new ones made and fitted by Swedair and the fuselage structure was strengthened locally. The fitting of the Bofors Bantam missile installation had been carried out at Shoreham under the supervision of Bofors but, on inspection, it was discovered the missile mountings made at Shoreham were installed back to front so presumably the missiles would have fired backwards! The mountings were modified so that the missiles would point the right way and the 'butchering' of the installation made the whole thing look rather tatty. The missile control box was installed at the top centre

The second prototype was only partially completed by Beagle when they collapsed and was completed at Prestwick. *(via FL)*

of the instrument panel just below the compass.

Before the skis were fitted Judge demonstrated the aircraft to the head of Flying Training Personnel. The Colonel was enthusiastic with his only real criticism being that the acceleration on takeoff might be a bit too exciting for a young pupil. As Judge said, "you can't win."

On arriving at Vidsel, the base to be used for the trials, Judge carried out two handling flights with an SAF pilot, with the wheels still fitted. On the first of these the trial nearly came to an abrupt end when the SAF pilot elected to carry out a long spin from 3,000 feet over a snow-covered frozen lake. He apparently lost his height reference and, despite Judge's urging, delayed his recovery until 750 feet was indicated on the altimeter and in the pullout they were virtually on the surface. Judge had to apply power to clear the trees skirting the lake.

In an unheated open-ended blister hangar with snow and ice covering the floor and a temperature of -15°C, the fitting of the skis was a slow process. The skis which had been sourced by Beagle from the American company, Finidyne, were rejected in favour of Finnish-built skis recommended by Lutab, a consultancy from Stockholm who carried out the ski design calculations. As was normal with skis, even with Teflon coating, the stationary aircraft froze to the snow and 2,200 rpm was required to get it moving, or slightly less if the rudder pedals were treadled. Once

moving, about 1,300 rpm was needed to keep the aircraft moving at slow taxi pace. Directional control was surprisingly good. Closing the throttle to idle at slow taxi speed resulted in a distance of approximately 15 feet to bring the aircraft to a halt. A number of accelerations were carried out with a Volkswagen minibus in formation as chase vehicle. At maximum power rather more rudder than customary was necessary to keep the aircraft straight and this might have limited the crosswind capabilities. Handling at rotation, takeoff, and landing did not differ appreciably from the wheeled aircraft.

Five minutes flying time from the base at Vidsel a frozen lake, Lake Grunträsket, provided ideal conditions for the snow trials and Victor 71 remained at Vidsel for two weeks of test flying with skis. On a typical takeoff, in 80 cms of soft virgin snow, the aircraft ploughed forward at low speed, gradually rising up on the skis until it got up 'on the step', accelerated and took off normally. The takeoff run would be about 425 metres and the time from start to unstick would be 40 seconds. The ease with which the Bulldog coped with the snow was underlined when a ski-equipped Army Super Cub attempted to take off on the same snow runway that the Bulldog had used. The Cub's skis dug in and the aircraft became hopelessly bogged down, tipping onto one wingtip and nearly onto its nose.

Bulldog prototype G-AXEH is seen here during the ski trials. In service, only the Swedish Army employed the skis - and it was far from common. *(GJ)*

Overnight, with the aircraft in the open without covers, it was given a cold soak and the following morning a cold start was attempted at -32ºC without the assistance of pre-heat or external battery. The propeller lever was frozen fully forward, the mixture lever was stiff and the control cables were very slack. The starter motor turned the engine readily but it would not fire, probably as the fuel was too cold to vaporise properly. After a half-hour pre-heat and an external battery plugged in, the engine fired, initially on one cylinder but with the others joining in quickly. After seven minutes of running at increasing rpm the engine was up to temperature and pressure and ready for takeoff.

The head of the FC wanted to see the aircraft put through a one-turn spin programme in all flap configurations and throughout the centre of gravity range (CG) with skis fitted. This would permit the aircraft to carry out the 'Artillery Manoeuvre', a sort of 'split-arse' stall turn, without fear of getting into any handling difficulties. Although Judge agreed to carry out these tests, subject to John Larroucau's agreement, it was decided to leave them in abeyance until the Army had completed its evaluation at Östersund.

The aircraft was handed over to the Army and was flown to Östersund for a week's evaluation on skis. The frozen lakes surrounding Östersund provided more varied snow conditions than Lake Gruntrasket. Sometimes the snow was sparse, giving sudden decelerations, and sometimes hard-packed. At the request of the Army Staff, a race from standstill to 1,000 feet was staged between the Bulldog and a Super Cub 150, both with full fuel (an attempt by the Cub pilot to go off with half fuel was discovered and thwarted) and two occupants. The Bulldog flew first and clocked 73 seconds. It flew a circuit and positioned just behind the Cub as it commenced its takeoff run. The Cub was easily outpaced and was credited with 77 seconds, although this was probably optimistic, as the Cub called 1,000 feet as the Bulldog passed that height and they were well ahead of and above the Cub.

With the Army trials completed, the aircraft returned to Vidsel and the spin trials with skis commenced. At some CG positions it was difficult to get the aircraft to spin and it repeatedly entered a spiral dive instead. As well as the ski trials, 16 successful firings of wing-tip pylon-mounted Bofors wire-controlled missiles were carried out confirming the Bulldog's ability to perform the role of missile-firing trainer in conjunction with ground forces. The trials resulted in several proposed modifications. The standard Pup seats were to be redesigned with the squabs removed so that the occupants could sit on parachutes. To enable a second student to observe from the rear a third seat would be required, positioned on the starboard side. On the Army version the rear windows were to have a hinged lower section to facilitate aerial photography. These modifications were never implemented by Beagle and became the responsibility of SAL when the project transferred to them.

Judge left the Bulldog in Sweden for the Swedish to continue the trials and returned home by scheduled flight on 23 February. Fifteen weeks later, on 8 June, 1970, he returned to Sweden, again by scheduled flight, to collect G-AXEH and fly it back to Shoreham via Hamburg and Rotterdam. The prototype had been away for almost five months. The Shoreham to which the aircraft returned in June was very different from when it had left in mid-January, shortly after the government axe had fallen. The departure of staff had continued steadily during the first half of the year and the numbers were now much reduced. Unsold aircraft crowded the hard standings and filled the hangars. Testing of the Bulldog came to a stop and the prototype did no further flying until 7 July when Judge did the necessary test flying in connection with the renewal of the CofA.

Three days later, on 10 July, Judge flew the prototype for the last time when he took it to Gatwick to meet John Blair, SAL's Chief Test Pilot, who had come to collect the aircraft. After returning to Shoreham Blair took the controls for a familiarisation flight before flying the aircraft to Prestwick.

Swedish Army Bulldog Fv61010 on its Finnish-made skis. Built as an Sk61A it was later modified as an Sk61D. *(via FL)*

Scottish Aviation climbing high ~ with the Bulldog

The Bulldog will become a classic. This opinion comes, not from Scottish Aviation, but from independent aviation experts. It will be a classic aircraft because it fulfils completely its role as a tough military basic trainer. Quality control is meticulous. The design guarantees efficiency and reliability. The Bulldog is now being produced in quantity by Scottish Aviation who have drawn upon their 37 years of experience combined with every modern facility not only to produce the aircraft, but to provide the "after sales service" required by today's Air Forces.

The Bulldog Military Basic Trainer is fully aerobatic and will perform the most demanding Air Force training operations. It can carry comprehensive instrumentation and avionics and is already being delivered to Air Forces in Europe, Africa and Asia.

So the Bulldog is aptly named. It is tough, reliable and exactly right for the job it has been carefully designed to do. These qualities make it a leader. And the Bulldog's lead is firmly held by Scottish Aviation, who are now climbing higher than ever. Right to the top, in fact.

Scottish Aviation Limited,
Prestwick International Airport, Scotland.

CHAPTER FOUR

BULLDOG RESCUE AND SALE

In December, 1969 the future for the Bulldog looked bleak and was going to depend very much on the outcome of the Beagle receivership. The Receiver, Kenneth Cork, took on the responsibility of managing Beagle so as to maximise the assets and achieve the maximum settlement for creditors. It would be his decision whether to sell the company either in whole or part or to close down any part that was unprofitable or unsaleable. Because of the unusual corporate status of Beagle and the fact that the Government had made it known that all creditors would be paid in full the Receiver's task was more straightforward but MinTech, on the other hand, representing the sole shareholder, played a very active part in the receivership process, particularly where the future of the Bulldog was concerned. The Foreign Office was also to play a major role in the fate of the Bulldog as it sought to minimise the damage to relations with the three countries, Sweden, Kenya and Zambia, to which Beagle had a contractual commitment. The Treasury was keen to see a solution to the Bulldog predicament which would not involve the Government in any outlay but, as it transpired, it was to be sorely disappointed as the solution to the Bulldog problem turned out to be very expensive.

It was soon clear that, having taken the closure decision to bring to an end the constant outflow of funds politicians had overlooked the consequences of the breach of Beagle's contracts with the armed forces of Sweden, Zambia and Kenya. Apart from the financial penalties damage would be done to the UK's prestige if a Government-owned company was seen to renege on international deals. It would have been prudent to have had a rescue plan in place for the Bulldog before wielding the axe. The order

for Sweden, by far the largest, would be the most problematical and the FMV found themselves in a highly embarrassing predicament as it had stood firm in the face of intense domestic pressure and insisted on the Bulldog in preference to the Saab MFI-15. It was quick to voice its concerns and to seek assurances that the British Government had some other means of fulfilling the contract. The Kenyan Air Force, with its comparatively small order for five aircraft was also quick to react. Only the Zambians, who had ordered eight, seemed fairly ambivalent, being more concerned that they would not lose the UK Government aid that was being used to pay for the aircraft. The three orders, for a total of 71 aircraft, were worth £743,000 even without the additional value of spares and support.

ORDER POSSIBILITIES

These three early orders were to have been the springboard that would bring the qualities of the Bulldog to the attention of other Air Forces around the world. Already talks were ongoing with the Australian Department of Air about a large order for the mid-1970s. 50 Bulldogs were required quickly by Canada to enable them to make use of available funds and this was significant as the UK was poised to sell Nimrods to the Canadians, a valuable deal that would be put at risk if the Government reneged on the

Bulldog contracts. The Royal Thai Air Force was also in talks about placing an order. The knock-on effect could affect deals with the Governments of Iraq and Iran, both of whom had purchased Pups and were potential customers for the Skyvan and Harrier. The Swedish made a veiled threat that they might have to adopt a policy of not to committing to any orders with UK companies that relied on any degree of financial support from the British Government given there were orders in the pipeline for defence equipment potentially worth almost £30 million.

MinTech was the Government department responsible for the management of Beagle's affairs with the responsibility for monitoring the day-to-day operations. It bore the ultimate responsibility for commercial decisions and was at fault in not making it clear to the Treasury that severe financial penalties would result from the breach of the three Bulldog contracts. Mintech should have had in place a means of isolating the Bulldog from the rest of Beagle and continuing production.

As the furore surrounding the Bulldog escalated the Government and the Receiver remained convinced of the need to find a buyer for Beagle as a going concern with no consideration being given to the possibility of saving just the Bulldog project and liquidating the rest of the company. It was always going to be a far harder task to find a buyer for the company as a whole

The Royal Canadian Air Force had a large fleet of DHC-1 Chipmunks and the Bulldog would have been a strong contender - but it was not available in time. *(RS)*

given that, prior to the Bulldog, the only commercially viable part of the company was the sub-contracting arm. Before the appointment of the Receiver, Beagle had been in talks with Ling-Temco-Vought, and, in Beagle's view at least, those talks were making good progress but the appointment of the Receiver brought those talks to an abrupt halt. The Receiver contacted every British aircraft manufacturer from the largest to the smallest who might be capable of putting together a serious bid and received a number of enquires, some more serious than others. Only two were to develop into anything meaningful - from George Miles and from Hawker Siddeley Aviation (HSA). Apart from the sub-contracting work, the Bulldog, with its potential for orders for 400 or more aircraft over the coming years, was the only asset of real value so losing the three Bulldog contracts would cause a significant decrease in the value of the company.

There was some brief optimism when HSA said it might take on the Bulldog providing it was protected against any financial loss and this brought it home to the Government that to stand any chance of getting the Bulldog built they would have to provide some form of financial assistance. HSA considered the only way the Bulldog would work for it was if it was built at Rearsby with Rearsby's overheads so they suggested that HSA might manage Rearsby as the Government's agent, initially perhaps for twelve months after which they would have a better idea as to whether it was worth continuing. Neither the Receiver nor the Government saw this as an attractive solution, not least as it would involve the Government continuing to absorb the day-to-day running costs.

Interest was not confined to British companies and one suggestion proposed a tripartite American-European-British association between the Government and a consortium comprising Piper and Messerschmitt-Bölkow-Blohm (MBB). Initially the Bulldog would be the consortium's sole project but in due course the programme would be expanded to include the products of the US and German companies. There would be advantages all round and the Government would get the Bulldogs built and Piper and MBB would gain a foothold in the British market. Both Piper and MBB had been in talks with Masefield in the weeks leading up to the receivership but the talks had foundered as the Government had refused to countenance any plan that involved it retaining any part of the equity or in providing any working capital. The consortium's new proposal was to create a new company with each of the three parties investing an equal sum to acquire the assets of Beagle. Working capital for the Bulldog would be provided by the Government, to be repaid from future profits. As the new proposal varied little from that already discussed with Masefield the same objections applied and the idea was swiftly rejected.

Among the companies that did not respond to the Receiver's approach was Scottish Aviation which was in the midst of one of its frequent financial problems and struggling to stay afloat after the failure of Handley Page left it with an unpaid £2.2 million debt.

ISSUES WITH MILES

With the rebuttal of HSA's proposals it seemed only Miles was sufficiently interested to take the discussions further. In fact it was two days before the Receiver was even appointed that George Miles wrote to Beagle advising them of his interest in acquiring the company, in whole or part. But, following the Receiver's appointment, there was reluctance from the Government and the Receiver to engage in discussions with Miles, although Miles's staff were given access to Beagle's financial records. Evidently the Miles brothers were seen as lacking sufficient substance to be taken seriously.

The Government and the Receiver had agreed a deadline for closing down Beagle at the end of December, 1969 and as that date approached, and with Miles seemingly the only party prepared to consider an offer on a basis that would be acceptable to both the Receiver and the Government, the Receiver proposed the liquidation of all the Shoreham assets whilst allowing the Pup and Bulldog work to be carried out at Rearsby until such time as either an offer could be accepted or the decision was taken to cease production altogether. The deadline passed but nothing changed and the Government continued to fund the outgoings into January. To reduce the running costs a large number of the workforce at Rearsby and Shoreham were made redundant and work on the Bulldog slowed.

Masefield then approached the Receiver, proposing to cut back Beagle to a level just sufficient to complete the Bulldog orders and continue the profitable sub-contract work. Taking the opposite line to the Receiver he wanted to close Rearsby and concentrate the Bulldog and the sub-contract work at Shoreham, giving up production of the Pup and the B206 altogether. He had not costed his scheme but MinTech estimated that completing the

The management of Beagle pinned its hopes on large scale production of the B.206 Basset for the RAF but, in the event, only a small order was placed and few were sold commercially. This is one of the RAF Bassets sold off to private owners. (RS)

Bulldog would incur a loss of £320,000 (a figure difficult to comprehend given the value of the Swedish order of £640,000). It can only be that it was recognised that there was still a lot of development work to do before the Bulldog could enter production. The fact that after SAL took over the Bulldog it took 13 months to complete development work before the first production aircraft was completed is proof of this. The Government found itself in a potentially tricky predicament. If it agreed to let Beagle complete the Bulldog orders it would highlight the fact that it had precipitously closed down the company without considering the implications. MinTech's forecast of a loss of £320,000 may have seemed large but it paled into insignificance when it considered the likely damages that the Swedish would be entitled to. Although a precise figure could not immediately be calculated as it was dependent upon which aircraft the Swedish selected as the replacement, it was evident that it would be much more than the loss that was forecast for Masefield's scheme. Early estimates came up with a figure of £730,000 if the Piper PA-28-180 Cherokee was chosen as the alternative. If Saab's MFI-15 was chosen the figure could be as much as £1,090,000 and for the SIAI-Marchetti SF260 it could be £1,350,000. There were also the damages due to the Zambians and Kenyans which, whilst comparatively minor, could still total £75,000. The magnitude of these figures demonstrates once again the complete absence of any consideration of the effects of the decision to summarily close down Beagle. By now, even if the Receiver found a manufacturer to complete the three contracts, some damages would still have been due to cover the loss of the deposit and the delay in deliveries.

DAMAGES ASSESSMENT

MinTech was appalled at the scale of potential damages and, in its panic, suggested to the Foreign Office that it might like to persuade the Swedish to waive their claim to any damages. It would be asking the Swedish to relinquish their contractual rights, absorb their losses and earn the approbation of their politicians and the public. This would be to enable the British Government to walk away unscathed despite it being the sole architect of the problem by making an ill-considered decision to cease providing funds to a company it owned. Furthermore, it was the threat of damages that was the FMV's biggest lever in their attempts to get the Government to take the Bulldog situation seriously. Needless to say, the Foreign Office declined to take up the suggestion.

Masefield persisted with his plan and, having realised the size of the potential damages, MinTech was prepared to listen whilst he refined his ideas. He was now proposing to continue Pup production up to c/n 250 (it presently stood at c/n 169) as well as completing the three Bulldog orders and keeping the sub-contract work going. MinTech revised its calculations accordingly and estimated that the loss would increase to £510,000, still considerably less than the likely minimum damages figure of £805,000. Although not part of Masefield's plan an alternative to continuing Pup production would have been to increase substantially the profitable sub-contract work. Each completed Pup incurred a substantial loss and would continue to do so until the break-even point was reached after many hundreds more had been built. Other than completing partially-built aircraft and using up stocks of parts there seems little point in Beagle prolonging the losses on the Pup. The supply of parts not already in stock would have been problematical as most suppliers would already have been owed money and would have insisted on these debts being paid before agreeing to any further supplies. Then they would, no doubt, have insisted on payment up front – or, at the very least, payment being guaranteed by the Government. The complexities of

insolvency law would probably have meant a new company would have had to be formed leaving the insolvent company in the hands of the Receiver but as the Government had by now publicly announced that no creditor would be unpaid, the only loser would be the one and only shareholder, the Government themselves.

Despite MinTech's concerns, the Receiver quite liked Masefield's refined plan but was worried that unless substantial orders for the Bulldog and the Pup were forthcoming before any RAF order, which was at least four years away, the steadily diminishing workload would affect morale and could result either in the departure of the skilled staff or a deliberate slowing of production to stretch out the completion of orders. Buyers of both types would have a genuine worry that, if Beagle only remained in existence for a defined period, it might not get the future technical support and spares they would need. But once again the Government had failed to grasp what might have turned out to be a workable solution and refused to sanction any scheme that would necessitate continuing Government finance. The Government's intransigence suggests that such decisions were being led by the Treasury rather than MinTech and there must have been a sense of frustration at MinTech that nothing other than an outright sale of the company was ever going to happen. Having reached this point MinTech felt that there was no alternative but to wind up Beagle and, on 13 February, 1970, advised the Swedish, Zambian and Kenyan Governments of this decision. It acknowledged that a means of building the Bulldog might still be found, but at that time there was no certainty that it would happen.

OTHER SUITORS FOR THE BULLDOG

Just as it seemed that Miles and Masefield were going to be the only parties preapred to make serious proposals, the Receiver received

A number of Chipmunk operators around the world were obvious customers for the Bulldog. One of those was Ghana, one of whose Chipmunks is seen here, who acquired 13 Bulldogs. *(RS)*

enquiries from two new quarters. Sport-Air, an American company based in Florida, was interested in taking on the Bulldog and the Pup, using Rearsby as its base. It was prepared to assume responsibility for the £210,000 deposit paid to Beagle by the Swedish and for the overdraft of £100,000. It was prepared to pay the Receiver £150,000 for the rights to the two types together with the jigs, tools, stock and work-in-progress. It anticipated it would take a further £800,000 to upgrade the facilities at Rearsby to enable production to adopt a modern flow-line system. This massive investment, totalling

£1.26 million, seen against the risks of the loss-making Pup and the lack of certainty of future orders for the Bulldog, suggests either a lack of commercial reality or an alternative agenda that was not being made apparent. Perhaps, wary of the offer, it was the Swedish rather than the Receiver who vetoed Sport-Air's proposal on the tenuous grounds that they did not like the idea of the production of the Bulldog being controlled from America.

The second approach was from Shorts. A team arrived at Shoreham from Belfast in February and included in the team was Tom Carroll who, until his resignation in

1966, had been Beagle's Chief Designer. Straight away Shorts made it clear that they were not interested in the Pup, seeing it as having no commercial future. It thought the price for the Bulldog in the Swedish contract was £4,000 under-priced, a judgement later borne out when SAL in due course raised the price by about this amount. It was even critical of Beagle's profitable sub-contract work claiming it was all short-term. It was clear to the Receiver that, despite having been sent a full briefing, the Shorts team had arrived at Shoreham woefully unprepared and without any real grasp of the situation.

At the beginning of February, 1970 the Piper/MBB consortium resurfaced but its fresh proposals differed very little from those already rejected in December and as it still involved continuing investment by the Government it suffered a similar fate. With Masefield's proposals no longer being taken seriously it was beginning to look as if the interest shown by Miles was going to be the only route to saving the Bulldog.

Most of the Bulldogs delivered to the Royal Jordanian Air Force flew in the red and white colour scheme but this one, RJAF.406 was painted in camouflage. After it was declared surplus it was sold to a private owner in France. *(Juanita Franzi)*

CHAPTER FIVE

SWEDEN – AND MILES

When news broke of the British Government's refusal to continue providing financial support to Beagle, Swedish officials were appalled that it had abandoned a company which, only three years earlier, it had set on its feet. They suggested that it was unwise for any Swedish Government Department to commit to orders with British companies that depended on financial or other support from the British Government and Swedish officials were told not to pursue negotiations with the British until the Bulldog situation was satisfactorily settled. Orders in jeopardy totalled nearly £15 million including £300,000 for cameras, parachutes, rocket propellants and tyres, £4 million for cluster weapons, £8 million for the possible purchase of ten Sea King helicopters and a possible future procurement of infra-red Linescan equipment for the Viggen, Draaken and Saab 105.

A delegation from the Swedish Air Board met with the Receiver and MinTech in mid-December, 1969 seeking an assurance that a way would be found to fulfil the Bulldog order but the Receiver was unable to go that far and could only tell them that talks were taking place with interested parties. Meanwhile MinTech advised Sweden, Zambia and Kenya not to cancel their contracts until the situation became clearer. The Swedes saw the decision to close down Beagle as political rather than commercial but the Government insisted Beagle was a commercial entity subject to the same corporate rules as any other company and, according to those rules, was insolvent. The Swedish took the view that the directors at Beagle had been appointed by the Government and had a duty to undertake the long-term planning and financing of the company. They saw Beagle as a Government-owned company and they had placed their order considering they were secure in the knowledge that the financial resources required would be made available.

The FMV continued to harass the Government for a commitment to complete their order and by the third week of January, 1970 was threatening to terminate the contract and seek damages but the Receiver could offer the Swedish no assurances. The Swedish continued to investigate alternative aircraft. Saab's MFI-15, fell far short of the Bulldog's specification and the basic MFI-15, priced at £8,000, would require extensive modification to match the Bulldog's specification including increasing the cabin volume and headroom, increasing the volume of fuel tankage, increasing the engine power, structural changes to permit increased weights at the required acceleration factors, inverted flight capability and other minor changes such as 28 volt electrics. The list constituted more of a complete re-design than modification and the cost of incorporating the changes would raise the unit price to £17,500, substantially more than the Bulldog.

The cheapest alternative aircraft was the Japanese Fuji FA200-180 but this too fell far short of the Bulldog specification and making the changes to meet the Bulldog specification raised the unit price from £8,000 to £14,000. Another expensive alternative was the SIAI-Marchetti SF.260, already in use by the Belgian Air Force, and, although this would require less extensive modification, the basic unit price of £14,000 would rise to £20,000. Timing was every bit as important and the MFI-15 was 18 months away from entering service (although the Air Force maintained it could be as much as two to three years), the SF.260 could be operational within six to nine months and the FA200-180 within 12 to 15 months. Consequently, the Swedish had little option but to continue to put pressure on the British Government and the Receiver to find a company willing and able to build the Bulldog.

During January and February, 1970 Miles' staff had continued trawling through Beagle's papers, poring over company accounts and carrying out stock checks and equipment inventories, prior to the making of a firm offer. The Receiver had made it clear that at this stage he intended only selling Beagle as a whole and was not prepared to consider breaking it up and Miles had made it

A strong contender in the international trainer market was the SIAI Marchetti SF260. The Belgian Air Force had a large fleet as illustrated by this four-ship air show team. *(RS)*

clear that he was prepared to buy the whole company. However, Miles had to find the money. Various Miles subsidiaries were producing products such as plastics, actuators, simulators, and electronics, but these were small scale operations. Finding the financial backing that Miles needed was at least partially resolved when Geoffrey Edwards, who had made his money as an agent for the British Aircraft Corporation and several defence equipment companies, came forward. Through his company, Strathaven, he was prepared to join forces with Miles to put together a bid for part or all of Beagle. To act as adviser and go-between he appointed Jim Charlton, deputy managing director of the International Management and Engineering Group, another of Edward's companies whose career had been spent largely at English Electric.

It was clear that a project such as the Bulldog would warrant some form of launching aid from the Government and Miles quickly put out feelers to the Ministry of Aviation whose response was encouraging and went as far as mentioning that a figure of £200,000 might be available. It was also confirmed that the Government would assume responsibility for the repayment of the deposit paid to Beagle by the FMV and the purchaser would be absolved from any responsibility for any additional costs that might be incurred through Beagle's breach of contract, including the damages for late delivery. By this time the Receiver seemed to have had a change of heart over his wish to sell the company as a going concern. He put it to Miles that he was prepared to sell the Bulldog project, the spares for the Pup and B206, and the sub-contract work-in-progress, for the sum of

£375,000. He intended keeping back the complete and partially-complete Pups and B206s in the hope that buyers could be found for these separately, either singly or in bulk. They did sell eventually although it took 18 months before the last aircraft was sold. As part of the deal the purchaser would be expected to take on responsibility for the service and support of the Pup and B206. It would get the leases at Shoreham and Rearsby although at Shoreham the lease would be for the buildings only as someone, most probably the Shoreham School of Flying, was in discussions to take over the airfield.

MILES CONTACTS WITH SWEDEN

Miles made direct contact with the FMV which conceded that it would not be averse to discussing a higher price per aircraft with whoever took on the contract but they said this knowing they would be able to reclaim any costs over and above the original contract price in the form of damages against the Receiver. The FMV also made it known that it would be prepared to discuss whatever detailed contract amendments Miles felt were necessary. Miles saw the Bulldog as a stand-alone project and produced figures that showed that, based on 100 units, the average build cost of each Bulldog would be £12,814 (excluding any profit) which was considerably more than Beagle's contract price of £10,565. The Ministry of Aviation came up with its own figure for the build cost of £14,190. Miles concluded that the Bulldog was a viable proposition and by offsetting the launching aid and the down-payment against the

outgoings, it would be cash flow neutral. For this to work there would have to be launching aid of £250,000 and the Receiver would have to accept an offer of between £200,000 and £250,000, payable in instalments, for the project. In response to the Receiver's figure of £375,000 for the whole company Miles told the Receiver he was prepared to pay £350,000. He attached two conditions to his offer; that none of the three existing Bulldog orders were to be cancelled and there had to be an assurance that eventually there would be an order from the RAF. Whilst able to concede that, so far as he was able to influence the other parties, the three contracts would not be allowed to lapse, neither the Receiver nor the Government could guarantee any RAF order. The Receiver, as well as insisting on an unconditional offer, imposed his own conditions. He now wanted to exclude the lease of the Rearsby site including the plant and equipment and part of the lease of Shoreham, namely the airfield, control tower and sufficient hangarage to accommodate a flying school. The lease at Rearsby would have been of no consequence to Miles but the restrictions on the use of Shoreham would have concerned him greatly as one of his prime intentions was to get back control of what he felt was his by right. For the Receiver to hamper his attempts to broker a deal to dispose of the company by introducing the potential stumbling block of the restricted use of Shoreham is difficult to understand especially as the occupation of part of what was primarily an industrial site by a flying school was a comparatively insignificant issue.

In the end, following the Receiver's rebuff and a further backtrack by MinTech on its previous statement that launching aid would be available for the Bulldog, Miles abandoned his bid. But the situation changed at the end of February, 1970 when, to the Receiver's undoubted relief, a new potential purchaser made an approach to MinTech.

The Swedish Air Force used the Harvard IIb as an unlikely liaison aircraft and it was to be replaced with the Safir. (SS)

CHAPTER SIX

THE DEAL WITH SCOTTISH AVIATION

In January, 1970 after Miles had made his unsuccessful offer of £350,000 for the whole company, he wrote to Dr Gordon Watson, SAL's Director of Engineering, to tell him how his talks with the Receiver had fared. His reasons for disclosing this information are not clear but SAL had acknowledged previously that, although it was not interested in any form of acquisition of Beagle, in whole or part, it would be interested in a partnership of some description should Miles be successful. Watson's rather downbeat reply was that he thought, wrongly as it turned out, the Swedish would not be prepared to renegotiate the Bulldog contract at a higher price nor, rightly, was there any likelihood of the Ministry of Defence confirming an RAF order in the foreseeable future. For these reasons SAL was no longer interested in any form of collaboration with Miles and, more tellingly, it would not be responding positively to any further approaches by the receiver. In the light of events shortly to unfold, it might be said that this last was a deliberate misstatement to mask the fact that SAL was, in fact, seriously contemplating taking on the Bulldog and was just a few weeks away from contacting the Receiver.

Only a few weeks after Watson had replied to Miles's letter, on 26 February, 1970 Jimmy Downey, the Under-Secretary Air at MinTech,

took a telephone call from Ranald Porteous, the sales manager at SAL to advise the Ministry that his company was interested in "accepting a contract" for the Swedish Bulldogs. Up to this point SAL had shown no interest in the Bulldog and the reason for this sudden change of heart is not clear but it is likely that the effects on the workload of the failure of Handley Page were beginning to be realised. No doubt rumours had reached Prestwick of Government aid being made available for the Bulldog and Downey confirmed to Porteous that any reasonable proposal for some form of launching aid would be considered. However, when Porteous said that, in the absence of launching aid SAL would lose £500,000 Downey immediately said the Government would certainly not look favourably on a figure of this size. Four days after that telephone call Porteous, accompanied by H W Laughland, SAL's Managing Director, called on Downey at MinTech's London offices on Millbank and explained that the failure of Handley Page would mean redundancies of between 350 and 400 out of a total workforce of 2,000 and taking on the Bulldog project would go a long way towards reducing this figure.

Its preliminary investigations of the Swedish contract had revealed

conditions that they considered onerous including the requirement to provide mandatory modifications for fifteen years, penalties for not meeting the performance specification, and penalties for late delivery, and that meant that it would cost £1.25 million to complete the contract. Given the contract figure of £640,000 there would be a shortfall of £610,000 to be paid either by the Government or the FMV but Downey reiterated that the Government would not contemplate providing assistance of this magnitude. He pointed out that it should view this as a project with a commercial future and any launching aid would only be in respect of the Swedish contract and in the form of a loan repayable by a levy on the sale of further aircraft produced after the Swedish contract had been completed. Once the Swedish contract had been completed it would be on its own and would have to make the Bulldog commercially viable. In what turned out to be a fairly accurate forecast, SAL estimated it could sell 400 Bulldogs in ten years. In parting, Downey suggested SAL looked at the potential earnings from spares and from the support of the B206s and Pups rather than just the Bulldog in isolation, but the meeting was constructive and in marked contrast to the obstructive

Scottish Aviation already had a good track record with the Swedish Government, having converted a number of ex-Royal Navy Douglas Skyraiders for target towing. One of these is seen here outside the hangar at Prestwick. *(RS)*

Nigeria received 37 Bulldog Model 123s and NAF238 (c/n 282), seen here, was delivered in 1974. It remained in service until 1990. *(Juanita Franzi)*

nature of the discussions that had taken place between Miles and the Receiver.

SAL moved quickly and within a couple of weeks its team, led by commercial director, David McConnell, had looked closely at the contract between the FMV and Beagle and put forward details of the amendments they would be seeking. Certainly the Swedish had no qualms about the involvement of SAL as they had worked closely with the Prestwick company in 1962 when SAL overhauled the Swedish fleet of Douglas Skyraiders. At this point, before any actual figures were discussed, the only point of principle that could be a possible stumbling block was SAL's insistence that the financial aid be in the form of a non-repayable grant rather than a repayable loan.

OFFERS ON THE TABLE

SAL's first offer amounted to £175,000 for which it wanted the manufacturing rights of the Bulldog, the Pup and the civil and military B206s (although at this point its intention was to build only the Bulldog), together with all jigs, tool, plant and equipment and work-in-progress. It was prepared to take on the support of all the Beagle types. The amount of launching aid that SAL had in mind was now £420,000 based on an estimated loss for each of the 58 aircraft of £4,000 plus £175,000 to cover the cost of the amendments

to the contract conditions. The deposit paid to Beagle would have to be paid over to them. Seemingly it had by this stage conceded that the launching aid would be in the form of a loan as it proposed repaying the £420,000 by a levy of £350 per aircraft from the 101st aircraft onwards. This was an indirect inducement for the Government to place an order for the RAF in due course. However, it was seemingly an unattainable goal as paying back £420,000 would necessitate selling 1,200 aircraft after completing the Swedish order. It would also have to pay the Government 5% of the sale price of all spares manufactured at Prestwick to Beagle's drawings. It was not interested in completing any of the partially-built Pups and B206s nor in buying any spares for them although it would be prepared to sell the spares on behalf of the Receiver. Production of the Bulldog would be at Prestwick which would incur substantial costs in moving jigs, tools, equipment and work-in-progress from Shoreham to Scotland. This transfer would also cost time and delay the start of production thereby increasing the damages to be paid to the Swedish by the Receiver. It was estimated that the transfer of the project to SAL would delay the delivery of the first aircraft by ten months but Beagle's contract with the FMV required the first Bulldog to be delivered to the SAF on 31 August

1970, just six months later, a date which was by now impossible. In fact it took SAL 13 months from date of order to supply the first Bulldog to Sweden so had Beagle continued in business and the Bulldog gone into production with them it would very likely have incurred substantial damages for failing to adhere to the contract delivery dates.

SAL's offer of £175,000 was half that of Miles and the main material difference was the exclusion of the sub-contract work from SAL's offer. Also, SAL did not require either of the leases of Rearsby or Shoreham but, being leases, they were of minimal value especially that of Shoreham which was nearing the end of its term and would soon need renegotiating. Why SAL chose to exclude the sub-contract work is not clear, given its profitability and the need to provide as much employment as possible at Prestwick to offset the Jetstream shortfall.

At this point, Miles returned to the fray and put in a firm offer of £250,000 for the whole of the Beagle assets, conditional on receiving launching aid of £300,000 to cover losses on the Swedish contract. The Receiver considered this attractive and "considerably better than that from Scottish Aviation", and recommended it be accepted. Miles was offering to buy the stock, work-in-progress and equipment and the title in the buildings erected by Beagle and

Miles at Shoreham, subject to the agreement of a satisfactory ground lease with the airport's owners. It also included the agreement of a direct lease with the airport's owners of all the buildings owned by them, the Bulldog aircraft and all work-in-progress and related items, Pup support operations excluding the work-in-progress necessary for the Receiver to complete current production, support operations for the B.206 and Basset and responsibility for the completion of partially-built Pup and B.206 aircraft on behalf of the Receiver. It also wanted the value of tax losses subject to the addition to the purchase price of 25% of the amount of such losses. The offer was made subject to the novation of the Swedish contract. To repay the launching aid Miles was proposing the Government would be entitled to receive a levy of £500 per aircraft on each aircraft sold in excess of 100, a figure arrived at bearing in mind the need to keep the price of the aircraft competitive to achieve the substantial sales abroad that Miles was banking on.

The Receiver had been especially adept at negotiating with both Miles and SAL simultaneously and undoubtedly each company thought it was the favoured bidder. However, the Receiver's problem was that neither company was seen as financially secure. SAL was in extreme difficulty and reliant for financial backing on its parent, Cammell Laird which was about to undergo a major reorganisation. Miles's lacked financial substance, so it could only finance a deal using outside finance of a somewhat suspect nature and the Swedish were increasingly concerned at Miles taking over the Bulldog because lease issues at Shoreham meant it might end up having nowhere to build the aircraft. The British Government too were wary of Miles and saw safeguarding jobs in Ayrshire as more politically beneficial than losing jobs in Sussex. For the Receiver the Miles bid was financially superior to SAL's and

Miles would not have to transfer equipment and documentation from Shoreham to Prestwick with the consequent five month delay. But, despite the Miles bid being the most favourable financially, in the end the Receiver decided that the SAL bid would be the better deal overall. MinTech must have gone along with the Receiver's decision and both must have felt that SAL stood a better chance of completing the three orders.

At this late stage Shorts reappeared on the scene but, given the political overtones always associated with Shorts, the Government seemed alarmed at its interest and reminded it that under the terms of the Government's partial buyout it was prevented from building entire aircraft. It also seemed that Shorts were seeking a quick profit from the Swedish order and had no interest in future sales. In the event, Shorts quickly withdrew.

The Receiver needed to consider the likely damages that might be imposed by the Swedish, although this was complicated by the unknown number of option aircraft for the Swedish Army. Accepting Miles' bid, the compensation would be between £140,360 and £152,735 and SAL's bid involved compensation of 163,050 to £284,550. The Receiver was authorised by the Government to negotiate the compensation figure and the Swedish began the process by asking for £230,000 as a once and for all settlement. The Receiver responded with an offer of £187,500 and a settlement was quickly reached at £200,000.

THE SCOTTISH AVIATION DEAL FIRMS UP

Settlement of the damages cleared the way for a deal with SAL and its offer of £175,000 was accepted, made up of £25,000 for the Bulldog rights, £50,000 for materials and work-in-progress, and £100,000 for tooling. Launching aid of £393,000 was agreed between the Receiver and the Government, and

the Receiver would pay this sum to the FMV together with the damages of £200,000. The launching aid would be passed on to SAL by the FMV together with a deposit of £204,000 that was to be lodged in a separate account and drawn on when required. The deposit would be subject to a bank guarantee and the whole contract would require a performance guarantee backed by Cammell Laird, a requirement that would subsequently prove problematical. A new company, Scottish Aviation (Bulldog) Limited (SABL), would be created with share capital of 100 £1 shares, 99 owned by SAL and one by the FMV who shrewdly ensured they had the right to acquire SAL's shares at par in the event of the failure of SAL or Cammell Laird. It transpired that the single share was not bought by the FMV but privately by a purchasing director of the Defense Materielverk. The Defense Materielverk was subsequently censured having been deemed to have acted incorrectly by participating in the formation of a limited liability company without the permission of the Swedish parliament.

The launching aid and damages that the Government were forced to pay out, totalling £593,000, is a measure of the folly of its decision to close down Beagle without an in-depth study of the consequences. Whilst it was quibbling with the Receiver about continuing to pay Beagle's running costs of £20,000 per week it laid itself open to paying a huge sum to extricate itself from the serious contractual mess it had caused. Whilst the £593,000 was a lot less than the £6 million that Beagle was asking for to enable them to stay in business, it would have gone a long way towards financing a 'minimalist' Beagle to complete the three Bulldog contracts and possibly continue thereafter with Bulldog production.

With all parties in agreement the way seemed clear for the contract to be signed and work to get underway but the Industrial Reorganisation

Corporation (notional owners of SAL's parent, Cammell Laird) emerged with the view that insufficient allowance had been made in the SAL/FMV contract for future increases in labour and material costs. Eventually through intervention by the Receiver and agreement with the FMV the final figure was increased by £20,000. SAL was now negotiating revised contract terms with the FMV. Most significantly the price of each aircraft was agreed at £17,820, a substantial increase on Beagle's figure of £11,045 and a measure of how much trouble Beagle would have found itself in had it proceeded to production. The revised price was based on adding the launching aid spread over 58 aircraft. In considering the FMV's willingness to accede to SABL's figure it has to be remembered that any additional cost incurred by the FMV would be recoverable as damages under the contract between the FMV and Beagle. Ten spare engines were to be included in the contract at £1,550 each. Without the launching aid the total value of the contract, excluding spares, would be just under £1,050,000. SABL agreed detailed amendments to the contract the most significant being delivery dates and lateness penalties and the supply of spares. SABL also acquired manufacturing rights for the Pup and the B.206 but, unsurprisingly, did not proceed with either. On 29 May, 1970, the Government confirmed that SABL had been awarded the contract for the Bulldog by the FMV and the task of transporting the jigs, tools and materials from Shoreham to Prestwick began.

THE ZAMBIA AIR FORCE ORDER

Back at the time in mid-1969 when the FMV contract was signed, Beagle had received two further orders for the Bulldog. Firstly, the Zambian Air Force ordered eight aircraft, worth £89,200, to replace its Chipmunks with delivery of the first two aircraft to be in the third quarter of 1970 and the remainder in the fourth quarter. Then the Kenyan Air Force ordered five aircraft, worth £55,750, to replace three Beavers and five Chipmunks used by the Kenya Flying Training School (FTS), with four to be delivered in the second quarter of 1971 and the last in the third quarter. The likely cancellation of these orders provoked differing reactions from the Zambians and the Kenyans.

While the Swedish officials maintained a courteous and sympathetic discourse with the British Government and the Receiver the Zambians were not so straightforward. They were uncommunicative and seemingly quite prepared to disregard diplomatic protocols by ignoring the contract that existed between their Air Force and Beagle and unilaterally sourcing a replacement for the Bulldog. In fact, the British Government was funding the Zambian's Bulldogs with a Defence Aid Grant so the money for the Bulldog was not their own. It seemed that the principle objective of British foreign aid was to dissuade emerging countries from turning to Soviet bloc countries for assistance.

To the Zambians the Bulldog was just another in the long list of British commercial misadventures. By closing Beagle with no regard to the contractual consequences, the British Government had ignited embers of growing dissent within Zambia for the British Government and British companies and the whole Bulldog episode was to have a major effect on international relations. Initial support for the Zambia Air Force had come from the RAF including the setting up of an FTS and Technical Training School but, by the end of the 1960s, Italy, Yugoslavia, China and the Soviet Union were also providing finance, aircraft and personnel. In 1970 the Italians were appointed to run the Zambia Air Force, a decision that had a heavy influence on future aircraft orders. Shortly before the Bulldog order was placed the Italians had provided Agusta-Bell helicopters and during the 1970s Chinese and Soviet influence was to grow with a proliferation of aircraft from these countries operated by the Zambia Air Force.

The Zambia Air Force attached great importance to its pilot training programme and concerns over violation of its airspace by Portuguese and Rhodesian aircraft prompted the rapid build-up of an effective Air Force. Any hindrance to this aim from failure of the Bulldog contract would be viewed very unfavourably in Lusaka and worsen the already delicate relations between Britain and Zambia. That the Zambian contract for the Bulldog was being financed through the British Foreign and Commonwealth Office Aid Budget made it a double headache. A Defence Aid Grant of £2 million had been made to the Zambians for defence equipment that included, as well as the eight Bulldogs, six Shorts Skyvans worth £650,000. The fact that the British Government owned a large stake in Shorts did not go unnoticed in Lusaka. What the Government had done to Beagle they could also easily do to Shorts. A 30% down-payment of £26,760, had been made to Beagle by the Crown Agents and the status of this payment in the liquidation process was uncertain, so, would the Crown Agents become just another Beagle creditor? As well as endangering the Skyvan order the Bulldog fiasco was putting at risk a potential future order for 12 BAC Strikemasters worth £2.8 million and other contracts for an HS748, and Rapier missiles. The Zambian's aggressive attitude soon became evident and its approach to the problem quickly hardened. The Defence Minister refused to purchase the Skyvan so the ripples caused by the Government's abandonment of Beagle were certainly growing larger and spreading further than anyone ever imagined.

The Zambians were soon in talks with SIAI-Marchetti about the SF260M and on 9 June, 1970 a telegram from Lusaka announced "Bulldog contract in course of cancellation through diplomatic channels." Ranald Porteous, anxious to avoid losing a customer, contacted the Air Commander of the Zambia Air Force to plead the case for the Bulldog but earned a rebuke from the Foreign Office for his efforts. Eventually, nine SIAI-Marchetti SF.260Ms were delivered to Zambia in 1970/71 and served in the flying training role until they were withdrawn from service in 1976. Ironically they were replaced with the Saab MFI-15-200 Safari. Zambia never did order any Skyvans although they did buy the replacement HS748 which was the last British aircraft it acquired.

BULLDOGS FOR KENYA

Kenya had also received assistance from the UK to establish its Air Force and this was reflected in its purchasing the Chipmunk, Strikemaster and Hunter. As with Zambia, political relations between the UK and Kenya were difficult but the Kenyan government took a more pragmatic stance and seemed prepared to await the outcome of the Receiver's efforts to find a solution to the problem. However, Kenya was becoming increasingly disillusioned with Britain and the West and was looking to form closer ties with the Soviet Union. A contract for six BAC Strikemasters, signed just a few months earlier, in October, 1969, and worth £1.662 million, was almost lost as a consequence of the Bulldog situation and only the strongest political pressure from Prime Minister Harold Wilson and a generous inducement of reduced charges for training prevented the cancellation of the contract. A potential order for four Shorts Skyvans was almost certainly lost as a consequence.

The initial order of five Bulldogs for the Kenya Air Force was only won after an exhaustive evaluation of the type against the Saab Safir. Perhaps like the Swedish, the Kenyans realised that the Bulldog would be the ideal primary trainer and they would have to wait to see if the Receiver could find a company to fulfil the contract. Eventually the order for the five aircraft was completed and the Kenyans patience even extended as far as permitting the aircraft for the Royal Malaysian Air Force (RMAF) to jump the queue. It was not until July, 1972, almost three years from placing the order, that Kenya took delivery. There is no record of any damages for late delivery having been paid by the British Government and such was the Kenyan's satisfaction with the type that nine more Bulldogs were delivered four years later.

The Kenyan Air Force had a batch of ex-RAF Chipmunks which needed replacement. Kenya eventually acquired 14 new Bulldogs. *(RS)*

CHAPTER SEVEN

BULLDOG TESTING AND DEVELOPMENT

In June, 1970 with the Swedish ski trials completed, the Bulldog prototype arrived back at Shoreham but no further test flying took place and, other than the airworthiness tests in July to renew the aircraft's CofA the aircraft remained in the hangar. Beagle's association with the Bulldog came to an end on 10 July, 1970 when John Blair, SAL's Chief Test Pilot, flew by scheduled service to Gatwick. He was collected by Judge in the Bulldog and flown to Shoreham where, later that day, he flew with Judge for a check ride. This was the last time Judge was to fly the Bulldog and it must have been a poignant moment for him as he walked away from an aircraft that he had been the first to fly and had nurtured through its test flying programme. It must have been obvious to him that the Bulldog was going to have a successful future, a success that he had already played no small part in, and now he was having to witness it being relinquished to another company. The following day Blair flew the Bulldog to its new home at Prestwick. The remainder of SABL's acquisitions followed by road.

John Blair served his apprenticeship with Blackburn and started his flying training with the RAF Volunteer Reserve (RAFVR) at Brough on the Blackburn B2 trainer, Hawker Hart and Fairey Battle. During the war he first served as an instructor in Canada and then flew Liberators with Coastal Command. He joined Scottish Aviation in 1947 flying as a captain on Scottish Airlines on DC-3s and civilianised Liberators. He transferred to production test flying in 1956 and in 1974 was awarded the Queens Commendation for Valuable Services in the Air and the R P Alston Medal for practical achievement associated with the flight testing of aircraft and his particular contribution to the development and certification of the Bulldog.

With its investment in the Bulldog, Scottish Aviation (Bulldog) Limited (SABL) acquired not just the production rights but also the two prototypes, the fully completed and flying G-AXEH and the partially-completed G-AXIG, together with a third airframe for static testing and all the jigs and tooling and the uninstalled components. The fuselage and wings of the second prototype had been largely completed by Beagle between June and October 1969, as had the fin, ailerons and flaps. The manufacture of the tailplane, elevators and rudder, and the final assembly was completed by SABL between October 1970 and February 1971. When the prototype arrived at Prestwick it was given a thorough inspection. Part of the team began defining the production build standard whilst the technical office looked at what needed to be done to complete certification. As Beagle had produced the first prototype by taking a Pup fuselage from the assembly line and modifying it, much of the design information that had arrived from Shoreham was in the form of numerous Design Office Instructions (DOIs) defining a whole range of changes which had been required to convert a Pup to a Bulldog. Not only had these DOIs to be converted to drawings of production standard but subsequent changes, instigated by SABL itself, had to be incorporated as well as the changes called for by the SAF. Fortunately, the Beagle drawing and modification protocols were to the SBAC (Society of British Aircraft Constructors) standard format making SABL's task more straightforward.

Accounts differ as to SABL's reaction to the Bulldog after their first appraisal. At the beginning of September SABL informed MinTech of their concerns about the technical claims made by Beagle regarding the Bulldog's capabilities. This is at odds

G-AXEH is seen here in its Scottish Aviation blue and white paint scheme with the SAL logo on its first public airing at Farnborough in 1970 where it put on an impressive performance at the hands of John Blair. *(PB)*

with the comments made by those at SABL who had been involved in the completion of the design programme and who paid tribute to the work done by Beagle to produce a fine aircraft, and especially to the painstaking efforts of Pee Wee Judge which resulted in the aircraft's exemplary handling characteristics. At pilot level, John Blair was always the first to give credit for the aeroplane to Judge. Although SABL did not regard the Bulldog design as finalised for production, very few changes actually had to be made to Beagle's original design. These were only minor changes, both to simplify production and to complete certification. The initial claim denigrating the aircraft's capabilities may have been more to do with SABL reserving their position with MinTech in case of future problems fulfilling their contract with the SAF.

One press article referred erroneously to the need for SABL to strengthen the aircraft to improve the stress loadings to meet the SAF's specification of +6g -3g. In fact, both prototypes were limited to +4.4g -1.75g at 2,150 lbs but this was a restriction applicable to the prototypes only and production aircraft were cleared to the higher figures without any strengthening work being necessary. In a letter to the author, John Chalmers, SABL's Head of Project Department, maintained that George Miles claimed to have designed the Bulldog and had used this claim to assert his right to the project. It was also reported that he was somewhat critical of SABL's capabilities.

The test flying programme was halted briefly in September, 1970 to enable the prototype to be displayed at the SBAC show at Farnborough, the first opportunity SABL had to showcase its new project. Sadly, this was to be the show at which Pee Wee Judge, who had flown the prototype in its early days at Beagle, lost his life in the Wallis autogyro. At the time of his death, Peter Masefield was negotiating to get Judge a job on the test flying team at Scottish Aviation.

The 31 minute first flight of the second prototype, late in the afternoon of 14 February, 1971, during which it performed faultlessly. *(DC)*

COCKPIT CANOPY ISSUES

One item that was taking up a great deal of the flight test team's time during development flying was the jettisoning of the canopy. There had always been conjecture as to the likely trajectory of the canopy after it had been jettisoned during spinning which was the most likely situation in which it might require jettisoning. It was essential to establish whether the canopy's trajectory might damage either the aircraft or its occupants. SABL had recruited Jim Waddington from Beagle who had been with G-AXEH from the beginning of its test flying at Shoreham and was present during the cold weather trials in Sweden. Waddington was seconded to the small team investigating the canopy operation. A series of physical jettisons, over a wide range of speeds, were carried out in the late summer of 1970 in the blower tunnel at Boscombe Down using the ex-Beagle fuselage mock-up modified by the addition of engine cowlings. The structure and jettison mechanism of the mock-up's canopy were updated to represent the installation on G-AXEH. When the canopy was closed it was retained by four spigots engaging with fittings on the lower rails, but when the canopy was partly opened it was retained on the lower rails and upper rear rail by shoes that could be released by withdrawing pins. During the blower tunnel tests the canopy was jettisoned by pulling on a cable that was attached to a loose socket slipped over the jettison handle. The sequence was filmed with a high-speed cine camera and the ejected canopy was caught by a trapeze wire to prevent

it falling to the ground at the end of its trajectory. The tunnel at Boscombe Down was powered by four Rolls-Royce Merlins and the noise produced at full speed was quite something. Test jettisons were carried out at various speeds from the Vne (the not-to-be-exceeded speed specified for the aircraft) of 178 knots down to 50 knots and with the canopy closed and partly open. The mockup was also set up at an angle of attack of 45 degrees and tested at a speed of 50 knots to simulate spinning conditions.

Most of the tests were successful and it was established that in normal flight attitudes and at speeds above the stall the aerodynamic lift on the canopy was sufficient to lift it cleanly off the rails. The trajectory in every case was sufficient to clear the fin even in yawed flight when the canopy tended to roll as it left the fuselage. At higher speeds the canopy developed a considerable amount of lift and the release from the aircraft was sufficiently violent to distort the canopy framing. The tests simulating spinning were less conclusive. The tunnel could not be tilted to the vertical and so the mockup was positioned nose up rather than nose down and when the canopy was released it simply slid down the rails until it hit the rear stops. However, it was thought from the results of the other trials that there was a good chance that the canopy would lift clear if the nose was pointed downwards as it would in a spin. However, most importantly, it was discovered that when the canopy was jettisoned from the partly opened position it was necessary to release the canopy nose first. When the canopy was partly opened the leak of air from

The Swedish Army operated this FPL61C (FV61066) which was delivered in October 1972. It was later transferred to the Swedish Air Force. *(Juanita Franzi)*

the cockpit destroyed the smooth airflow over the canopy resulting in much reduced lift as well as moving the centre of the lift rearwards. In this condition the canopy tended to lift tail first and immediately pitch nose down causing it to dive forcibly into the cockpit with the inevitable consequences to the crew.

The tests also revealed another problem which required the jettison mechanism to be modified. The handle had a double action, the first action unlatched the canopy but used all of the normal rotation of the pilot's wrist so the second action of pulling the handle down and aft to release the canopy from the rails was difficult to complete because the pilot's shoulder was constrained by the seat harness. The handle could not be used to push the canopy upwards as it just folded back to the starting position. Also, as the latch hook worked on the horizontal plane it was prone to catching the windscreen arch as the canopy left the aircraft. A redesign of the mechanism was obviously required. The latch hook was made to work in the vertical plane and designed so that, even if the canopy lifted early, the latch roller would kick clear of the windscreen arch structure. This also meant that the canopy could be closed by a simple slam instead of a slam and twist.

The jettison handle was changed to a simple lever rather like a car handbrake and it also incorporated a ratchet system so that it stayed

down when pulled and could be used to lift the canopy clear of the aircraft at the low speeds that would be experienced when the aircraft was spinning. The ratchet teeth were not evenly spaced but were positioned so that each part of the rigging sequence could be checked for timing by moving the handle to the relevant tooth position. The handle was retained in the up position by a shear pin to avoid accidental operation and to speed up the action as a determined force would have to be applied to shear the pin and start the handle moving. Also, a jacking claw was incorporated in the rear release pin to pull the canopy aft and off the lower spigots as the handle was pulled down. To meet the "canopy partly open" case, the timing of the withdrawing of the claw retaining pins was changed to ensure that the front of the canopy was released first so that it would always pitch up into the airflow. The canopy rails were altered to incorporate removable stops on the bottom rails and a cut out was added in the upper rear rail so that the canopy could be lifted off the aircraft in a fully rigged condition making servicing easier. There were other minor changes to the canopy seals and mechanism cables and the whole modified canopy installation was incorporated into the second prototype, G-AXIG, which was shortly to enter the test flying programme.

When G-AXIG joined the test flying programme testing could continue using an aircraft of virtually production standard. Unfortunately, the early tests with the canopy showed that there were still problems. When the canopy was closed after being opened a few inches in flight, the rear spigots failed to re-engage in their housings at the rear of the lower rails. It was realised that, as the canopy moved forward to within about an inch of being fully closed, the disturbed airflow reattached and the suddenly applied lift loads sprung the rear of the canopy to an increased width. As this situation meant that the canopy was not fully attached to the aircraft it would have failed to eject satisfactorily had it been jettisoned. The amount of distortion in the canopy was measured in flight and the problem was overcome by building the rear arch of the canopy about 1½ inches narrower than the nominal dimension. Nylon rubbing strips were added to the rear fuselage to force the canopy to the correct width when closed on the ground and the built-in force was sufficient to overcome the air loads when the canopy was closed in flight. It had still not been proved conclusively that the canopy would leave the aircraft cleanly in a spin and so G-AXIG was prepared for a series of tests. Although not keen to lose an expensive canopy, it was decided to see what would happen if the canopy was deliberately unlatched during a spin. Unfortunately, all this test achieved was to create confusion as to the best escape method. The centrifugal force of the spin caused the canopy to run back to the fully open position and then close again as the spin was stopped in the nose down attitude. This would present serious problems if the pilot was in the throes of leaving the aircraft when the canopy began to slide shut. The pilots asked for a hook to be added to the rear of the rails to catch the canopy and hold it fully open. However, it was argued that this was not foolproof and instead the problem was overcome by decreeing that the escape sequence, regardless of speed or attitude, had to be 'grab the handle – pull down fully – then push up'. The blower tunnel tests had shown that at speeds above the stalling speed and with the canopy closed the pilot would not have time to complete the action, the canopy would be gone before he had the chance to push the handle up. With this in mind, to prevent the handle catching in clothing or equipment as it departed rapidly, it was designed to be of small diameter and completely smooth. The finished production aircraft were subjected to a ground test where a vertical load was applied to the canopy to simulate an air load and the handle was pulled to prove the integrity of the jettison mechanism.

Vindication of the amount of time and effort spent ensuring the efficient operation of the jettison mechanism came shortly after delivery of aircraft to Sweden. Two SAF instructors went off to explore the aircraft's handling including spins. During a spin there was some confusion as to how many full turns were to be attempted and, as the aircraft continued to spin approaching the safety height above the ground, the non-flying pilot jettisoned the canopy which disappeared cleanly over the tail. The flying pilot recovered from the spin whilst restraining his colleague from climbing out. They flew back to base in a draughty aircraft and a short time later a call was received from a farmer who had found the canopy. There was only slight damage to the lower metal skirt that was easily repaired and only three new release shoes were needed before the canopy was refitted to the aircraft.

Unfortunately, there were to be quite a few cases of the Bulldog being abandoned in the spin but it appears the canopy departed correctly every time. It is not certain whether the canopy was ever jettisoned in straight and level flight although possibly there was one instance when it may have been released just before a forced landing. There was one case where there was a doubt about a clean release when two crew members had successfully abandoned the aircraft in a spin but when the aircraft was found in a field the canopy was still sitting on the rear fuselage. After talking to the crew and carefully examining the dents in the fuselage it was concluded that the canopy had indeed separated cleanly and then followed the aircraft down and parked itself back on the fuselage. This had been an escape at very low altitude and the crew were lucky to survive as their parachutes barely had time to deploy.

Wing static bending tests were completed in November, 1970 with loadings up to 9g being achieved and, by the end of 1970, SABL's production plans were ready for work to commence early in the New Year. Whilst the design team was busy 'productionising' the drawings, test flying was proceeding towards final certification.

THE SECOND PROTOTYPE FLIES

The second prototype, G-AXIG (c/n B.125.002), partly assembled by Beagle and completed by SABL, made its maiden flight on 14 February, 1971 in the hands of John Blair. The flight lasted for 31 minutes and was followed later in the afternoon by a second flight of 1 hour 16 minutes. A number of minor defects were reported, such as the cockpit noise level, but nothing of significance. G-AXIG was equipped to SAF standards and wore SAF colours with the spurious Swedish serial 61000 and code '5'. A team from the SAF arrived at Prestwick to carry out the final acceptance trials and, after a month of flying, the final modifications were agreed. There was little required in the way of aerodynamic

The second prototype, G-AXIG at Gatwick in June, 1971 en route to Paris and displaying Swedish, Kenyan and Malay insignia below the cockpit. (KB)

CHAPTER EIGHT

THE BULLDOG INTO PRODUCTION

The first Bulldog for the Swedish Air Force was the only one delivered with a full paint finish. (PH)

Bulldog production was established in one of Scottish Aviation's hangars at Prestwick, with the door clearly labelled "Bulldog Country", and 150 employees were involved directly on the production line with a further 250 in the machine shops and foundry as well as in the design offices. Production was phased in gradually to reach six aircraft per month. A full Type CofA was awarded to the Series 100 on 30 June, 1971. At 10am on 26 July, 13 months after the design was acquired from Beagle's Receiver and three weeks ahead of the contract programme date, the first two production aircraft, G-AYWN (c/n BH.100-101) and G-AYWO (c/n BH.100-102) left Prestwick for Manston, flown by John Blair and Angus Clydesdale, en route to Malmö where they were handed over to the SAF. That it took a year to finalise the design to a production standard, as well as incorporating the SAF's requirements, is a measure of the amount of detail work that was necessary. It was also in line with the delivery period that Beagle envisaged when it stipulated the first delivery date in its contract with the FMV. As the aircraft were owned by SABL until they were handed over to the SAF, they had to be British-registered as they could not be ferried out of the UK on a B Conditions registration. Only the first six aircraft for Sweden left the production line completed

operational standard. The remainder were delivered unpainted and with removable ferry avionics for the completion by the SAF.

SABL's numbering system used a Series number (the original specification Bulldog being the Series 100) and a Model number (the aircraft for the SAF being the Model 101). John Chalmers, Head of the Project Department, had wanted to designate the initial Bulldog as the Series 1100 and the Swedish version as the Model 1101 but he was overruled by the Technical Director, Dr Gordon Watson, who decreed that the Series 100 and Model 101 system be adopted. The Series 100 was built

for Sweden, Malaya and Kenya with c/n BH.100-198 being the last of the Series. For the RAF specification, and for all customers thereafter, the aircraft became the Series 120. Eventually the Series 200 project, with retractable gear and Lycoming IO-360 engine, was intended to evolve as the Series 2100 as the military version in the trainer/very light strike roles and the Series 2200 Bullfinch civil tourer. The sole Bullfinch built was designated BH.200-381 and is described later. SABL also planned a larger development of the Series 200 with a 300hp Lycoming IO-540 engine, which was designated the Series 3100 and, in 1981, there were plans for a Series 420/440 range, all with retractable gear and the IO-360 engine, to include the Series 420 two/three seat side-by-side trainer and the Series 440 two-seat tandem trainer. SABL's numbering system showed some inconsistency as it slipped between using four digits for some Series (Series 2000, 3100) and three digits for others (Series 420/440). Three digits were used exclusively for individual aircraft serial numbers (e.g. BH.100-101).

The typical panel layout of a Swedish Bulldog as seen on Fv61016, later SE-LLD. (PH)

CONTINENTAL
ENGINE PROPOSALS

Production Bulldogs were fitted with the Lycoming AIO-360-AIC engine rated at 200 hp. Rolls-Royce was planning to extend the range of Teledyne Continental Motors engines manufactured under licence at Crewe by introducing a six-cylinder Continental IO-360 rated at 210 hp. They were keen for SABL to adopt its new engine in the Bulldog and in February, 1972 they proposed that the Ministry of Defence authorise Scottish Aviation and Rolls-Royce to carry out a joint engineering appraisal of the feasibility of installing the Continental engine. Rolls-Royce had already contracted Miles Aviation (R & D) Ltd., which was carrying out design, installation and prototype flying of the 0-240 in a Cessna C150 Aerobat, for Reims Aviation to design and install the IO-360 in a Cessna aircraft. George Miles, with an eye on future development work, attempted to persuade the Ministry of Defence to insist on the Continental engine

but the advantages of the Continental over the Lycoming were not considered sufficient to warrant pursuing Rolls-Royce's proposal. Inevitably there would have been additional cost, delay and general disruption to SABL's production programme and the configuration of the engine would have compromised the cowling lines significantly. At this time SABL's Technical Director, Dr Gordon Watson, and John Chalmers, head of the Bulldog project team, entertained George Miles to lunch at the Waldorf Hotel in London. Miles's case was that an RAF aircraft should have a British-made (albeit under licence) engine and Chalmers wanted to make an issue of Miles's interference but Watson forbade it.

Although the Bulldog production line was predominately turning out the 58 Model 101 aircraft for the SAF there was still the other order inherited from Beagle, for eight aircraft for Kenya, to be fulfilled. However, work on the Kenyan Model 103 aircraft did not begin until early in 1972 with the first

aircraft ready for delivery in May. Before the Kenyan aircraft were begun the 15 Model 102 aircraft for the RMAF (which was the first order received directly by SABL), seem to have be given preference and were slotted into the production run after only 14 of the Swedish aircraft had been begun. Eventually the Kenyan aircraft were completed and, on 24 July 1972, all five were airfreighted from Prestwick to Kenya on Cargolux CL-44 TF-LLI.

By August, 1972, twelve months after the first aircraft had flown, the last of the 58 aircraft for the SAF had been delivered. In the meantime, the Swedish Army had decided to order just 20 of the 43 aircraft for which it had an option under the contract and work began on these immediately following the Air Force aircraft. The last of these was flown for the first time in January, 1973 thus finally fulfilling the contract first entered into between Beagle and the FMV three and a half years before in June, 1969.

An impressive lineup of Swedish Bulldogs at Ljungbyhed. *(LL)*

CHAPTER NINE

NEW ORDERS

Even after the appointment of the Receiver, Beagle had continued to receive interest in the Bulldog. The Royal Thai Air Force, with money to spend, had just bought 16 North American Rockwell OV-10 Broncos for use in the COIN role and was also looking closely at the Skyvan and at the Bulldog which could replace its Chipmunks. However, perhaps because of ongoing uncertainty over the future, it did not pursue their interest with SAL and, as with Zambia, instead ordered 18 SIAI-Marchetti SF.260s.

Although SABL's prime objective was fulfilment of the contracts already entered into by Beagle with the Swedish FMV and Kenya Air Force, foremost in the minds of the directors was the potential for further substantial orders. The Bulldog was unique in its class and was the only non-American primary trainer designed specifically for the purpose. Its attraction for Air Forces around the world had to be exploited to the full to justify the investment at Prestwick as well as safeguarding the jobs of the Bulldog workforce for as long as possible. The sales team was led by David McConnell, SABL's Commercial Director, who had been the principal player in the tripartite

negotiations with the Receiver and the Swedish FMV that led to the company acquiring the Bulldog. Ranald Porteous, who had joined SABL from Beagle as Sales Manager and then Marketing Director, began a campaign to bring in further orders. Porteous began by pursuing the Zambian Air Force in a doomed attempt to persuade it not to cancel the order for 15 aircraft. Inevitably many of the seeds sown by Porteous and his team fell on stony ground. But SABL cast the net wide and demonstrations were given to the Air Forces of Ecuador, Canada, Botswana, Ireland, Lebanon, Kenya, Ghana, Nigeria, Jordan, Greece, Saudi Arabia, Botswana, Singapore, Hindustan, United Arab Emirates, Chile, Denmark, and China.

It took SABL a year from acquiring the Bulldog rights to win their first firm order. In May, 1971 the RMAF placed an order for 15 Bulldogs, worth £320,000. Although production of the SAF's Bulldogs was the priority, for no lesser reason than that damages would be incurred for late delivery, the production plan was adjusted to insert production of the Series 102 Malaysian aircraft. This pushed back not only completion of the Swedish order but also the commencement of the Kenyan

Bulldogs. Manufacture of the Malaysian aircraft commenced with c/n BH.100-115 and the first two aircraft came off the production line in November 1971. All the Malaysian aircraft were dismantled after flight testing and taken by road to London Docks from where they went by fast ship to Port Klang (formerly called Port Swettenham) in Malaysia. They were then transported by truck to the Supply Depot on the old Sungei Besi airfield at Kuala Lumpur for assembly. Assembly took about a week and the first aircraft, FM 1220, was flown for the first time in its new environment by Angus Clydesdale of SABL on 24 January, 1972, accompanied by Squadron Leader Khong, the Chief Instructor of the RMAF Flying School. Clydesdale flew three times that day and the aircraft came through the tests with only minor snags. Each time it taxied out, the Bulldog passed Twin Pioneer FM1001, the first aircraft to enter service with the RMAF - which had originally been delivered from Prestwick 14 years before as G-APJT and was now grounded and destined for the RMAF museum.

The following day Clydesdale and Khong loaded the aircraft to maximum weight with fuel and baggage and took off at noon, in a temperature of 100° F, for the

The Royal Malaysian Air Force had 15 Model 102 Bulldogs. FM1221 was one of those withdrawn from service in 1990 and was passed over to the Kedah Flying Club at Alor Setar. *(Juanita Franzi)*

RMAF EFTS at Alor Setar, 300 miles to the north, where the Bulldogs were going to take up their duties as replacements for Hunting Provosts. The next four weeks were spent on conversion flying and ground instruction.

SABL, in common with most manufacturers, employed a team of flight test pilots who, besides production testing, supported the sales and marketing departments with demonstrations and pilot conversions. These would either be carried out at Prestwick or at the customer's base and could consist either of single flights or detachments. Almost invariably customer's pilots were given ground school training at Prestwick and awarded a Certificate of Compliance. Occasionally this aspect of training was truncated and pilots were cleared to operate the aircraft prematurely with the consequent decline in competence. One foreign team leader, having concluded training at Prestwick, wanted to carry out a formation flight of his five Bulldogs. Being short of a competent formation pilot, Len Houston agreed to take part and, flying over Ayr, he spotted opposing traffic heading directly towards the formation at approximately the same height. The formation leader seemed oblivious to the situation and so Houston called for an emergency break and the formation dived rapidly, pulling out almost at rooftop height.

The busy production line in the Bulldog hangar at Prestwick with 12 aircraft in various stages of build. *(GJ)*

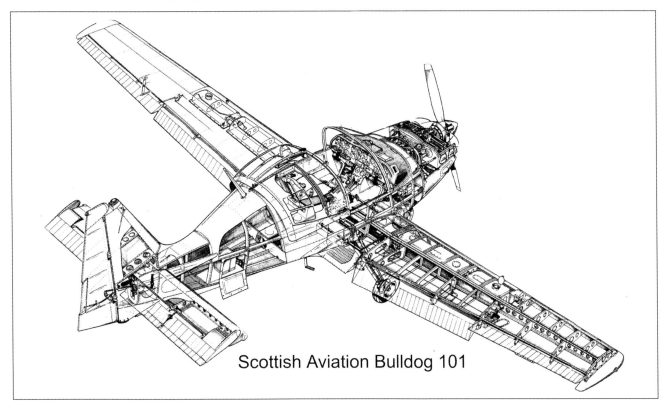

Scottish Aviation Bulldog 101

This cutaway drawing shows the structure of the Bulldog as delivered to the Swedish Armed Forces. *(FM)*

CHAPTER TEN

THE ROYAL AIR FORCE

When the Bulldog entered service in 1973 the RAF was about to undergo a major reorganisation of its flying training regime and the Bulldog was intended to play a prominent role. There had been, and would continue to be, three stages to pilot training – primary, basic and advanced. Flying training accounted for 50% of all the sorties flown by the RAF and about a third of all the flying hours in the RAF worldwide. It followed that a significant proportion of the cost of running the RAF went on flying training and it was imperative that the steadily rising costs were contained by improving efficiency without prejudicing standards. Entry into pilot training was by one of two routes – direct entry (i.e. those entering straight from civilian life), and graduate-entry through one of the University Air Squadrons. Of the two Groups within Training Command, No 23 Group, based at RAF Linton-on-Ouse, was responsible for primary and basic flying training of direct-entry students and the advanced flying training of all pilots, both direct-entry and graduate-entry. The RAF College at Cranwell had Group status and was responsible for the 16 UASs existing at the time, serving 46 universities and other degree-awarding establishments. The Central Flying School (CFS) at RAF Little Rissington, another establishment with Group status, was responsible for the training of flying instructors and also incorporated the Helicopter FTS.

Membership of the University Air Squadrons consisted of either RAFVR members who were undergraduates interested in flying who might in due course join the RAF, described as direct entry students, and RAF entrants sponsored through university under the Cadetship Scheme. Direct entry students were not commissioned and held the rank of Officer Cadet whilst RAF entrants were commissioned as Acting Pilot Officers, and paid as such, becoming Junior Officers in the RAF on conclusion of their university course.

The flying syllabus comprised 95 hours of flying over three years covering general handling, pre-solo and circuit training, instrument flying, navigation, formation practice, and low-level navigation. Aerobatics were part of the general handling component, hence the requirement for the Bulldog to be fully aerobatic.

Until the introduction of the Bulldog primary flying training had been undertaken in the de Havilland Chipmunk. Having been in service with the RAF since 1949, the Chipmunk, was nearing the end of its useful life. In its turn it had replaced the Tiger Moth as the RAF's primary trainer and initially it was allocated to the Oxford and Cambridge UASs and No 22 Reserve FTS. By the end of 1951 most of the University Air Squadrons and Flying Training Schools had been equipped and the last of the total of 740 aircraft that

passed through the RAF's hands was delivered in 1953. By the time the last Chipmunk was retired from the UASs in 1974 a substantial number had had to be withdrawn from service because of metal fatigue but, after extensive refurbishment, some were allocated to the Air Experience Flights (AEFs) where they were intended to stay until 1990.

The Chipmunk was currently used for the primary training of RAF Direct Entry and University Entrant pilots and Royal Navy Helicopter Specialist pilots. It was also used for cadet air experience flying, with the Army Air Corps (AAC), the Royal Naval College Flight and for a few miscellaneous tasks within Strike Command and RAF Germany. During the 23 years of service the Chipmunk remained fundamentally unaltered and only with an expensive refurbishment and upgrade would it be able to continue in service beyond the 1970s. Even then the Chipmunk would fall short of the desirable attributes and flight safety aspects of a modern primary trainer in a number of major respects. The RAF no longer favoured the Chipmunk's tandem configuration and the type was noisy, draughty, poorly equipped and lacking in sophistication. The gap between the Chipmunk and the aircraft used for the next level of training, the Jet Provost, soon to be replaced by the BAe Hawk, was a large one. In the late 1960s the RAF began the search for a new trainer, ideally one with side-by-side seating, a better avionics fit and some degree of sophistication.

NEW TRAINING REGIME

The existing training regime involved 30 hours of primary training flying during a six-week full time course at an FTS. For graduate entrants the training was

The Bulldog XX689 was originally delivered to RNEFTS but was transferred to the Central Flying School (CFS) in 1984 still with its original code "3". *(RS)*

This Bulldog, XX694, displays the un-military tail logo of East Midlands UAS. *(PH)*

spread over the student's three-year university course and a student would receive 95 hours of primary training with the UAS. The increased flying hours were necessary because of the discontinuity of the training. After primary training all students undertook a basic flying training course on the Jet Provost involving 145 flying hours for direct entrants and 120 hours for UAS graduates – fewer hours of basic training flying compensating for the higher number of primary training hours flown by graduate students. Thereafter students were streamed for specialist training depending on the type of aircraft they would fly at the operational conversion stage.

Under the new pattern of training the primary training would be omitted for direct entrants and the flying content of the basic flying training course would be reduced to 100 hours. As basic training on the Jet Provost could not be given in a university environment, graduate entrants would continue to receive primary flying training at their UAS and when graduates moved on to basic flying training it was anticipated that the flying hours on the Jet Provost could be reduced to 25 hours. It was also anticipated that when the Chipmunk was replaced with an up-to-date primary trainer a much larger part of the basic training of graduate entrants could be carried out whilst still at university.

The new primary flight trainer would also be needed at the CFS to train primary flying instructors. The task of providing preliminary flying instruction for future Royal

Navy helicopter specialist pilots would be carried out by the RAF on behalf of the Royal Navy at the Royal Navy Elementary Flying Training School (RNEFTS) attached to CFS and the new primary trainer would also fulfil this role. The less demanding air experience role would continue to be carried out by suitably refurbished Chipmunks although some Bulldogs serving with UASs shared their role with AEFs.

To be able to meet the requirements of these new training regimes the primary trainer of the future would have to possess five essential characteristics. It would have to have a better rate of climb so as to increase productivity, it would have to have a side-by-side seating configuration to provide direct supervision by the instructor and it would have to be more manoeuvrable and have a better aerobatic capability to enable more demanding aspects of flying to be demonstrated and practised. It would require an avionics fit that would permit safe operation in the

changing air traffic environment and, in common with most service aircraft, it would have a tricycle undercarriage to improve landing and taxying qualities in high winds and crosswinds.

When the Bulldog entered service with the RAF Training Command in 1973 it was one of three new types introduced that year as part of the strategy to re-equip the Command with up-to-date types. Whilst the Bulldog would take over from the Chipmunk in the primary training role, the Scottish Aviation Jetstream T.1 would supersede the Varsity as the navigational trainer and the Westland Gazelle HT.2 would replace the Sioux and Whirlwind for rotary training. A fourth type, the Hawker Siddeley (BAe.) Hawk T.1 would enter service in 1976 to replace the Jet Provost.

Beagle Aircraft was building the B121 Pup 150 and several foreign air forces had shown an interest in it as a military trainer. In March, 1968, at the request of MinTech, A&AEE undertook a preview assessment of the Pup 150 as a potential primary trainer for the RAF. Using G-AVLN (c/n B121/004), the trials took place at Beagle's base at Shoreham and the report concluded that the Pup-150 was a well-designed sporty little aircraft with very pleasant handling characteristics and well harmonised controls. The company was already addressing the minor criticisms that the trials raised and it was suggested

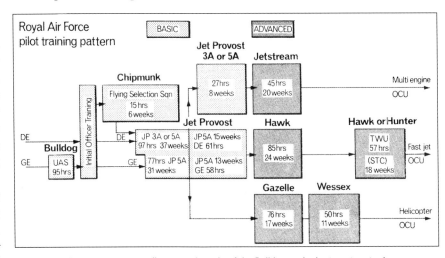

The RAF's pilot training pattern illustrates the role of the Bulldog as the basic trainer in the new system.

XX517 is one of the RAF's Model 121 aircraft and was delivered in April, 1973. Shown here in service with CFS it also flew for the Royal Navy Elementary Flying Training School. *(Juanita Franzi)*

that a clamshell or sliding canopy could be fitted in place of the side doors. At this time Beagle was in the process of installing a 200 hp engine in the Pup-100 prototype to assess the effects of the more powerful engine on handling and performance. This was a prelude to the introduction of the military Pup, the B121T, which had been envisaged when the Pup range had first been mooted. No doubt Beagle would have taken the opportunity of showing the team from A&AEE the mockup of the B121T.

The Army too was showing an interest in the Pup-150 as they also sought a replacement for its Chipmunks. In February, 1969 G-AVLN was delivered to the Army Aviation Centre at Middle Wallop for evaluation. The AAC was aware that the Bulldog prototype was nearing completion and was just a few months from flying. The Bulldog was of greater interest to them but they were happy to assess the suitability of the Pup-150 as an

elementary trainer. At the same time it would look closely at the specification for the Bulldog to see how it would improve on the Pup. Like the RAF, the Army found the Pup-150 to be a great improvement on the Chipmunk. It was more comfortable, easier to land and taxi, possessed superior aerobatic and spinning performance, had a higher cruising speed, and had the all-important side-by-side seating. Like the RAF, it too felt the Bulldog when it appeared would be a much better aircraft for its needs.

RAF DEMONSTRATIONS

Only a few days before the decision was taken by MinTech to withdraw financial support from Beagle, Pee Wee Judge was busy demonstrating the prototype to potential customers. On 24 November he flew, accompanied by Eric Greenwood, Beagle's head of military sales, to CFS at Little Rissington to show the aircraft to

officers of the Examining Wing. He made four flights, with the Wing Commander, two Squadron Leaders and one Flight Lieutenant from the Wing. One of the Squadron Leaders was writing the RAF's new flying training syllabus and, much as the Statement of Requirement for the Anson replacement had been written around Beagle's contender for the order, the Basset, so the new flying training syllabus was being written around the Bulldog. Judge made sure he operated with a full fuel load, with only one refuelling being required at lunchtime, to demonstrate that, despite being fully equipped and instrumented, the Bulldog was still capable of aerobatics within the aircraft's maximum all-up weight, and was pretty lively with it. Many light aircraft, including the Pup, had to restrict the fuel load to be capable of aerobatics with two up. The RAF had been looking at the Victa Airtourer 150 but was critical of its inability to spin (it went into a spiral dive with rapidly increasing airspeed and a risk of damage to the airframe with full up elevator and rudder full on) as well as its poor cockpit layout, central control column, and imprecise elevator trimmer. By comparison, the CFS staff were impressed with the Bulldog, appreciating its classic handling. They were especially taken with its spinning characteristics which fitted in perfectly with current training techniques, with the slight tendency

The Beagle Pup G-AVLN was used for evaluation by the Army Air Corps. *(MA)*

for the rate of rotation to speed up during recovery providing evidence to the pilot that recovery was under way.

The day after the visit to the CFS two officers of the Royal Australian Air Force arrived at Shoreham to be shown the aircraft. One, Squadron Leader Dunn, was on the staff of the CFS and a member of the Red Arrows display team and was shortly to take up his duties as Chief Flying Instructor at the RAAF Central Flying School. The other visitor was an engineering officer. Squadron Leader Dunn flew with Pee Wee and was given the "full treatment". Judge always emphasised that the Bulldog was not a "tarted up" light aircraft but had been developed as a military primary trainer. Three days later, it was the turn of the Iraqi Air Force when the CFI of its Primary Flying Training School, accompanied by an engineering officer, arrived at Shoreham to look at the Bulldog and the Series 5 Pup as potential replacements for its Provosts and Chipmunks. Whilst Ben Gunn, a Beagle demonstration pilot and member of the sales team, took the CFI aloft in the Bulldog, Judge flew Pup G-AXDU with the engineer and then they swapped passengers. Inevitably, of the two aircraft the CFI was most impressed with the Bulldog especially its performance, constant speed propeller, excellent visibility and useful disposable load. However, both officers were disconcerted to learn that the Bulldog would be using an American Lycoming engine and expressed concerns that they would be left exposed if at some time the Americans were to cut off supplies of engines or spares to the Arab countries.

The appointment of the Receiver did not prevent the RAF from carrying out Preview Handling Trials at Shoreham on 22 and 23 December, 1969 with the intention of making a brief handling assessment at representative training loading. The trials took place only a few weeks after the Receiver's appointment, and had no doubt been arranged some time before. So, by the time the report was published, it was looking likely that production of the Bulldog was to be continued by SABL and therefore the outcome of the trials was felt to be of relevance. Ironically, had this rush of interest and enthusiasm for the Bulldog by the RAF occurred several months earlier it may have made the outcome of the Government's decision to withdraw support for Beagle somewhat different.

The report of these trials compared the Bulldog with the Preview, Performance and Handling Trials of the Pup-150 carried out by A&AEE in March, 1968. A letter from A&AEE Boscombe Down to MinTech of 5 February, 1970 reported that

"The overall impression of the aircraft was most favourable, and in our view it is well suited to the military training role. No handling problems were encountered and the handling characteristics were even better than those of the Pup. The aircraft was easy to fly while providing scope to achieve precision. Ground handling was excellent, pedal forces being lighter than on the Pup. Stability and control were good about all axes. Stalling tests showed that the controls were effective throughout and recovery was prompt. The aircraft could be made to spin more easily than the Pup and the rate

of rotation, though fast, was acceptable in view of the stable nature of the spin. Aerobatics were if anything better than on the Pup due to the clear view canopy, constant speed propeller and larger rudder. Recommendations are made for improving the cockpit layout."

On engineering matters, the report concluded that Beagle had taken advantage of experience with the Pup and improved items such as the brakes and the fuel tanks. There were still some items to be addressed and it was recommended that an operational reliability trial be undertaken together with canopy jettison tests. These latter tests would eventually involve SABL in considerable head scratching before they were satisfactorily concluded. The Bulldog was a competent primary trainer which enabled the student to acquire the basic techniques of flying. Apart from its constant-speed propeller it was a relatively unsophisticated aircraft with a fixed undercarriage and a minimal avionics fit. As such there was a considerable gap between the Bulldog and the Jet Provost or Hawker Siddeley Gnat basic trainers which the students would be flying on the successful completion of their primary training - albeit the gap was going to be smaller than when the Chipmunk was the primary trainer. In 1972, before the Bulldog entered service, the RAF was already looking for ways of reducing this gap with an upgraded Bulldog with improved avionics and a retractable undercarriage.

For SABL the jewel in the crown was always going to be the order for the replacement of the RAF's Chipmunks. The negotiations with Beagle's Receiver to take on the Swedish contract had been conducted very much with this potential order in mind. The Swedish order was an excellent launch pad but it was the RAF that would provide the means of turning the venture into a profitable enterprise. In its customary fashion the RAF was uncertain how to proceed. It had been operating about 200 Chipmunks as the ab

The Australian-built Victa Airtourer was one of several types considered by the RAF as a Chipmunk replacement but it was quickly pronounced unsuitable. *(RS)*

initio trainer, for the UASs and AEFs. A review of flying training had concluded that, until the Hawk entered service, the Jet Provost would have to remain in service because the gap was felt to be too great between the Bulldog, or whatever the next primary trainer was to be, and the Gnat and Hunter advanced trainers. By 1970 the Chipmunk had been in service for 20 years and, although it was thought to have a further ten years of service life, it would require expensive refurbishment and other improvements. The figure of £7,500 per aircraft was put forward as the likely cost of refurbishment plus an additional £4,500 for modernisation - a total of £12,000 when the cost of a new fully-equipped Bulldog was over £20,000, including spares.

RAF BULLDOG ORDER

The Long Term Defence Plan Costings made provision for 323 aircraft of the Bulldog type to be delivered from 1980/81 onwards. An alternative plan bringing delivery forward by five years was for 242 aircraft for delivery from 1975/76. However, at this early stage SABL had concerns that, given its other commitments, it would not be able to have aircraft ready for delivery that soon. The Preview Handling Trials which took place at the end of December, 1969 were very brief, lasting just two days, and intended only as a preliminary assessment of the aircraft's capabilities. Between 26 October and 17 November, 1971 the second prototype, G-AXIG, underwent more comprehensive trials at A&AEE. These trials, which comprised 32 sorties totalling 35 hours 5 minutes flying, covered the practical CofG range and the design flight envelope and included night and instrument flying. The report of these trials, (AAEE/963) said

"The results confirm the favourable opinion gained during the preview and it is considered that the Bulldog is extremely well suited to the military primary training role. The aircraft, although very easy to fly, required some degree of skill to achieve

The Sportavia RF-5 was briefly evaluated by the RAF for use by the Air Experience Flights. *(RS)*

precision. This and the need for positive spin entry were features liked in a primary trainer. The test aircraft for these latest trials differed from the first prototype used in the preview trials thus: A1B6 Lycoming installed instead of the A1C as the A1C had a rotational speed restriction for the engine/propeller combination, longer exhaust stack, a flat base on tip of rudder to accommodate the optional relocation of the anti-collision beacon, trailing edges of the wing centre sections had been re-shaped to follow the taper of the trailing edges of the outer wings."

Despite the favourable reports from A&AEE for the two trials, there was still indecision on the part of the RAF, which was still insisting that an order for the Bulldog was not a foregone conclusion. However, as the Swedish had found following the collapse of Beagle, in reality there was little choice. Indeed, when the Central Flying School looked at the prototype Bulldog at Shoreham in November, 1969 it pointed out that the new flying training syllabus was being written with the use of the Bulldog in mind. Following the appointment of the Receiver at Beagle the Ministry of Defence considered the feasibility of buying up all the Pup-150s in various stages of completion, which it was presuming would otherwise be scrapped. It was thought that this option might be cost-comparable with the refurbishment and modernisation of the Chipmunk. The Pup-150s, of which about 60 would be required, would be used by the University Air Squadrons and Air Experience Flights. Other alternatives for the AEF role had

been considered, including the Fournier RF5, being marketed by Sport-Air for about £4,800 – 6,000, depending on equipment, and the Scheibe Falke motor glider costing £3,758.

On 23 November, 1971 Anthony Barbour, the Chancellor of the Exchequer, announced in the House of Commons that over 100 Bulldogs would be ordered for the RAF. At the beginning of December it was confirmed that the Bulldog had been selected by the RAF for the UAS and AEF requirements. The order, for about 130 aircraft, would be worth more than £1.5 million. The first 60 aircraft would be required in 1973 and the balance in 1974.

Air Staff Requirement 401 (ASR401) was issued on 15 August, 1972, for a 'Primary Pilot Training Aircraft,' to be followed shortly by Specification No 282 which was entitled "Bulldog Series 100 Model 104 Primary Pilot Trainer." The designation 'Series 100 Model 104' would have been the next in the Series 100 sequence but, subsequently, the differences between the Series 100 and the RAF's specification were considered sufficient to warrant the new designation of 'Series 120'. The RAF aircraft became the Series 120 Model 121 and the Series 100 Model 104 designation was reallocated to the civilianised second prototype, G-AXIG. Although G-AXIG, had been built to SAF standard it was subsequently re-equipped with an instrument layout representative of the Malaysian and Kenyan aircraft and, most importantly, for the potential

RAF order. Specification No 282 required the aircraft to be constructed and equipped to the standard of the Series 100 Type Specification as amended by the requirements of the Ministry of Defence. These requirements were driven partly by the general requirements for service aircraft and partly by specific requirements for the Bulldog in its role as a fully aerobatic trainer. Compliance with the requirements of the Ministry of Defence specification resulted in an aircraft with significantly different details to the Series 100.

ASR 401 acknowledged that the evaluations carried out at Boscombe Down and CFS had shown that the Bulldog would be eminently suitable for the RAF tasks. It also stated that no other British-built aircraft would fulfil the requirements and that no other aircraft had been given serious consideration. Of the 200 Chipmunks currently employed by the RAF, 129 were used for training. Under the new training regime, with direct entry students commencing training on the Jet Provost, the primary flying element of No 2 FTS at RAF Church Fenton would be phased out, thereby reducing the overall number of aircraft required. It was calculated that, on a one for one replacement basis to meet the needs of the UASs, the CFS, RNEFTS and the miscellaneous role requirements of Strike Command and RAF Germany, a total of 132 Bulldogs would be needed. The target date for delivery of the first Bulldog was set as April, 1973 and the last during 1974/5.

At the time the ASR was issued Treasury approval was obtained for a total unit aircraft cost of £20,300. This included an allowance for avionics, for which there was no standard fit, and a fatigue meter. Allowing for inflation the unit aircraft cost at June, 1972 was forecast as £21,180. These were Ministry of Defence figures, not the company's and SABL's quotation was not expected to be received until the end of 1972 but it was anticipated that it would not be substantially different from the

As with he RF-5, the Scheibe Falke was a possible contender for the Air Experience Flights but it was felt that a motor glider would not give the same flight experience as a traditional powered aircraft. *(RS)*

Ministry's estimates. Based on the Ministry's figures, by the time the last Bulldog had been delivered, the order would have cost £4.46 million (approximately £70 million at 2018 prices). In a little over two years since SABL had renegotiated the unit aircraft cost in the contract for the SAF the figure had increased by 50%.

FIRST RAF BULLDOG FLIES

The first flight of the first RAF aircraft, XX513 (c/n BH.120-199), was on 30 January, 1973. In a ceremony on 12 February this first RAF Bulldog was handed over ceremonially by the Duke of Hamilton, SAL's President, to Air Vice-Marshall Cook at Prestwick. XX513 went first to Boscombe Down for trials and assessment before being attached to the Southampton University Air Squadron.

Between March and August, 1973, A&AEE carried out CA Release Handling and Performance Trials at Boscombe Down using XX513 for the majority of the flying but with spinning trials carried out on XX526, XX529 and XX536 with XX529 also being used for night flying trials. XX513 had completed 14 hours of flying before its arrival at Boscombe Down. Apart from cockpit lighting, the aircraft was to full production standard. A modification (Mod1) incorporating a strake over the leading edge of the flaps was

introduced part way through the test programme. This was because it had been discovered during production flight testing at SABL that some aircraft showed a tendency to roll markedly when flaps were moved to the fully down position. Investigations showed that this was due to premature asymmetric separation of the airflow over the flaps just before the flaps reached the fully extended position. Modifications to cockpit lighting were also incorporated and evaluated on XX513 and XX529.

After completion of the Release Trials and the issue of the CA Release Recommendations, a report was received from the Service that two aircraft had exhibited unsatisfactory behaviour during spins. In one incident a high rotational rate steep-attitude spin had developed from a normal entry. In the second incident the rate of rotation had increased and the aircraft had shown a reluctance to recover using normal recovery action. The two aircraft were flown by A&AEE pilots to establish the reason for the unusual behaviour. They found that it was possible consistently to reproduce a high rotational rate unstable condition during the spin if a delayed entry technique was used. Instead of full rudder followed smartly by elevator the rudder would be applied slowly. The resulting unstable spin could be disorientating but in every case it

Bulldog XX529 was one of the Bulldogs used for evaluation of the type's cockpit lighting. *(RS)*

The Bulldog XX700 was repainted in an experimental grey camouflage scheme. It is seen here at Wyton in May, 1981 but the proposed paint scheme was not adopted. *(RSh)*

reverted to a normal spin after one to three turns and recovery was not affected. The likely cause of the delayed recovery was thought to be the pilot's failure to maintain full pro-spin rudder during the spin. As a result of these additional trials additional advice on spinning was incorporated in the Aircrew Manual.

Production for the RAF continued steadily throughout 1973, at one stage reaching six aircraft per week, with breaks to accommodate the five aircraft ordered by the Ghana Air Force and the 20 for the Nigerian Air Force. XX525 (c/n BH.120-211) took part in the Paris Air Show in 1973, flying non-stop from Prestwick to Le Touquet, and in 1974 it was the turn of XX522 (c/n BH.120-208) to appear at the Hanover Air Show.

The resolution of engineering issues encountered in service was an ongoing process and testing and modifications were a normal occurrence. From January, 1977 through to 1980 SABL pilots were carrying out empennage fatigue measurements involving 45 hours of flying over 37 flights. Other tests looked at the potential for crank case cracking in the Lycoming IO-360 engine which resulted in the engine mounts being modified to counter any risk of vibration-induced cracking. There had been instances of engine stoppages in the spin and tests were carried out to establish a cause. Tests of specific issues such as these would have resulted from concerns raised by the engineering department of a particular user and the information gleaned would have been disseminated through the entire Bulldog fleet. SABL also carried out testing on their own behalf to explore other uses for the Bulldog such as banner towing and the use of smoke generators for display flying.

In 1974 the first prototype, G-AXEH, was fitted with a three-bladed Hoffman metal propeller to see if this would produce a better performance. In July the aircraft was flown to Germany and returned with a three-bladed wooden propeller which was also fitted to

the Nigerian Air Force's G-BBPD (c/n BH.120-280). The Swedish Army was known to have carried out trials of a Hoffman three-bladed propeller but the outcome was not known. It was established that there was insufficient improvement in performance with a three-bladed propeller to justify the additional cost.

By the end of 1976 the first prototype was nearing the end of its useful life and it was due for its CofA renewal which, because of its non-standard background at Beagle, was not going to be straightforward. So the aircraft was grounded and in January, 1978 was used by the Ghana Air Force as an instructional airframe for ground engineers. By November that year it was withdrawn from the register bringing to a close a career lasting almost nine years during which it had formed the backbone of the test programme and it was donated to the National Museum of Flight at East Fortune.

Unlike the Basset, the only other Beagle-conceived aircraft to enter military service, the Bulldog was well respected and highly thought of by the RAF. Serviceability was never an issue and the aircraft was considered highly suitable for the task it had to perform. The RAF Bulldogs reached the end of their service life in 1989 and, over the next 11 years, they were all struck off charge and put up for sale on the civil market where they found willing buyers.

The Bulldog prototype, G-AXEH was fitted with a three-bladed Hoffman propeller but the performance improvement was negligible. *(DC)*

CHAPTER ELEVEN

THE FINAL BULLDOG ORDERS

With the RAF order well in hand it was important that new orders materialised in time to prevent the production line from slowing and in March, 1973 it was announced that the Ghana Air Force had ordered six Model 122 aircraft, worth over £200,000 with spares, for delivery by the end of June. The last aircraft was completed in July, 1973 and all the aircraft left Glasgow Docks for Ghana. A second order from Ghana, for a further seven Model 122A aircraft, was received in October-December, 1975 and these aircraft were ferried rather than shipped. They were fitted with a ferry tank modification which provided just over 50% additional fuel which greatly benefited the planning of routes and provided extra assurance and greater flexibility. Without the ferry fuel tank a typical route, Prestwick to Takoradi, Ghana, would have taken 43 flying hours over 20 legs but with the tank fitted a typical route, Prestwick to Nairobi, Kenya, took 45 hours flying time over just 12 legs.

Just two months after receiving the order from Ghana, the Nigerian Air Force ordered 20 Model 123 Bulldogs, worth £750,000, with delivery of the first aircraft in October and the final aircraft in March, 1974. The aircraft were ferried via Gatwick in January, 1974 by West London Air Charter, one of whose pilots, Janet Ferguson, had originally ferried B206s for Beagle including the three aircraft for the Royal Flying Doctor Service of Australia. Many of the Bulldogs were ferried under contract with ferry companies and flights were led by an experienced ferry pilot, such as Janet Ferguson, who were used to navigating and dealing with the issues of refuelling, diplomatic clearances, and terrain. The flights were organised in groups of three aircraft flying in loose formation. On one delivery flight, in G-BBJM (c/n BH.120-262), Janet Ferguson was on the downwind leg of an approach to Bathurst in The Gambia, when a buzzard struck the right wing. She landed safely and subsequently flew the Bulldog on a further 400 miles to Freetown, Sierra Leone, with the aircraft handling satisfactorily despite wing displacement and leading edge damage - which was a testament to the Bulldog's strength. At Freetown the aircraft was declared unserviceable and a replacement wing was sent out.

The first three Nigerian Bulldogs arrived at Kaduna on Monday 4 February, 1974. They had suffered frustrating delays on the journey out caused by weather, Christmas holidays and the oil crisis. These 12-day flights, often led by Janet Ferguson, routed down through France and Spain and on down the west coast of Africa before turning left for Nigeria and were mostly routine apart from some fuel sourcing problems.

Len Houston occasionally took part in ferry flights when his test flying duties permitted. On one trip to Nairobi, flying at 8,500 feet over the Ethiopian mountains, the engine of Houston's aircraft shut down completely. After a methodical cockpit check and an unsuccessful attempt to restart he contemplated a forced landing in a steeply-sided valley with no apparent flat ground. Fortunately, he became aware of an obstruction by his right elbow which proved to be a piece of carelessly loaded luggage that had fallen on to the ferry tank 'on/off' switch, selecting 'on'. The ferry tank had emptied on the leg after takeoff and was feeding air into the main pipes. Turning off the ferry tank allowed fuel to start flowing again and the engine restarted immediately.

BULLDOGS FOR JORDAN, LEBANON AND HONG KONG

Interest in the Bulldog showed no sign of abating and the next order received, for 13 Model 125 aircraft,

Wearing classic Bulldog red and white colours, the Ghana Air Force's G105 was one of the first batch of Model 122 aircraft delivered in July, 1973 and operated until the mid-1990s. *(Juanita Franzi)*

was from the Royal Jordanian Academy of Aeronautics, based in Amman, the first from a civil training school. These were ferried to Jordan in March, 1974 by pilots of the Academy. It was agreed that SABL would lend the Academy the demonstrator, G-ASAL, to enable its instructors and ground crew to gain some experience of the aircraft. Squadron Leader Ivor Gallwey, who had joined SABL's flight test team, was deputed to fly the Bulldog to Jordan, accompanied by John Lucas of the Product Support Department, who was to look after all the documentation as well as tending to the aircraft en route and to remain with the aircraft in Jordan. After two days delay, they left Prestwick on 7 May 1974 with their arrival expected in Jordan on 10 May. Having left at midday they only made it to Gatwick and overnighted there before proceeding via Troyes, Valence, Nice and Rome. Crossing the Apennines on the way to Brindisi they encountered severe icing but they decided to press on and reached Brindisi safely.

They continued to Athens, Rhodes and Nicosia where they paused to consider the latest situation of the Syrian/Israeli war. They were told that all aircraft over-flying Syria had to land at Damascus and the direct route between Damascus and Beirut was closed. The only way into Damascus was from Tanf, 110 miles east of Damascus. The planned route of Nicosia to Damascus was therefore not possible as the large dogleg now required meant that there was no alternative but to land at Beirut for fuel. Air Traffic Control at Beirut

L-145 was one of the six Bulldogs delivered to the Lebanese Air Force. This aircraft was displayed for a while at the Lebanese Air Force Museum but later returned to service with 1 Squadron Aviation School at Beirut. (4A)

persuaded the Syrians to allow the Bulldog to fly at 13,000 feet over the mountains instead of the minimum height of 23,000 feet, and also to cut the corner at Tanf. They approached Damascus from the east over surface to air missile (SAM) sites and gun emplacements. The proposed route from Damascus to Amman meant returning to Tanf before turning for Amman but the Syrian Air Traffic Ccontrol pointed out that, as the military never started before 8 am, an early start would enable them to miss out the Tanf leg and save almost two hours flying. However, once in the air and despite the early start, the military decreed that they had to go the long way but luckily it soon relented and allowed the shorter sector. Their arrival at the Academy in Amman before 8 am caught everyone unawares but G-ASAL was safely delivered and handed over.

During 1975 SABL built six Model 126 aircraft for the Lebanese Air Force and these were delivered in October of that year. Various Air Forces began placing repeat orders, or taking up the option for additional aircraft written into the original contracts. These included the Ghana Air Force (seven Model

122A ferried in May, 1976 following short-term storage at Prestwick), Kenya Air Force (nine Model 127 ferried in July and November, 1976 by West London Air Charter), Nigerian Air Force (first twelve Model 123 ferried in June, 1978 followed by a further five in June/July, 1978, originally intended to be shipped but eventually reassembled and ferried), Royal Jordanian Academy of Aeronautics (nine Model 125 delivered in June to August, 1982 in a C-130H Hercules). A new customer was the Royal Hong Kong Auxiliary Air Force which ordered two Model 128s, worth £100,000 including spares, for use in the basic training role and to assist in search and rescue. The Botswana Air Force was another new customer ordering six Model 130s. However, space at Prestwick was coming under pressure as the area originally used for the Bulldog production line was now in use for Jetstream work so production of the aircraft for Nigeria and Jordan was carried out on jigs at the side of the hangar.

By 1977 SABL found it necessary to build Bulldogs on spec to prevent the production line from slowing and 17 aircraft were started before firm orders were received for them, although 11 of these were soon sold to the Royal Malaysian Air Force in January 1977.

The Hong Kong Auxiliary Air Force acquired this Bulldog in 1977, serialled HKG-5. It was sold back to the UK in 1988 and became G-BULL but retained its Hong Kong colours. (RS)

CHAPTER TWELVE

BULLDOG WEAPONS PLATFORM

In February 1971, whilst production of the Bulldog for the SAF was at its peak, Rolls-Royce was declared insolvent owing SAL £300,000 for sub-contract work on the Griffon engine and for repairs and overhauls on the Derwent which was a massive loss for the small company to suffer. Financially SAL was in a fragile condition, relying on a bank loan and the guarantee of its parent company to remain afloat. When the go-ahead was given by the Government in 1970 for SAL to take on the Jetstream, the design department, much reduced in numbers, found itself too hard pressed to devote much time to development of the Bulldog save for the necessary work to satisfy specific customer requirements. Nevertheless, one area that SABL did devote design time to was exploring the Bulldog's role as a weapons platform.

Several customers recognised the Bulldog's potential as a light ground attack aircraft and various air forces had expressed an interest in the aircraft being modified to perform this role. The development of light armament capability presented SABL with a relatively inexpensive means of increasing the potential of the Bulldog. An early customer, the Swedish Army, intended the Bulldog to be fitted with Bofors Bantam wire-guided missiles and SABL incorporated wiring and the Swedish Army installed the missile packs. The Botswana Air Force required its Bulldogs to be capable of carrying 68mm rockets and a single 7.62 mm machine gun. The Rheinmetall MG3 belt-fed gun (a derivative of the famous wartime MG42), which was, essentially, a weapon intended for infantry use but adapted for installation in aircraft, was proposed as this was lighter and had less drag than the Portsmouth Aviation twin FN CPMG pod. A Browning M2HB 12.7mm gun was also considered but dismissed on account of its weight and recoil force.

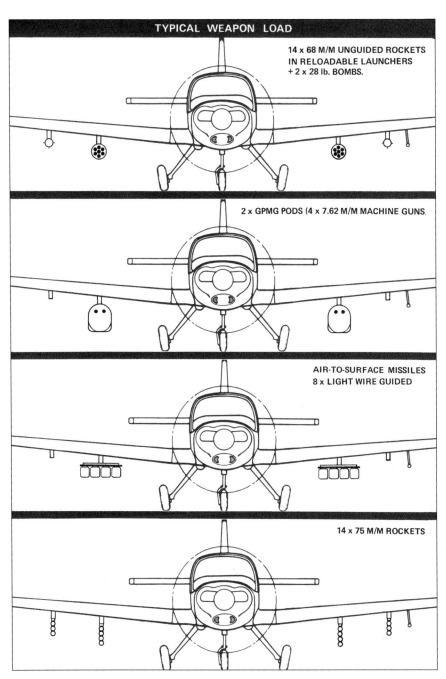

Taken from a sales brochure promoting the Bulldog as a weapons platform, this diagram illustrates the range of weaponry the aircraft could deploy.

HARDPOINT MODIFICATIONS

The modifications to the structure to provide the underwing hard points and the electrical firing systems were designed and, initially, G-AXEH was modified to provide a temporary installation to allow preliminary weapons trials to be carried out. The location of the ammunition packs for the machine guns is not known and, as the inboard sections of the wings were spoken for by fuel tanks, finding a

suitable position for these bulky, and heavy, installations would have been difficult.

Test pilot Len Houston, no stranger to weapons testing, carried out the testing and live firing trials. Tests began with dummy rocket pods attached to underwing pylons and showed that the aircraft's handling characteristics were not detrimentally affected. Although G-AXEH had been fitted with temporary hardpoints to carry out trials with a rocket pack, it was decided that the production aircraft needed a more robust set of fittings that could be more easily adapted to the variety of weapons which might be carried. At each hardpoint wing station vertical, lateral and fore-and-aft loads were carried by a two-lug fitting at the main spar and vertical and lateral loads were carried by a single lug at the front spar. The demonstration aircraft, G-ASAL, was built to this standard. A weapons control panel was added to the instrument panel and arming and firing switches were added to the top of the control column. A stiff bracket was fitted to the glareshield on which was mounted the "single point" sight.

Len Houston was formerly Chief Test Pilot at Ferranti where for nine years he had been flying the development trials of a weapon aiming system involving the use of intercept and terrain following radar, laser and navigational/attack systems. Among the types he flew on this work were the Lightning, Buccaneer, Harrier, Canberra, Meteor, Hunter as well as the Dakota. Much of the work involved flying at altitude at speeds approaching Mach 2 as well as contour flying at 100 feet and 600 mph. He had started his flying career with the Edinburgh UAS from where he joined the RAF.

On 15 August, 1974, using G-ASAL, two flights were carried out at Prestwick, one to establish the aerodynamic effects of a single pod attached to the starboard wing and the second to examine the effects of two empty Matra pods. The aircraft behaved well in the tests, so testing moved on to the West Freugh range to clear the initial firing and pod release functions. It then went to BAe Holme-on-Spalding Moor, a few miles from the Donna Hook shore firing range, where the firing of dummy and live stores could take place. In order to establish the integrity of the jettison system and the behaviour of the stores once release had taken place, and in case the predictions were wrong and the stores flew into the aircraft, tests were carried out by dropping two dummy stores, light and heavy weight, on the range. The intention was to recover the stores and, if undamaged, repeat the test with the pods on the opposite wings. Both units released cleanly without striking the aircraft and Houston flew back over the dropping zone to examine the impact area. The large number of fragments of the two stores that were spread over the impact area confirmed that no further tests would be taking place using those dummies.

A few days later the first live firing took place. The gunsight, the Single Point Sight, was a simple device selected for its size and weight that allowed it to be easily installed on the instrument glareshield with minimum modification to the aircraft. The device enabled one of the pilot's eyes to see the target while the other looked into the reticule. Being an optical device no electrical connections were necessary, the display consisting of an aiming pipper and vertical aiming line, with a facility for adjusting elevation angle to take account of the gravity drop of the weapon. This calculation was based on time of flight of the weapon, firing range and angle of attack and the adjustment being the only moving part, had to be preset by the pilot for the particular attack profile he had decided upon.

The aircraft was positioned in the Safety Arming Bay and 12 rockets with practice heads were installed in the pods. The targets were six upright 10-ft square panels positioned on the beach so that the attack heading pointed seawards. A noticeable increase in aircraft weight extended the takeoff run but the aircraft handled well. Arriving at the dive position, and the range having given the clearance to fire, the mechanical trigger guard was released and the firing trigger held tightly. The five second countdown began and at zero the first rocket left the aircraft. With an aircraft speed of 160 knots very little shock effect was felt and the rocket smoke trail soon came into view as the missile headed towards the beach. Following successful firings of individual rockets the sortie that day ended with the firing of a battery of six rockets from the starboard side. An automatic ripple mechanism in the pod selected each individual rocket in a pre-selected sequence so that each weapon was prevented from interfering with the trajectory of another. The aircraft yawed strongly as the firing occurred but returned to stable flight when the last rocket was released. The whole sequence took one-sixteenth of a second. Houston described the view from the cockpit as the twelve rockets left the aircraft as spectacular as was the sight of the large concrete-filled oil drums hurtling across the range. The Bulldog was in the attack business.

During the preparation of the Basic Type Specification, the development of the Bulldog as an Armed Light Aircraft was given special and detailed consideration. As well as the provision for rockets and machine guns the Specification provided for glider and target towing, forward air control, supply dropping, search and rescue, airborne reconnaissance, psychological

SAL's Model 120 demonstrator was at the SBAC show at Farnborough in 1976 with an array of weaponry and sporting the insignia of all the air forces operating the type. *(PH)*

operation, law enforcement, weapon training, target illumination and marking, and grenades.

In September, 1970, shortly after SABL had begun work on the Bulldog there was an approach from a South African company, Astra Aircraft Corporation, based in Johannesburg, who wanted to enter the light aircraft market, preferably with a British product. It was looking to order 200 sets of airframe components, based on the Pup or Bulldog design, which would be equipped and completed at its South African factory and sold throughout southern Africa. Such an order had a potential value of about £1.5 million and would have put Bulldog production on to an entirely different footing. However, as Beagle had already learnt to its cost back in 1966 when they had tried to sell the B206 to the South Africans, any deal with South Africa required political clearance and the absence of any further action by either Astra or SABL would indicate that these early discussions on the supply of kits came to nothing.

The third Bulldog Model 122 for Ghana, G-102 (c/n 226), is seen here at the factory before delivery in July, 1973.

This poor quality photograph shows three of the Bulldogs in the first batch for the Nigerian Air Force. G-BBJM, N and O, are seen here at Shoreham on 7 August, 1974 at the start of their ferry flight. (via KB)

CHAPTER THIRTEEN

THE BULLDOG SRS. 200, 300 AND 400

This illustration from a Scottish Aviation brochure of the time shows the original concept of the four-seat Bulldog 200.

In 1971, in an effort to keep ahead of the competition by exploring new projects and developing the existing ones, Scottish Aviation instigated a general study of the market to establish whatever potential there might be for development of the Bulldog. One possible way forward was a four-seat version and it was feasible that the installation of a 260 hp Lycoming IO-540 six-cylinder engine, together with an increase in strength and weight, would allow the accommodation to be increased to a full four seats with a baggage allowance of 25lbs per person. A full set of performance, weight and balance and price calculations followed and these showed that the proposal was viable. The maximum takeoff weight was set at 2,640 lbs. Price calculations gave a likely market price of £16,460 and the new design proposal was initially to be named the 'Wasp'.

In February 1971, South Africa's Astra Aircraft Corporation made a further approach when John Nash, Astra's Chairman, visited Prestwick to discuss another venture. This time he was looking to purchase 100 of a Bulldog derivative which was to have better performance than the Piper Cherokee 180 and

be capable of carrying four people and 100 lbs of baggage. This aircraft was to be fitted with underwing hardpoints to carry external armament but it was important that the type was always to be referred to as a civil aircraft and certificated as such. Again, Astra was asking for the aircraft to be delivered in kit form minus engine, propeller, instruments and avionics which would be supplied and installed by Astra in South Africa.

SABL started preliminary design work on Astra's specification which, although aproximating to the forecast figures for the Wasp, was given a new identity as the Stag Series 100. Shortly after, it became the Model 201 so that, at a later date, the universal aircraft could be defined as the Stag Series 200. The name 'Stag' was coined by Ranald Porteous although the reason for it is unknown except perhaps that it had Highland connotations. SABL hedged its bets by simultaneously working up design parameters for a 200 hp version, retaining the IO-360 engine and the Bulldog propeller. Subsequently, the plan to use the 260 hp IO-540 was dropped for the Series 200 but would be resurrected later for the Series 3100. SABL established that the 200 hp

version would still have the capacity for four seats and 100lbs of baggage within a maximum all-up weight of 2,575 lbs (1,170 kg). The additional cabin size to accommodate four seats necessitated a 10-inch forward fuselage extension. The IO-360 would be installed with an approved Lycoming extension shaft to 'sharpen' the entry and improve the nose appearance.

By the end of March, SABL was able to define the Stag Model 201 for South Africa as a civil aircraft with a maximum all-up weight of 2,600 lbs (1,182 kg) and maximum aerobatic weight of 2,250 lbs (1,023 kg) and provision for four occupants plus 100 lbs (45 kg) of baggage. Entry would be via gull wing doors (although a sliding canopy remained an option), instrumentation and avionics were similar to the Bulldog (although to be customer supplied and installed), the cowlings and engine mount were moved forward by nine inches (229 mm) to suit the optional 260 hp engine and it would have fixed landing gear. A month later this definition was incorporated into the Model 201 Variant Type Specification, the only differences to the original definition being slight reductions in the maximum takeoff weight to 2,579 lbs (1,172 kg) and maximum aerobatic weight to 2,205 lbs (1,002 kg).

By the summer, in the absence of any immediate response from Astra to its proposals for the Stag, SABL was having to look again at how it might take the Bulldog forward. For the Bulldog itself cost pressures were obviously starting to mount as the Project Department was considering instigating a value engineering exercise in the hope of reducing the labour element by 10%. There was still optimism that the Stag would be the way forward with the Series 200's high commonality with the Bulldog Series 100. With its genuine four-seat cabin and cowlings and mountings capable of taking up to a 300 hp engine, the type offered a range of options to suit several sectors of the market. At the other end of the scale it was suggested that the potential market for a low-powered version of the Bulldog, with simpler instrumentation, might warrant investigation. A further suggestion was to look harder at the ultimate development of the Bulldog with increased power, more weight, and a retractable landing gear. It was felt that the Bulldog Series 100 was a 'draggy' aircraft with better than calculated climb performance but poorer than expected cruise performance. This could be attributed largely to the fixed landing gear, so, by introducing retractable gear it might be expected that 15 knots would be added to the

level speed and about 100 to 150 ft/min to the climb performance. The improved sophistication of retractable gear would also make the type more attractive in the military training role. Increasing the engine size to 300 hp could increase the level speed to 172 knots and the rate of climb to 1,700 ft/min (8.59 m/sec). By increasing the fuel capacity by 17 imp. gallons (77 litres) the endurance of the 300 hp version would remain the same as the Series 100. The 300 hp version would be the basis of the range and the lower-powered versions would use the same structure, with the retractable gear fixed in the down position if required. This would give a family of four aircraft, namely the Type A (a 300 hp aircraft with retractable or fixed gear), Type B (200 hp with retractable or fixed gear).

Introducing retractable gear would entail widening the forward fuselage slightly to provide a nosegear bay and the wing centre section would have to be widened by 10 inches to accommodate the main gear. Effectively, a new forward fuselage would be needed which could be melded to the existing rear fuselage of the Series 100. There were concerns over the effect of the increased weight on the landing gear but it turned out that balance rather than weight was to prove the bigger problem.

Developing the Type A was considered the most cost effective solution but the development costs

were estimated at £200,000. By comparison the less favourable choice, developing the Type B, would only cost in the region of £120,000. The report by the Project Department recommended that the Type B should be considered for development, to be designated the Bulldog Series 200, eventually to replace the Bulldog Series 100 and the Stag concept. The standard aircraft should have retractable landing gear with the fixed gear being offered as an option. The Type B would have all the features and structure of the Type A aircraft, four seats, additional tankage, and extended cowlings. Should the 300 hp version subsequently proceed it was to be known as the Series 300, although the correlation between power and designation was unintentional. It was proposed that, if, for marketing reasons, it was important to distinguish between the civil and military types, the full designation could be the 'Bulldog Series 200 Stag' so that either the Bulldog (military) or the Stag (civil) could be omitted from the marketing literature. The model numbers would be prefixed with 'R' for retractable or 'F' for fixed gear. Confusingly, the military version would be designated the Bulldog Series 2100 whilst the civil version would be the Bullfinch Series 2200.

Subsequently, and also somewhat confusingly, SBAL stressed that the Series 200 was intended to be a development of, and successor to,

In more aggressive mode, the Bulldog 200 was portrayed as a two-seat ground attack aircraft with four underwing hardpoints.

the Bulldog Series 100 and not a development of the Stag. However, to add another layer of confusion, it was decided that the name 'Stag' would have to remain for the civil version of the aircraft as the name 'Bulldog' was now accepted as being the name of a military aircraft.

Despite the Type Specification for the Stag Series 201 stipulating a gull-wing door configuration, SABL seemed to be retaining the sliding canopy for the Series 200. This caused them to look at potential drag reduction on the present sliding canopy. In the new configuration the windscreen arch would be sloped forward and the rear frame sloped aft, allowing the canopy to drop into place using a flush upward-hinged system. If the sliding canopy configuration was adopted on the Series 200 and Series 300, then the 10-inch wider cabin would necessitate the canopy being given two spine tubes which would provide lateral stiffness and give a good base for the lateral loads to be carried by the upper hinge arm. Apart from providing the additional rigidity the new configuration would improve access to the seats. The downside would be a slight increase in weight imposed by the counter-balance system that would be required. The canopy would not be openable in flight either for ventilation or photography but this would be overcome by the provision of a camera port and an adequate cabin ventilation system.

After the SABL Board agreed to proceed with the design definition two draftsmen were allocated to look at the power plant and fuselage section lines. By 1 November, 1971 the first draft of the Preliminary Basic Type Specification was issued, followed closely by preliminary calculations of the retractable landing gear design parameters and definition of the gear geometry. It was decided that the gear would be a trailing link design and shorten by about 8 inches (203 mm) on retraction. A meeting with Lockheed Precision Products followed to discuss further

development work on the landing gear and Lockheed came up with some possible design solutions. Lockheed was given a weight limit of 131 lbs (59 kg) for the system, including wheels, tyres, and brakes, but they considered this was not possible. SABL decided to obtain quotes from other landing gear specialists and also considered the manufacture of parts of the system themselves. Enquiries were sent to seven companies but only Messier showed any sort of interest.

Further weight and balance and spin recovery calculations were carried out but this time with an increase in the tail arm to ease balance problems and improve spin recovery. This change came about partly due to the increase in the length of the aircraft to 25 feet (7.63 m) which was 20 inches (508 mm) longer than the Series 100.

By early 1972 SABL was able to give some thought to the possible programme for the manufacture of the Series 200. Because of its commonality it was theoretically possible to build the Series 200 alongside the Series 100 until the latter was phased out. The prototype would be built separately to its own timescale. It was proposed that the Series 200 would start coming off the line at the beginning of 1975 and that would set the programme for the building and testing of the prototype. To allow time for the design and manufacture of the prototype set of landing gear, the go-ahead would be needed by March, 1972. This was a tight schedule with further pressure added when it was decided that

tropical trials would be carried out in Cyprus around August, 1973. On the sales side, Ranald Porteous estimated that, over a ten-year production run, 800 aircraft could be sold and, of these, 200 would be the fixed-gear version.

In the Spring of 1972 SABL looked again at the balance problems it had identified earlier. The Series 100 Bulldog had inherited the somewhat limited CofG envelope of the original Beagle Pup. When it came to the Series 200, with its more varied role and hence loading conditions, this unfortunate trait became even more critical. When the loading conditions for the various combinations of occupants, with and without fuel, gear retracted and extended, were overlaid on the CofG envelope, it was seen that, in the single pilot case, the CofG was forward of the forward limit and, in the four- occupant case, the CofG was aft of the aft limit. Various iterations eventually concluded that the engine was too far forward and occupancy would have to be limited to three. With the optimum engine position only 2½ inches (63mm) ahead of the Series 100 position it was obvious that the IO-540 engine was not feasible. It was probably never going to be anyway for structural and operational reasons. Only by ballasting would the aircraft remain within the centre of gravity envelope and the position and amount of ballast would vary according to the role of the aircraft. The conclusion of the design team was that only military operators would accept this ballasting procedure and it would not be

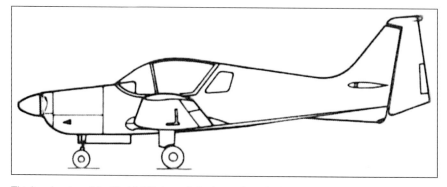

This line drawing of the Model 420 shows little change from the Model 120 other than the retractable undercarriage. *(IA)*

practical for civil operators. Technical Director, Gordon Watson, whilst accepting the facts did not accept the conclusion. He could see a case for retaining the engine position at 9 inches (229mm) forward of the Series 100 position and using ballast in the form of fuel in a 3-gallon tank in the fin. This solution would be complicated as the tank contents would have to be checked and drained or transferred to suit each loading condition. Calculations showed that the fin tank idea could be made to work and, at the same time, the weight and balance figures were adjusted to allow for the rear seats being moved 3 inches forward.

To illustrate the complications of using the fin fuel tank as variable ballast various roles would involve the following operating criteria. For the military training role with one pilot, the fin tank would have to be full and not used during flight. For the military training role with two pilots, the fin tank would have to be full and not used during flight except in an emergency. One can only speculate on the thoughts of the single pilot with a fuel emergency knowing he has three gallons (13.5 litres) of unused fuel that he is not permitted to use. Also, in this condition, if additional radio equipment was fitted it would have to be in the position of one of the rear seats and the other rear seat might need to be fitted. For the military liaison role with a pilot and passenger in the front seats the loading was similar to the training role. With three occupants the fin tank could be full and could be used in flight. With all four seats occupied the fin tank had to be empty. Finally, for the private touring role with one, two, three or four occupants the loading had to be as the military training role. Also, with one or two occupants in the forward seats at least one of the rear seats had to be fitted. Up to 440 lbs (200 kg) of baggage could be carried with one pilot but this would be marginal if a front-seat passenger was carried.

Doubts were beginning to emerge, not only about the wisdom of having an aircraft in the civil market which had a critical requirement to operate the fin fuel tank correctly, but also whether the Series 200 would ever be cost effective. The obvious market for such a rugged, adaptable multi-role aircraft was going to be the military. With the increasing workload on the Series 100 Bulldog and the Jetstream T.1 further work on the Series 200 was no longer a priority although design work did not cease altogether. Somewhat prematurely the Series 200 was announced at the SBAC Farnborough show in September, 1974 and brochures were available for prospective buyers.

When Jetstream work began to tail off in 1975 the opportunity arose for serious work to resume on the Series 200. Substantial redundancies in the factory had been mirrored in the design department so that it was a much reduced design team that revisited the Bullfinch. To keep a nucleus of design capability it was decided in April to build a prototype with the aim of getting the aircraft to Farnborough in September of that year. Although the company's enthusiasm was high the project was hampered by budget constraints. The only outside equipment cost was for the all-new retractable landing gear and the cost of that was shared with APPH, which had finally been selected as the landing gear and hydraulic equipment manufacturer. An electric screw jack was needed for the retraction gear, and this was taken from a Fairchild Republic A10 Thunderbolt II canopy on a long-term loan arrangement and, although it was far too powerful and far from ideal, it had to be used for cost reasons.

The fuselage lines were developed including the marrying of the new widened forward fuselage with the rear fuselage of the Series 100. The Series 100's outer wings, rear fuselage and tail unit were able to be used with only slight modifications. Because the rear fuselage was

mounted at a slightly different angle the incidence of the tailplane was altered to suit. Starting from the nose, the cowlings were extended to accommodate the Lycoming IO-540 engine that was to be used in production aircraft but, for cost reasons, the standard 200 hp IO-360 was installed because it was available. The propeller shaft was extended to enable the propeller to be mounted further forward. The forward fuselage was completely redesigned to incorporate four seats with a centre console wide enough to provide the nosewheel bay. The wing centre section was also reworked to increase the span by about ten inches to provide a mounting and wheel well for the main landing gear. To save space the main gear was designed to shorten as it retracted but it still used up the area that would normally be on the line of the rear spar. To overcome this the wing centre section was made a two-spar structure. The overall fuselage length was increased to lengthen the tail arm for improved spin recovery and improve the balance situation. The canopy was redesigned to be an up-and-over style with the windscreen arch sloping forward to allow the canopy to drop down into place. The windscreen glazing was cut down from the standard Bulldog layout and the canopy glazing was formed from two half sections of the standard canopy with the extra width being made up by a metal central spine. The canopy latching was by fore and aft shoot bolts on the top centreline but, although airworthy, this was not a success and it was realised that canopies need to be anchored at their skirts to avoid ballooning due to air loads. The counterbalance coil springs were heavy but lack of funds meant that gas struts could not be afforded.

The landing gear extension and retraction system posed design problems. It was realised that it was not possible to design for the jam situation as the A-10 actuator was much too powerful, so it just had to be accepted that if a leg jammed then something would break. The system comprised push rods, idlers and bellcranks to connect the actuator to the legs. Difficulties with rigging meant that the legs always reached the down and locked position but sometimes the main gear had to be helped into the uplocks by a short period of reduced-g. Those in the know would recognise the short hesitation in climb after takeoff for what it was. This problem could have been fixed by fitting stiff springs in the pushrod circuit but time was running out. Instead a small screw jack was fitted in series with the main actuator which was accessible through a small hatch in the centre console so that the pilot could use a small ratchet spanner to wind the legs down should the main actuator fail to move for any reason. The nosewheel steering was similar to the Bulldog except that a push-pull cable was used since the rudder circuit was designed from the outset to be a complete cable loop. As the nosewheel retracted the steering was automatically decoupled and the leg was centred to allow it to enter the bay. The main gear leg carried a small door to close off the lower wing surface but the wheels and tyres were left exposed. The nose gear bay was closed by a simple sideways hinged door that was closed by the leg as it entered the bay and all standard Bulldog instruments and avionics were used.

THE SERIES 200 PROTOTYPE FLIES

As the programme proceeded through July and August, 1976 the design team was hard pressed to stay ahead of the build. The first flight of G-BDOG (c/n BH.200-381), by now re-named the Bullfinch, again at Ranald Porteous' suggestion, took place on 20 August, 1976 and lasted just 17 minutes. John Blair was happy with the handling of the aircraft and the performance appeared to be as predicted. He complained of a draught coming in through the hole where the nose gear actuating

A fine air-to-air photo of the Bullfinch G-BDOG showing its sleek lines with the gear retracted. (DC)

rod passed through into the wheel bay and this was quickly sealed off with a fabric gaiter. On the third flight of the day a series of dummy go-arounds were to be carried out at altitude to check for trim changes. As the gear retracted on the first climb away there was a loud bang and the gear indication lights showed a red for the nose gear. Either the nose gear had failed to reach the up-lock or the micro-switch had failed. A fly-past showed that the main gear was up but the nose leg was hanging in an unlocked position and, more worryingly, the nose bay door was closed. Various ideas were postulated on how to get the nose gear into the down lock. There was no aerobatic manoeuvre that would throw the gear forward against the air load. A landing on the grass was suggested but there was the danger that the nose would dig in and the aircraft overturn causing the windscreen arch to collapse. The airport fire brigade stood by to lay a foam carpet but it warned this would only last a few seconds.

Len Houston took off in the demonstration aircraft, G-ASAL, to formate on the Bullfinch to get a closer look at the problem. Houston reported that the leg was swinging free and that he could get close enough to poke it down if he had a long pole. Despite his confidence nobody volunteered to fly with him to handle the pole. It was eventually agreed that one of the push rods from the actuator had failed but which one? A stress engineer did some quick calculations on the

strength of the rods and suggested a possible failure point. John Blair called a halt to the discussion by reporting a low fuel state. The decision was taken to ask Blair to attempt to lower the gear using the emergency screw jack warning him that the broken rod end might engage with the elevator drive levers applying down elevator. Blair wound the gear down slowly whilst checking for any control restriction and was able to report three greens and the aircraft landed safely.

Back on the ground an examination of the nose gear established that the nose wheel bay door was held open by a simple over-centre spring-loaded strut when the gear was down but the strut was sensitive to a critical frequency that caused it to fold. That frequency happened to be the blade passing frequency as the aircraft climbed away. The door had closed under the influence of the slipstream coming from the right and trapped the gear on the outside. Amazingly the rod end that engaged with the leg had suffered a lug failure and, as the gear had been wound down manually, the fabric gaiter that had been fitted the night before had guided the broken end into place to push the gear into the downlock. A guard tube was hurriedly designed to be attached to the right side of the leg so that if the door folded closed again it could not trap the leg outside the door.

With only days to go to the Farnborough show a tragedy overtook the project when the CAA pilot and observer who were to fly the aircraft to clear it for the show were killed whilst flight testing an aircraft in Germany. A replacement crew was allocated and the Bullfinch received its clearance and Len Houston flew it to and during the show. Ranald Porteous advocated a full-scale launch for the Bullfinch but by now there were serious misgivings about the projected costings. These showed that the price would have to be set well above the market level for aircraft of similar attributes. Instead, when the temporary CofA expired in December, 1976 it was not renewed and the aircraft was placed in storage. Although the military version would be slightly more viable as it would attract a price premium, any military interest seemed to have evaporated. After its return from Farnborough the Bullfinch was not flown again at Prestwick and the project was terminated in 1977. After a period of long-term storage, G-BDOG was sold to Dukeries Aviation in May 1980 who have operated it on a Popular Flying Association (PFA) Permit to Fly.

In 1973, whilst work on the Series 200 continued in the background, SABL began to look at a further development for a 2/3 seat training aircraft with retractable gear and a 260 hp engine. It is not clear how this aircraft, designated Series 3100, differed from the Series 200. There are no surviving records but it must have been sufficiently

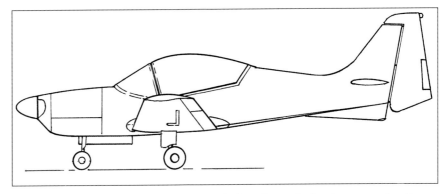

The Model 440's tandem seating arrangement resulted in a slimmer fuselage but presented problems with cockpit space. (IA)

different to warrant being given a new designation. SABL resurrected the name 'Stag' for the project but it seems to have got no further than very preliminary ideas.

It was not until 1981 that the design team resurrected the Bulldog project for the final time and it had in mind two ideas which it designated the Series 420 and 440. Both types would use the familiar 200hp Lycoming IO-360 and both would have retractable gear. The 420 would be simply another look at the traditional 2/3 seat trainer/ tourer along the lines of the Series 200 but the 440 would be a new departure with a tandem seating arrangement. Aware of the RAF's interest in the Embraer Tucano as an advanced trainer the design team began sketching a tandem configuration, not as a direct competitor to the Tucano, but as a basic trainer. It was recognised that, if advanced training was to be carried out in a tandem-seat aircraft, then it was logical that basic training

should be undertaken in an aircraft of a similar configuration. The RAF's reversion to tandem-seat training was a contradiction of their policy of favouring side-by-side seating which was one of the prime reasons why the Bulldog was chosen to superseed the Chipmunk.

The tandem arrangement presented many difficulties. It would be hard to achieve the length of cockpit needed and, although the cockpit could be narrower, the wing centre section would have to be the same width as the Series 200 to accommodate the main gear. The front pilot could sit astride the nose gear but a bit higher to provide room for the central control column. The rear pilot had to sit close behind the front seat and therefore there would be no room for his legs and the rudder pedals. The problem was overcome by making the cockpit slightly wider and creating side consoles either side of the front seat in which the pedals and the rear pilot's feet could

In later life the Bullfinch prototype had a cabin redesign as seen in this photo of G-BDOG at Shoreham in June, 2005. (RS)

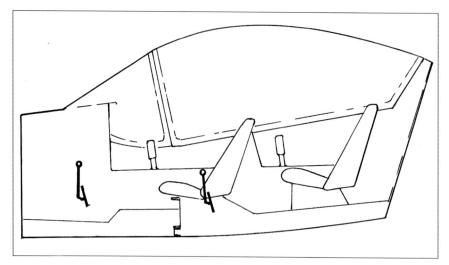

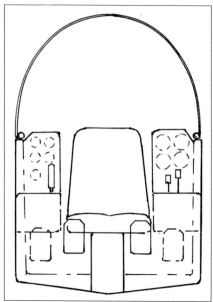

These two drawings illustrate the problem of how to accommodate the rear occupant's feet. *(IA)*

sit. This left very little room for the control column and for the instrument panel so it was suggested that a side stick be positioned on the right hand console and there should be a minimal instrument panel split in two and positioned on the rear face of each of the consoles. The landing gear retraction system was simplified. Instead of the single screw-jack on the Series 200 operating push rods three separate small jacks would be connected to each gear. A simple manual release pin would be used in emergencies.

The Series 420 canopy would be the same up-and-over design as the Series 200 but with the latches at the skirts instead of on the centre spine. The smaller and narrower Series 440 canopy could have been hinged on one side with quick-release hinges to jettison. Much of the Series 200 wing structure, rear fuselage and tail unit would be retained.

Whilst the design team was able to cobble together a solution to the rear seating arrangement the problem remained of the routing of the control cables to the rear of the aircraft. The seats, wing structure and the main landing gear obstructed the route and there seemed little that could be done about it. The NDN Firecracker had been in existence for a few years and had shown that a tandem arrangement was possible with adequate space for controls and panels. The Firecracker's seats were raised sufficiently above the wing structure to allow routing of the control cables to the rear and the normal positioning of the control column. The Firecracker had a slightly humped-back look but the fuselage was longer than the Series 440. Whilst the span was less the low-aspect ratio wing provided the necessary handling and probably ensured a wider CG range. A mock-up of the tandem layout would have helped to solve the various problems but the project was dropped and with it ended any further development of the Bulldog.

The NDN Firecracker had a tandem seat layout which incorporated a higher seating position. *(RS)*

CHAPTER FOURTEEN

SAL'S JET TRAINER PROJECT

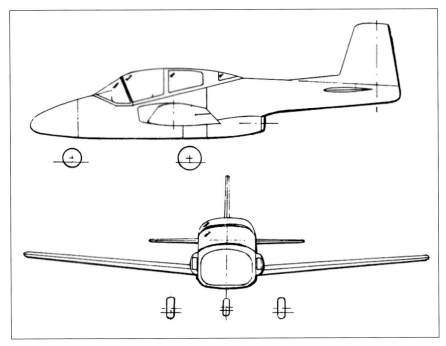

SAL investigated the production of a small jet trainer as a possible successor to the Bulldog and came up with the attractive lines of the Don. *(IA)*

Whilst the Series 200, 300 and 400 could justifiably be said to be true developments of the original Bulldog, sharing much of the original airframe and engines, it is probably unrealistic to describe SAL's project for a jet-powered trainer as anything but a completely new design and as such it might be thought to be beyond the scope of this book. However, the design would have put to good use SAL's experience of designing and building small military trainers and, had it progressed to production, it would have become the only jet aircraft to be designed from the outset in Scotland and joined the Jetstream T.1 in ensuring that SAL's name remained associated with military trainers for a few more decades.

The idea of a small jet trainer was first mooted in 1974 when SAL drew up an ambitious plan for a range of eight types utilising a variety of engines. SAL realised that orders for the Bulldog would eventually begin to dry up. The operating costs of piston-engined aircraft had become extremely sensitive to the price of aviation fuel and the oil crisis of 1973 had resulted in disproportionate increases in the cost of AvGas. The Bulldog, and the Bullfinch, the only derivative to have made it to the flying stage, found themselves competing against small jet trainers and turboprop aircraft. The eight proposed variants comprised the Type 1 (2/4 seat multi-role aircraft with two unspecified 400lb thrust turbojets), Type 2 (two-seat trainer with a Marboré VI turbojet), Type 3 (2/4 seat trainer with a 285 hp Continental O-285-B turbocharged piston engine), Type 4 (four-seat trainer with a 300 hp Continental O-320 turbo-charged piston engine), Type 5 (2/4 seat trainer with a Dowty-Rotol ducted fan with a Continental O-320 turbocharged piston engine), Type 6 (two-seat trainer with an unspecified 904lb.s.t. high bypass turbofan), Type 7 (two-seat trainer with a 1,289 lb.s.t. Lycoming AT 170 2.2 turbojet) and Type 8 (a 2/4 seat version of Type 7).

It was decided to concentrate on the Type 1 and it was given the name 'Don'. It was to be a very small jet, not much bigger than the Bulldog, with a 30ft span wing and 27ft length. Although some scheme drawings were produced the project did not get as far as selecting an engine although the Turboméca Palas was mooted. It was felt that two small engines would suit the size of the airframe better than one larger engine and the width needed to accommodate four people would have permitted a side-by-side engine arrangement, possibly

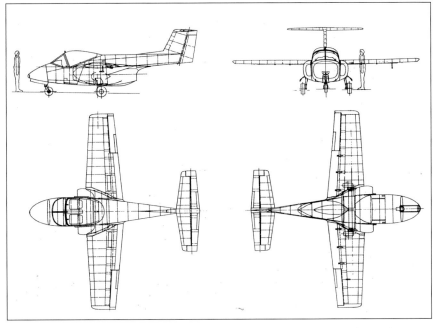

The Sapphire was another prospective venture to replace the Bulldog but it got no further than a preliminary sketch. *(IA)*

sharing the same jet pipe. Fuel tankage to provide sufficient range would probably have been a problem.

Little progress was made on the Don until, in 1975, a market was identified for a small jet trainer which was also capable of performing additional roles such as weapons training and ground attack, a role defined as 'LUMPS' – light utility multi-purpose system. In November, 1975 work began on a redesign of the Don utilising the newly-introduced Lycoming ALF101G twin-spool by-pass fan engine which, being very light, would reduce operating costs without sacrificing performance. It was named the Sapphire by John Chalmers from 'SA' for Scottish Aviation and 'PPHIRE' for fire in the belly. For the light strike function it was designed as a battlefield utility support system (BUSS) in the roles of Gun-BUSS, Bomb-BUSS and Rocket-BUSS, depending on the armament carried. Side-by-side seating was chosen as, at the time, this was favoured by Bulldog users and required by the USAF for basic pilot training although the RAF was beginning to favour tandem

seating. Introducing side-by-side seating shortened the fuselage length and enabled the wing to be raised and the large intake ducts for the turbofan to be positioned below the wings. The slimmer rear fuselage resulted in a design that began to look tubby.

The initial and only design of the Sapphire, the Series 1100, did not have ejection seats although the ability to fit them was designed in later when it was realised that their absence might have prejudiced its operational advantages. With its high speeds and altitude limits the Sapphire was a sophisticated aircraft and its retractable landing gear and air brakes would have introduced students to the sort of advanced systems they would meet in the later stages of their training. The Sapphire was clearly able to offer a higher level of performance, and a more rigorous training regime, than the later derivatives of the Bulldog.

The Sapphire project was progressed to a very detailed standard but when, in 1980, SAL became part of British Aerospace (BAe) and Prestwick had been designated as the civil aircraft factory, the project was transferred to the military division at Brough.

A cockpit mock-up was built as part of a presentation to the RAF but the decision to revert to a tandem seating configuration for training aircraft meant there was no interest from that quarter. An attempt to interest the USAF for their basic flying training requirement also came to nothing and the project was abandoned in February, 1980.

In September, 1978, SAL was required to assess the Miles M.100 Student as a potential BAe product. A comprehensive engineering, flight and operational assessment was carried out by the Project Department on the Student prototype, G-APLK (later G-MIOO). The assessment paid especial attention to the Student's performance against the projected performance of the Sapphire as well as civil certification and current basic pilot training requirements. It was concluded that the aircraft was somewhat dated and the claims made regarding its performance were optimistic. There were potential certification problems and it did not comply with the current concept of a basic trainer. It was not considered to be a suitable BAe project.

SAL took a look at the Miles M100 Student as a possible follow-on to the Bulldog but it was not considered commercially viable. *(MA)*

CHAPTER FIFTEEN

BULLDOG CIVIL DISPOSALS AND OPERATIONS

Large numbers of Bulldogs were assembled at Shawbury where they were eagerly snapped up by private buyers at auction. *(IG)*

As the 1990s drew to a close the main military operators were looking to replace their ageing fleets. The RAF decided on the Grob G.115E Tutor as its new type and in the early months of 2001 Tutors started to be delivered and the Bulldogs were gradually phased out.

From mid-2000 Bulldogs were being taken to RAF Shawbury and elsewhere for disposal. Whilst some were sold direct to private buyers, many were sold by auction. The auctions were carried out by Phillips, Auctioneers with the first taking place on 16 March, 2000 where five aircraft were sold (XX523, 551, 561, 616 and 630) and, generally, these and later aircraft fetched prices of between £9,000 and £12,000. This auction was followed by others on 29 November, 2000 (5 aircraft), 24 May, 2001 (24 aircraft) and 25 October, 2001 (10 aircraft). Not surprisingly, these found a ready market in the UK and most Bulldogs continued in civil hands painted in their original attractive red and white RAF livery and often with their individual unit markings. Purchasers of the aircraft had to ensure that all required modifications and airworthiness directives (ADs) were up to date and appropriate cockpit placards and emergency

markings, as defined by notices BH-194 and BH-195, were applied to the aircraft. In cases where British civil registrations had been given to aircraft at the time of delivery, these could be re-adopted if the aircraft was returned to UK registry. For Bulldog owners, technical support is provided in the UK by de Havilland Support Ltd. which issues service bulletins and provides a source for spares. Most UK Bulldogs are operated on a CofA through de Havilland Support but at least two (G-CBCB and G-DOGG) are on a Permit to Fly through the Light Aircraft Association (LAA) and this may be a lower cost option due to self maintenance but it has the disadvantage that a permit aircraft needs individual permission to fly outside the UK and has to be

individually authorised for IFR and night flying.

Fatigue life of the Bulldog airframe is a particular issue. All the RAF aircraft, which had already flown an average of 8,153 hours, were fitted with a fatigue meter and this allows the health of the airframe to be tracked through a fatigue index (FI) with a maximum value which must not be exceeded. Bulldog pilots are obliged to record the fatigue meter readings after each flight and have this record reviewed annually. It should be noted, however, that a given FI number does not necessarily reflect the actual flight hours and a Bulldog which is carefully flown may have quite high hours but an FI below the mandatory maximum of 114 FI. Other production Bulldogs were not fitted with a fatigue meter and their maximum allowable airframe flying time has been set at 5,000 hours. There is a modification (BH.193) to strengthen the mainspar joint at the point that the dihedral changes and if this is fitted the life can be increased to 8,760 flying hours. However, this involves complex installation of replacement joint straps and spar doublers with adjustment to bolt holes which can be expensive and may be impracticable for some aircraft. There is also a 15,000 hour limitation on the life of the tailplane. Brakes are another Bulldog issue with some owners opting to replace the Goodyear

A number of SAF SK61A Bulldogs were given an avionics upgrade and redesignated SK61D or SK61E and transferred to the Lund School of Aviation to train civil pilots. Upgraded aircraft had "D" or "E" on the tail. *(PH)*

Having been decommissioned, the Nigerian Air Force's Bulldogs were stored at Kaduna in various states of disrepair. Eventually, a number were sold to New Zealand. *(AM)*

Bulldog XX620 served with Yorkshire UAS and East Lowlands UAS before being sold to the USA in 2000 where it became N621BD. *(RS)*

brakes fitted to RAF aircraft with Cleveland wheels and brakes. This has been prompted by scarcety of spare parts but does not apply to the Swedish Bulldogs which already had the Cleveland units.

In Sweden, the military training syllabus had moved to all-through jet training in 1987 and most of the Bulldogs began to be phased out. Some SK 61s were equipped with a more comprehensive avionics fit for the training of civilian commercial pilots of the Trafikflyghogskolan

(now part of Lund University School of Aviation) (TFHS) also located at Ljungbyhed. These aircraft were designated either SK 61D or SK 61E depending on the equipment fitted. Later a total of 27 Bulldogs were transferred to the civil register, given registrations in the SE-LL- and SE-LN- series, and modified to civil regulations in 2000/2001. The Bulldogs of the TFHS were sold in batches with the last being disposed of in 2006. As the SK 61 was phased out some were distributed among the

Air Force Wings and continued in service as liaison aircraft until 1998 but most were stored at Ljungbyhed. The flying clubs associated with the Air Force were initially promised 25 Bulldogs but nothing came of the plan and instead the aircraft were sold on the civilian market with most going to the USA, Hungary and the UK. Twelve Air Force Bulldogs were taken on by the Flygvapenmuseum (Swedish Air Force Museum) some of which were allocated to technical schools as instructional airframes. One aircraft, Fv61025 SE-FVX c/n BH100-130 was donated to the Swedish Historic Flight at Satenas and a second, Fv61015 c/n BH100-117 went to the Flygflottij 15 Museum, Soderhamn.

A large batch of Swedish aircraft was sold to Avia-Rent in Hungary and many remain there in civil operation. Among other original military users, the Botswana Air Force sold its remaining five Bulldogs to AW Aviation in the UK who sold them on to private owners and the Ghana Air Force also released its in the mid-1990s, again with these ending up back in Britain. The survivors of the Nigerian Air Force's 37 strong fleet were offered for sale in 2012, having been in withdrawn

Safely delivered by Joe Drury across "The Pond", the Swedish Bulldog now flies in Florida registered N1004N. *(RS)*

ACROSS THE POND

Of the many ex-military Bulldogs sold to buyers in the United States, most were dismantled and shipped by sea. However, a few embarked on the long trip across "The Pond". One such was the Swedish Bulldog, SE-LNP which made its epic delivery flight in August, 2005 in the hands of Joe Drury who was facing his first experience as a ferry pilot. The first leg through gloomy weather was to

Wick in the UK where Andrew Bruce of Far North Aviation assisted with fitting large auxiliary tanks. This left not much room and survival equipment seemed to take up most of the remaining space. Hard to also fit a suitcase, food, maps and Joe himself into the already cramped cockpit. But, with a total North Atlantic flying time of 45 hours and individual leg times of 7 hours, he needed to be comfortable!

And then - off to Iceland and aeroplane was sluggish but clawed her way into the air and took half an hour climb to 6,000ft. Joe lost ATC contact and was left listening to the airliners while concentrating on navigating precisely to Keflavik. A long time later, he spoke to "Iceland Radio" where the woman controller sounded wonderful. The Bulldog landed in a howling gale. It was only a brief overnight stop, then back in the cockpit, heading west north-west over the Denmark Strait to Kulusuk. There was no alternate airport if Joe couldn't land at his destination, Kulusuk. The PNR (point of no return) came and went. As the Bulldog neared the coast it flew into cloud and instantly accumulated ice. Propeller to full low pitch and carburettor heat. The weather was awful and the airfield invisible - but a condition at Kaduna for several years and a number of major components including fuselages and wings were sold to Milsom Aerospace in New Zealand and may be refurbished and made airworthy in the future.

Quite a number of Bulldogs were sold to United States buyers, with a batch of 18 Swedish aircraft being acquired by Robert Garretson and sold on to American buyers. These were regarded as being specially desirable as they had the third rear seat, an average of only 4,000 flying hours and modern avionics including an ADF and DME. One particular buyer was Thomas L. Bragg of the Bulldog Aircraft Company at Peter Prince Field, Pensacola, Florida. He was a pilot for KLM and his Bulldog acquisitions included at least a dozen ex-RAF aircraft and a batch of seven from Jordan. In the USA, spares support is provided by SA Bulldogs USA run by Sherrill Greene at North Fort Myers, Florida. This organisation, which acquired all the SAF spares holding, also supplies spares to owners outside the United States. The Bulldogs in America are operated under the Experimental Exhibition category which permits IFR night

flying. In practice, these aircraft are maintained to normal CofA standards but cannot be used for flight training.

While most civilianised Bulldogs have been operated by private owners for sport and leisure flying, there have also been some specialised applications. One aircraft, G-BCUO, has been employed by Cranfield University's NFLC (National Flying Laboratory Centre) as a flight test research vehicle. It has been used for research into advanced in-flight instrumentation including fibre optic pressure and strain sensors. This project started in October, 2010 with the Bulldog being certified and flight tested in

July, 2014. Another notable outlet for the Bulldog's attributes has been in providing access for flying to disabled pilots through the Aerobility organisation based at Blackbushe in the UK. In 2003, Prince Feisal of Jordan gifted four Bulldogs (c/n 417, 432, 433 and 435) which had been in service with the Royal Jordanian Air Force, to the British Disabled Flying Association. Still remaining in service is the final production aircraft, G-DISA (c/n 435) which was operated by Aerobility in the south of England until 2012 when ownership passed to Ian Whiting and it now flies from Ashaig Airfield on the Isle of Skye providing flying for the disabled.

Originally registered G-BCUU, this Model 122A served with the Ghana Air Force as G-111 and then returned in 1996 to join the fleet at Cranfield University as G-CCOA. Following damage from a practice forced landing the fuselage is now displayed on the Isle of Wight pained as G-AXEH. *(RS)*

kind Danish pilot waiting to depart saw the Bulldog's landing lights and guided him down to the gravel runway. Joe's relief was immense.

Then onwards to the Greenland capital, Godthåb (or Nuuk as it is correctly known in Inuit) climbing to 14,000ft to clear the icecap, and cruising for around five hours over featureless terrain. Now to start the descent. But suddenly there was a loud bang and the engine started coughing. A petrol smell. It transpired that the aft auxiliary tank had imploded, soaking the floor with fuel. Fortunately this was followed by a safe landing. Joe had little time to rest before the long night flight to Goose Bay in Canada, across the Davis Strait - his longest water crossing. Fuel calculations were re-done following the loss of the auxiliary tank. Once

airborne, darkness fell over the Davis Strait and no radio contact was possible. It was time to change batteries in the Garmin GPS, but with chilled fingers he dropped the batteries. In the middle of a freezing ocean, three hundred miles from land with no GPS it was essential to fly a really accurate heading. Then, after three long hours a faint Morse code Y-Y-R heralded the radio range station at Goose Bay. To his complete surprise, Joe was only 30 miles off course! He was a happy man to get into the warm terminal building, having just flown thirteen hours in a day.

There were many miles still to do across the wild Canadian back-country, then half of the United States to traverse and the Rocky Mountains to fly over. The Bulldog was turning heads, as they were

extremely rare in North America. Overhead Mount Rushmore National Memorial in the Black Hills Joe photographed the Presidential sculptures. Then it was on over the Rockies and a struggle to reach 12,000 ft., clearing some of the ridges with only 50 or so feet to spare. Finally, the Bulldog touched down at Compton Regional Airport. Her new owner waiting - delighted to see his new acquisition which Joe had managed to give a good polish at a recent fuel stop.

The epic flight with SE-LNP was achieved at an average speed of 91 knots. It took 62 flying hours to fly the 6,517 miles. The Bulldog now wears a new registration - N1004N and continues to give great flying satisfaction to its American owners.

CHAPTER SIXTEEN

FLYING THE BULLDOG

Botswana Defence Force Bulldog OD-1 was one of six supplied. Following storage in Malta it returned to the UK in 1994 to become G-BHXA. *(RS)*

I can feel the flying controls firming up, airspeed must be above 120 knots by now. In my peripheral vision I see the runway threshold flashing by 500 feet below but my concentration is only on the Bulldog about 10 metres to my side, and two others beyond, drifting up and down as we all make minute control movements to stay in place. I'm waiting for the leader to pull into a 60-degree bank away from the formation, curving round and descending to the runway to roll wings level just before landing, mindful that there will be three other Bulldogs close behind, all aiming to land on the same runway a few seconds behind each other...

Somehow, a Bulldog in civilian markings always looks a bit out-of-place to my eyes. There is something purposeful about the 'dog, even just sitting on the ground, that tells you it's been built to do more than fly in straight lines from A to B. First impressions walking around the airframe confirm the solid build, surprisingly slim and graceful wings and an over-sized vertical tail - no wonder it's got a 30-knot crosswind limit. Climb up onto the wing, pull the canopy back, step down into the cockpit and the military feel is reinforced. There's great all-round visibility, and plenty of room behind the two seats if you do feel the need to haul baggage around.

The wide instrument panel has plenty of room for all the instruments and avionics a pilot could reasonably ask for, the flying controls fall easily to hand, and even at over six feet tall I have no trouble getting comfortable thanks to the adjustable rudder pedals.

Start-up is, again, military in feel, with a starter button rather than key turn, but, provided you don't over-prime the engine (a common gotcha for new Bulldog drivers), you'll usually be rewarded with the engine bursting into life eagerly after a couple of propeller blades have flicked past. Once on the move the direct nosewheel steering and good all-round visibility make taxiing straightforward and, checks complete, we're on the runway and ready to roll. The throttle goes forward, the noise level goes up, and just a bit of rudder is needed to keep straight as we accelerate briskly down the strip. Raise the nosewheel at 50 knots, lift-off at 60 knots and accelerate towards 80 knots for the climb. In most conditions we'll have used no more than 400 metres as we pass 50ft.

First impressions are of responsive controls, slightly more firm than the Pup and, perhaps because of the Bulldog's greater weight and wing loading, not as feather-light on the stick as the Chipmunk. Just like its predecessors trim is precise and there's no excuse not to be able to put the airspeed just where you want it.

Levelling out in the cruise and you need to decide how far you want to go and how quickly you want to empty your wallet. A 120 knot cruise means that you're burning through the fuel at 50 litres an hour and you'll need to be thinking about landing after not much more than two hours airborne. Throttle back a bit to 108 knots instead and you'll burn around 32 litres an hour and so can fly quite a bit further. With a relatively small fuel capacity no-one would accuse the Bulldog of being a classic long-range tourer, and if you throttle back too much you start getting overtaken by Cessna and Pipers and even Chipmunks - and there's no fun in that. Nevertheless, she'll bore straight lines in the sky quite happily and she also makes a stable platform for instrument flying.

Slow down and as you get towards the stall the Bulldog gives plenty of warning that things are getting uncomfortable - the controls become sloppy but still reasonably effective, there's a very light buffet as the airflow starts to give up the struggle and breaks away from the wing. Persist in bringing the stick back further and even then the Bulldog rarely bites - instead the nose pitches down lazily and unless badly provoked it's unusual for there to be a significant wing drop.

Anecdotally, spinning can be a different matter and like most Bulldog pilots I've read some scary stuff about the Bulldog spin, but in my (limited) experience, the spin entry, the spin itself and recovery are all straightforward. There again, I have a personal rule that I only spin the Bulldog if I have three assets in hand:

- At least 7,000ft between me and terra firma;
- An experienced ex-RAF Bulldog instructor in the other seat - and
- A parachute.

Standard aerobatic figures are easy to fly in the Bulldog. Although there's probably not quite enough power and just a bit too much drag to explore the more advanced figures, it's been my privilege to watch ex-RAF pilots pirouetting my Bulldog around the sky in gentle and graceful manoeuvres, always with plenty of control margin to spare and rarely going beyond 3g. The roll rate feels just right, and somehow the Bulldog always wants to turn at 60° angle of bank rather than 30°, control forces rise progressively as "g" builds up. No doubt you can take the Bulldog by the scruff of the neck and throw it around the sky, but somehow she doesn't feel suited to that sort of controlled violence.

Around the circuit the wide range of potential level flight speeds (80 - 120 knots) and relatively high limiting speed for the first stage of flap (135 knots) makes it easy to fit in with other traffic. The 'dog is stable and responsive in the approach configuration, and the good elevator controllability right down to the stall makes properly 'held-off' touchdowns easy to achieve, though the military-grade main undercarriage will cope with most mis-handled landings. Again, in most conditions landing to full stop requires no more than 400 metres. If the Bulldog does have one Achilles heel in this phase it's the gliding performance. Close the throttle fully and even at best glide speed she comes down fast. Get the speed wrong (especially too slow) and the 'dog glides like a brick – it can catch out someone used to the glide performance of an average Cessna or Chipmunk.

In short, the Bulldog does a lot of things rather well - there are not many aeroplanes that are equally happy as a trainer, tourer, aerobatic mount or instrument flying platform, but there is just one area, above all others, where she seems to really come into her element - and that is formation flying. The combination of precise and responsive flying controls, a reasonable reserve of power, good stability and great all-round visibility make this a machine that loves company - in twos, threes and fours (and sometimes more) there's little to beat the precision flying, team work and camaraderie of Bulldog formation flying. For my money, flying a tail chase under blue skies and over green fields is some of the best fun you can have in an aeroplane.

And so here I am, nudging the stick and throttle to hold station with the formation, waiting for the moment to snap over into a steep turn, then easing into a gliding curve to the runway 500ft below. In this moment, there is no aeroplane I'd rather be in.

"Green formation. Break. Break. GO!"

Jeremy Pratt

Jeremy Pratt, proprietor of the well known aviation retailer, Airplan Flight Equipment (AFE) acquired two of the ex Botswana Bulldogs. G-BHXA is currently airworthy and G-BHZS is held in storage as a spares source. *(RS)*

SAL BULLDOG – GENERAL ARRANGEMENT DRAWINGS

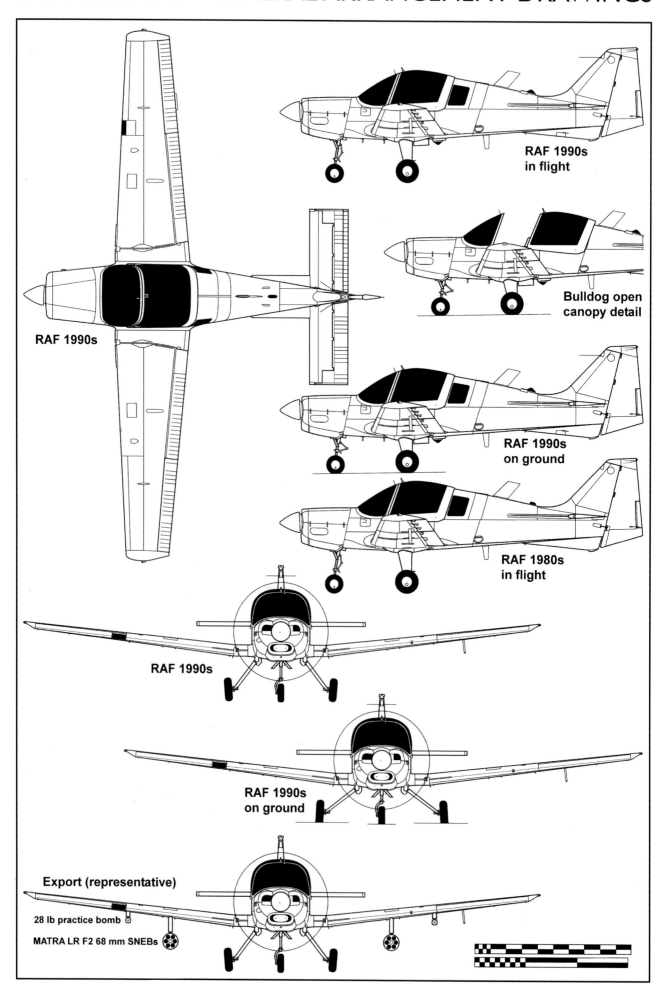

RAF 1990s
in flight

Bulldog open
canopy detail

RAF 1990s

RAF 1990s
on ground

RAF 1980s
in flight

RAF 1990s

RAF 1990s
on ground

Export (representative)

28 lb practice bomb

MATRA LR F2 68 mm SNEBs

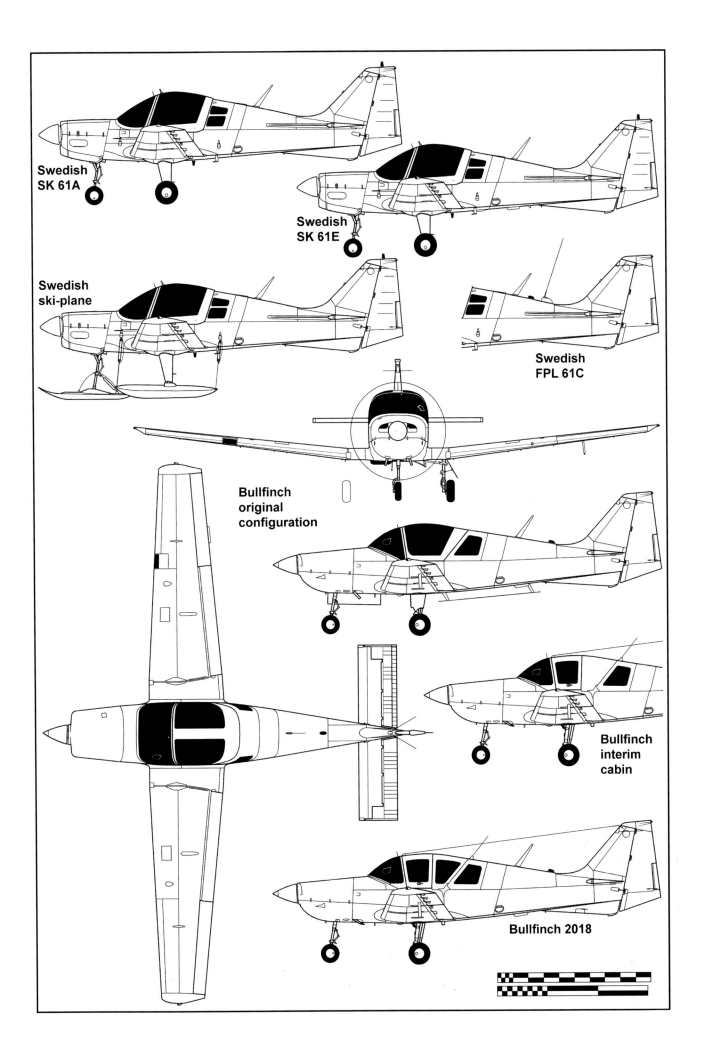

Swedish SK 61A

Swedish SK 61E

Swedish ski-plane

Swedish FPL 61C

Bullfinch original configuration

Bullfinch interim cabin

Bullfinch 2018

BULLDOG SPECIFICATIONS

	Bulldog Srs. 120	Bulldog SA-3-200 and Bullfinch
Powerplant	One Avco-Lycoming IO-360-A1A	One Avco-Lycoming IO-360-A1B6
	Fuel-injected and rated at 200 hp	Fuel-injected and rated at 200 hp
	Hartzell HC-C2YK-4/C7666A-2	Hartzell HC-F27R-1F-F7666A-2
	74-in (1,879 mm) diameter	74-in (1,879 mm) diameter
	metal constant speed propeller	metal constant speed propeller
Dimensions		
Wing span	33ft 3in (10.13 m)	33ft 10in (10.31 m)
Overall Length	23ft 3in (7.08 m)	24ft 11in (7.59 m)
Height	7ft 5.75in (2.28 m)	8ft 4 in (2.54 m)
Wing Area	129.4 sq.ft. (12.02 sq.m.)	133.5 sq.ft (12.40 sq.m.)
Wing Loading	18.2 lb/sq.ft. (89.3 kg/m.sq)	19.48 lb/sq.ft
Weights		
Max. Takeoff Weight - aerobatic	2,238 lb (1,015 kg)	2,293 lb (1,040 kg)
Max takeoff weight - semi-aerobatic	2,350 lb (1,066 kg)	2,601 lb (1,180 kg)
Empty Weight with std.equip	1,430 lb (645 kg)	1,810 lb (820 kg)
Maximum load with full fuel	679 lb (308 kg)	n/a
Performance		
(ISA, 2,315 lb.TOGW)		
Max level speed at sea level	130 kt (150 mph, 241 km/h)	150 kt (173 mph, 278 km/h)
Max Cruise Speed at 4,000ft, 75% power	120 kt (138 mph, 222 km/h)	141 kt (162 mph, 261 km/h)
Economical Cruise Speed, 75% power	105 kt (121 mph, 195 km/h)	n/a
Stall Speed, power off, full flap	53 kt (61 mph, 98 km/h)	55 kt (63 mph, 102 km/h)
Rate of climb at sea level	1,034 fpm (315 m/m)	1,160 fpm (354 m/m)
Service Ceiling	16,000 ft (4,877 m)	18,500 ft (5,639 m)
Takeoff to unstick distance	900 ft (275 m)	n/a
Takeoff distance over 50ft obstacle	1,400 ft (427 m)	1,280 ft (390 m)
Tactical spec takeoff distance	1,155 ft (352 m)	n/a
Landing distance from 50ft	1,189 ft (363 m)	1,238 ft (377 m)
Tactical spec landing distance	860 ft (262 m)	n/a
Gross landing run	500 ft (153 m)	n/a
Range with max fuel, 55% power	540 nm (622 sm, 1,000 km)	540 nm (622 sm, 1,000 km)
Endurance with max fuel, 55% power	5.0 hours	5.0 hours

Several Bulldogs are airworthy in the USA and this one, NX514XX is active with Tony Greene based at Fort Myers, Florida. *(RS)*

SCOTTISH AVIATION BULLDOG
PRODUCTION HISTORIES

Detailed histories of each of the Bulldogs are shown here, as far as they are known. As most of the aircraft still currently exist, the information is correct up to 30 November, 2018. It should be noted that, where there are dates in [square brackets], these give (where appropriate) the known earliest and latest dates. In particular, for RAF aircraft, record keeping moved from paper movement cards (which have been referred to) to computer files, where much information was over-written as matters changed, so no permanent record of the full history was retained. Consequently, many movements have had to be based on information recorded at the time in enthusiast magazines (notably *Air-Britain News*). Many of the Bulldogs supplied to the RAF units were also temporarily loaned out to other units from time to time for a few weeks. These loans have generally been ignored, as have movements to and from maintenance units for routine servicing.

With many of the overseas sales going to third world countries, details of their usage (and, more particularly, abusage and demise) remain unknown. Only one Bulldog was sold new into the civilian market, albeit to BAe's local representative in Venezuela, and its fate also remains unknown. Most of the ex-military aircraft, when disposed of, gravitated either back to the UK or to the USA, although many of the ex-Swedish Air Force specimens were sold to Hungary, where some still remain in store. Curiously, most of the Nigerian Air Force Bulldogs seem to have ended up in New Zealand, albeit none are yet known to have been made airworthy.

PROTOTYPES:

B125-001 B.125 Bulldog Model 1. Regd **G-AXEH** (CofR R10608) 25.4.69 to Beagle Aircraft Ltd, Shoreham. Ff 19.5.69. CofA issued 27.5.69. To Sweden 1.70 for demonstrations; painted as '71-FC'; latterly in Finland; returned to UK 8.6.70. Cld 29.5.70 & regd 27.7.70 to Scottish Aviation (Bulldog) Ltd, Prestwick; deld 10.7.70. Fitted with 3-blade Hartzell propeller & reflown 25.6.74 on trials. CofA lapsed 15.1.77. Regn cld 19.6.78 as pwfu. Stored Prestwick as ground trainer. Donated to Museum of Flight, East Fortune 23.12.84; removed from display [1.16] and stored.

The Bulldog prototype, still named Beagle Bulldog, seen at Shoreham on its return from the 1969 Paris Air Show. *(PD)*

B125-002 B.125 Bulldog Model 1. Regd **G-AXIG** (CofR R10975) 24.6.69 to Beagle Aircraft Ltd, Shoreham. Cld 29.5.70 & regd 2.2.71 to Scottish Aviation (Bulldog) Ltd, Prestwick. Airframe completed by SAL as Bulldog Model.100 and ff 14.2.71; painted in Swedish AF c/s as '61000/5'. CofA issued 16.2.71. To A&AEE Boscombe Down 22.6.71 for trials. Cld & regd 21.11.73 to George House (Holdings) Ltd (Alan Curtis), Farnham (based Blackbushe); deld 1.2.74; later Compton Abbas & op by Air Compton; returned to Blackbushe [95]. Regd 7.3.97 to Angus Alan Douglas-Hamilton (15th Duke of Hamilton), Edinburgh (based Archerfield Estate, Dirleton). Donated on death of owner to National Museums Scotland; ferried by air to East Fortune 23.2.11. Regn cld 21.4.11 as pwfu. To Headquarters Museum in Chambers St, Edinburgh & on display wef 7.11.

B125-003 Static test airframe completed by Scottish Aviation at Prestwick.

PRODUCTION AIRCRAFT:

BH100-101 Model 101 Regd **G-AYWN** (CofR R12183) 19.4.71 to Scottish Aviation (Bulldog) Ltd. Ff 22.6.71. CofA issued 5.7.71 (for 2 months); ferried to Sweden 26.7.71. Regn cld 29.7.71 as sold Sweden. To Swedish AF as Sk61A **Fv61001** 11.8.71 at Ljungbyhed. Wfu .01. To Ljungbyheds Aeronautiska Sallstap/Ljungbyheds Militarhistoriska Museum, Ljungbyhed.

The two prototypes and the first production Bulldog at Prestwick. *(DJ)*

BH100-102 Model 101. Regd **G-AYWO** (CofR R12184) 19.4.71 to Scottish Aviation (Bulldog) Ltd. Ff 14.7.71. CofA issued 19.7.71 (for 2 months); ferried to Sweden 26.7.71. Regn cld 29.7.71 as sold Sweden. To Swedish AF as Sk61A **Fv61002 23.9.71** at Ljungbyhed. Sold 10.04 to Avia-Rent Kft, Hungary. Regd **HA-TVB** 20.6.08 to Avia-Rent Kft, Budapest. Currently regd; based Kaposujlak.

BH100-103 Model 101. Regd **G-AYWP** (CofR R12185) 19.4.71 to Scottish Aviation (Bulldog) Ltd. Ff 1.8.71. CofA issued 2.8.71 (for 2 months); ferried to Sweden 6.8.71. Regn cld 7.8.71 as sold Sweden. To Swedish AF as Sk61A **Fv61003** 14.9.71 at Ljungbyhed. Sold 10.04 to Avia-Rent Kft, Hungary but not regd. Stored Kaposujlak [7.18].

BH100-104 Model.101. Regd **G-AYZL** (CofR R12266) 25.5.71 to Scottish Aviation (Bulldog) Ltd. Ff 18.8.71. CofA issued 23.8.71 (for 2 months); ferried to Sweden 25.8.71. Regn cld 27.8.71 as sold Sweden. To Swedish AF as Sk61A **Fv61004** 1.10.71 at Ljungbyhed. Sold 10.04 to Avia-Rent Kft, Hungary; stored Budaors. Regd **HA-TUJ** 12.10.11 to Avia-Rent Kft, Budapest; based Budaors; later Gyuro [1.12]. Currently regd; based Gyuro.

BH100-105 Model 101. Regd **G-AYZM** (CofR R12267) 25.5.71 to Scottish Aviation (Bulldog) Ltd. Ff 24.8.71. CofA issued 30.8.71 (for 2 months); ferried to Sweden 31.8.71. Regn cld 2.9.71 as sold Sweden. To Swedish AF as Sk61A **Fv61005** 6.10.71 at Ljungbyhed. To Trafikflyghogskolan (Lund University School of Aviation), Ljungbyhad (mod to Sk61D). To Svedinos Bil-och Flygmuseum, Ugglarp 8.04; on display [8.16].

BH100-106 Model 101. Regd **G-AZAK** (CofR R12293) 18.6.71 to Scottish Aviation (Bulldog) Ltd. Ff 10.9.71. CofA issued 14.9.71 (for 2 months); ferried to Sweden 15.9.71. Regn cld 17.9.71 as sold Sweden. To Swedish AF as Sk61A **Fv61006** 3.11.71 at Ljungbyhed. To Malmen. To Angelholms Flygmuseum, Angelholms 8.12; on display [2.17].

BH100-107 Model 101. Regd **G-AZAL** (CofR R12294) 18.6.71 to Scottish Aviation (Bulldog) Ltd. Ff 21.9.71. CofA issued 23.9.71 (for 2 months); ferried to Sweden 24.9.71. Regn cld 26.9.71 as sold Sweden. To Swedish AF as Sk61A **Fv61007** 11.11.71 at Ljungbyhed. Later mod to Sk61D. Regd **SE-LLC** 15.3.01 to Trafikflyghogskolan (Lund University School of Aviation), Ljungbyhed. Regn cld 6.9.02 as sold USA; ferried via Stapleford 20.6.02. Regd **N2077N** 13.9.02 to John R Stalick, Potomac, MD. Regd **N701BD** (reserved 1.11.02) 31.3.03 to Francis A Myers, Mendota Heights, MN. Regd [6.06] to Joseph E Simpson, Knoxville, TN. Regd 26.7.08 to Christian Johnsen, Tarzana, CA. Regn cld by FAA 22.8.12. Regd 28.7.14 to same owner. Regn cld 28.3.18.

BH100-108 Model 101. Regd **G-AZAM** (CofR R12295) 18.6.71 to Scottish Aviation (Bulldog) Ltd. Ff 28.9.71. CofA issued 30.9.71 (for 2 months); ferried to Sweden 2.10.71. Regn cld 3.10.71 as sold Sweden. To Swedish AF as Sk61A **Fv61008** 10.11.71 at Ljungbyhed. Later mod to Sk61D. Regd **SE-LLB** 5.12.00 to Trafikflyghogskolan (Lund University School of Aviation), Ljungbyhed. Regn cld 6.9.02 as sold USA; ferried via Stapleford 20.6.02. Regd **N108BD** reserved 16.9.02 to Morgan Tull, Derwood. CofA issued 3.9.02. Regd [6.06] to Bulldog Flyers LLC, Wilmington, DE; painted in Swedish AF c/s, coded '5'. CofA lapsed 30.6.13. Regn cld 24.12.14.

BH100-109 Model 101. Regd **G-AZAN** (CofR R12296) 18.6.71 to Scottish Aviation (Bulldog) Ltd. Ff 6.10.71. CofA issued 8.10.71 (for 2 months); ferried to Sweden 8.10.71. Regn cld 12.10.71 as sold Sweden. To Swedish AF as Sk61A **Fv61009** 11.11.71 at Ljungbyhed. To FMHS, Halmstad 10.5.93 as instructional airframe. Remains later to Gothenburg; then to Klas Andersson, Gotene 9.08 & stored [8.16].

BH100-110 Model 101. Regd **G-AZAO** (CofR R12297) 18.6.71 to Scottish Aviation (Bulldog) Ltd. Ff 12.10.71. CofA issued 14.10.71 (for 2 months); ferried to Sweden 15.10.71. Regn cld 18.10.71 as sold Sweden. To Swedish AF as Sk61A **Fv61010** 24.11.71 at Ljungbyhed. Later mod to Sk61D. Regd **SE-LLG** 5.4.01 to Trafikflyghogskolan (Lund University School of Aviation), Ljungbyhed. Regn cld 6.9.02 as sold USA; ferried via Stapleford 20.6.02. Regd **N747BD** 18.10.02 to Nigel Bird, South Boston, MA. CofA issued 8.8.02. Regd 16.12.04 to Raphael Jacobelli, Acton, MA; later Norwalk, CT. CofA lapsed 19.9.06. Regn cld 12.2.08 as sold Australia. Regd VH-CHU 8.8.08 to Charlie Tial Seng Chua, Wembley, Perth.

BH100-111 Model 101. Regd **G-AZAP** (CofR R12298) 18.6.71 to Scottish Aviation (Bulldog) Ltd. Ff 19.10.71. CofA issued 21.10.71 (for 2 months); ferried to Sweden 29.10.71. Regn cld 1.11.71 as sold Sweden. To Swedish AF as Sk61A **Fv61011** 30.11.71 at Ljungbyhed. Later mod to SK61D. Regd **SE-LLM** 4.10.01 to Trafikflyghogskolan (Lund University School of Aviation), Ljungbyhed. Deld 10.9.02 to Danish Luftfartsskolen, Roskilde. Regd 30.9.05 to ML Flygutbildning, Malmen/Vardsberg. Regd 27.10.17 to NAJ Aviation AB, Ornskoldsvik. Currently regd.

BH100-112 Model 101. Regd **G-AZAR** (CofR R12299) 18.6.71 to Scottish Aviation (Bulldog) Ltd. Ff 1.11.71. CofA issued 4.11.71 (for 2 months); ferried to Sweden 5.11.71. Regn cld 7.11.71 as sold Sweden. To Swedish AF as Sk61A **Fv61012** 14.1.72 at Ljungbyhed. Sold 10.04 to Avia-Rent Kft, Hungary but not regd. Last reported stored Kaposujlak [7.11]; probably still currently stored.

BH100-113 Model 101. Regd **G-AZAS** (CofR R12300) 18.6.71 to Scottish Aviation (Bulldog) Ltd. Ff 5.11.71. CofA issued 10.11.71 (for 2 months); ferried to Sweden 11.11.71. Regn cld 13.11.71 as sold Sweden. To Swedish AF as Sk61A **Fv61013** 10.12.71 at Ljungbyhed. Sold 10.04 to Avia-Rent Kft, Hungary but not regd. Last reported stored Kaposujlak [7.11]; probably still currently stored.

BH100-114 Model 101. Regd **G-AZAT** (CofR R12301) 18.6.71 to Scottish Aviation (Bulldog) Ltd. Ff 29.10.71. CofA issued 1.11.71 (for 2 months); ferried to Sweden 3.11.71. Regn cld 7.11.71 as sold Sweden. To Swedish AF as Sk61A **Fv61014** 1.12.71 at Ljungbyhed. Crashed Simmelberga farm, Kagerod 4.6.87; Kapt Staffan Hjelm killed.

A colourful Bulldog, FV66014 of the SAF. *(PH)*

BH100-115 Model 102. To Royal Malaysian AF as **FM1220**. Ff 25.11.71; roaded to London Docks 16.12.71 & shipped to Port Swettenham & erected at Kuala Lumpur; reflown 24.1.72. Deld 25.1.72 to Flying School, Alor Setar. Re-serialled **M25-01** mid 80s. Regd **9M-EMM** 12.99 to Kedah Flying Club, Alor Setar; painted in Northern Warrior c/s. Stored Alor Setar [3.17].

BH100-116 Model 102. To Royal Malaysian AF as **FM1221**. Ff 9.12.71; roaded to London Docks 16.12.71 & shipped to Port Swettenham. Erected at Kuala Lumpur & reflown 24.1.72. Deld 25.1.72 to Flying School, Alor Setar. To Air Force Technical College, Alor Setar; on display [4.96; 3.13]; still painted as FM1221.

BH100-117 Model 101. Regd **G-AZEN** (CofR R12427) 9.9.71 to Scottish Aviation (Bulldog) Ltd. Ff 9.11.71. CofA issued 10.11.71 (for 2 months); ferried to Sweden 11.11.71. Regn cld 13.11.71 as sold Sweden. To Swedish AF as Sk61A **Fv61015** 13.12.71 at Ljungbyhed. To Flygflottij 15 Museum, Soderhamn 11.99; on display [8.17].

BH100-118 Model 101. Regd **G-AZEO** (CofR R12428) 9.9.71 to Scottish Aviation (Bulldog) Ltd. Ff 15.11.71. CofA issued 17.11.71 (for 2 months); ferried to Sweden 18.11.71. Regn cld 20.11.71 as sold Sweden. To Swedish AF as Sk61A **Fv61016** 13.1.72 at Ljungbyhed. Later mod to SK61D. Regd **SE-LLD** 15.3.01 to Trafikflyghogskolan (Lund University School of Aviation), Ljungbyhed. Regn cld 6.9.02 as sold USA; ferried via Stapleford 20.6.01. Regd **N118BD** (reserved 17.9.02) to William G Ehrhorn, Marathon, FL. Regd 13.12.16 to Marathon Aviation Associates LLC (Steve Kortokrax), Marathon, FL. Regd 22.9.18 to Steven D Kortokrax, Roanoke, IN. Currently regd.

BH100-119 Model 101. Regd **G-AZEP** (CofR R12429) 9.9.71 to Scottish Aviation (Bulldog) Ltd. Ff 19.11.71. CofA issued 24.11.71 (for 2 months); ferried to Sweden 25.11.71. Regn cld 7.12.71 as sold Sweden. To Swedish AF as Sk61A **Fv61017** 12.1.72 at Ljungbyhed. Later mod to SK61E. Regd **SE-LNA** 5.12.00 to Trafikflyghogskolan (Lund University School of Aviation), Ljungbyhed. Regn cld 26.10.05 as sold USA. Regd **N4321B** 3.1.06 to Robert David Garretson, Ipswich (also of Long Beach, CA). CofA issued 12.8.06. Regd 13.4.07 to Sales Solutions Inc, San Ramon, CA. Regd 29.8.14 to Thomas L Klassen, Corpus Christi, TX. Regd 23.9.17 to Bob Livingston, Weston, FL. Regd 27.12.17 to John P Stone, Red Lion, PA. Regn pending 16.5.18 to Frank J Smith, Enola, PA

BH100-120 Model 102. To Royal Malaysian AF as **FM1222**. Ff 29.12.71; roaded to London Docks 17.1.72 & shipped to Port Swettenham. Erected at Kuala Lumpur & reflown 2.72. Deld 2.72 to Flying School, Alor Setar. Re-serialled **M25-02** mid 80s. To Kedah Flying Club .98. Regd **9M-ERR** and noted on overhaul at Kuala Lumpur/Subang [7.00]. To instructional airframe at the Malaysian Aviation Training Academy, Kuantan in 2012; extant [2.16].

9M-ERR was an RMAF Bulldog sold to the Kedah Flying Club. *(RS)*

BH100-121 Model 101. Regd **G-AZES** (CofR R12430) 9.9.71 to Scottish Aviation (Bulldog) Ltd. Ff 22.11.71. CofA issued 24.11.71 (for 2 months); ferried to Sweden 25.11.71. Regn cld 27.11.71 as sold Sweden. To Swedish AF as Sk61A **Fv61018** 14.1.72 at Ljungbyhed. Later mod to SK61E. Regd **SE-LNF** 22.1.01 to Trafikflyghogskolan (Lund University School of Aviation), Ljungbyhed. Regn cld 9.12.05 as sold USA. Regd **N68TL** (reserved 23.8.06) 2.9.06 to Mark J Riesterer, Chandler, AZ. Regd 7.10.06 to Shelldon Inc, (Wilmington, DE). Regd 23.6.12 to Andrew Jon Barkin, Los Angeles, CA. CofA issued 25.2.13. Sale reported 10.10.14. Regd 13.11.15 to James J Foskett, Merrimac, WI; painted in Swedish AF c/s. Regd 13.4.18 to James Shoenberger, Orlando, FL. Currently regd.

BH100-122 Model 101. Regd **G-AZET** (CofR R12431) 9.9.71 to Scottish Aviation (Bulldog) Ltd. Ff 29.11.71. CofA issued 1.12.71 (for 2 months); ferried to Sweden 2.12.71. Regn cld 14.12.71 as sold Sweden. To Swedish AF as Sk61A **Fv61019** 4.2.72 at Ljungbyhed. Later mod to SK61E. Regd **SE-LNN** 17.5.01 to Trafikflyghogskolan (Lund University School of Aviation), Ljungbyhed. Regn cld 6.10.05 as sold United Kingdom. Regd **G-AZET** 18.10.05 to Robert David Garretson, Ipswich. CofA not renewed. Regd 18.8.06 to Peter Spencer Shuttleworth, Derby; stored East Winch [5.07]. Regn cld 28.1.08 as sold Hungary. Regd **HA-BUL** 18.5.12 to Hidroplan Norf Kft, Hajmasker/Szentkiralyszabadja. Currently regd.

BH100-123 Model 102. To Royal Malaysian AF as **FM1223**. Ff 19.1.72; roaded to London Docks 12.2.72 & shipped to Port Swettenham. Erected at Kuala Lumpur & reflown 3.72. Deld 3.72 to Flying School, Alor Setar. Re-serialled **M25-03** mid 80s. To Kedah Flying Club .98 & regd **9M-EAO**. To Taunton, UK [11.11] as hulk for sale. Offered at auction 30.5.12; located Wellington, Somerset. Stored Kemble [1.18].

BH100-124 Model 101. Regd **G-AZHV** (CofR R12521) 4.11.71 to Scottish Aviation (Bulldog) Ltd. Ff 2.12.71. CofA issued 8.12.71 (for 2 months); ferried to Sweden 9.12.71. Regn cld 11.12.71 as sold Sweden. To Swedish AF as Sk61A **Fv61020** 14.1.72 at Ljungbyhed. Later mod to

SK61E. Regd **SE-LNB** 22.1.01 to Trafikflyghogskolan (Lund University School of Aviation), Ljungbyhed. Sold 12.05 to Robert D Garretson. Regn cld 8.12.05 as sold USA. Regd **N123MY** 23.6.06 to Robert David Garretson, Ipswich (also of Long Beach, CA); based Compton, CA. CofA issued 19.5.07. Sold 22.6.08 & regd 19.8.08 to Charles A Gehrmann, Atlanta, GA (based Cartersville, GA). Currently regd.

BH100-125 Model 101. Regd **G-AZHW** (CofR R12522) 4.11.71 to Scottish Aviation (Bulldog) Ltd. Ff 9.12.71. CofA issued 13.12.71 (for 2 months); ferried to Sweden 16-29.12.71. Regn cld 31.12.71 as sold Sweden. To Swedish AF as Sk61A **Fv61021** 16.2.72 at Ljungbyhed. Later mod to SK61E. Regd **SE-LNC** 5.12.00 to Trafikflyghogskolan (Lund University School of Aviation), Ljungbyhed. Deld 16.9.02 to Danish Luftfartsskolen, Roskilde. Damaged in heavy landing Ljungbyhed 7.6.04. Regn cld 1.6.05 as destroyed. To Aeroseum Museum, Save Airfield, Goteborg 6.06 (on display 8.16).

BH100-126 Model 101. Regd **G-AZHX** (CofR R12523) 4.11.71 to Scottish Aviation (Bulldog) Ltd. Ff 16.12.71. CofA issued 22.12.71 (for 2 months); ferried to Sweden 27.12.71. Regn cld 31.12.71 as sold Sweden. To Swedish AF as Sk61A **Fv61022** 4.2.72 at Ljungbyhed. Later mod to SK61E. Regd **SE-LNO** 4.10.01 to Trafikflyghogskolan (Lund University School of Aviation), Ljungbyhed. Regn cld 6.10.05 as sold United Kingdom. Regd **G-AZHX** 18.10.05 to Robert David Garretson, Ipswich. Regd **G-DOGE** 7.12.05 to William Peter Cooper, Orpington; stored East Winch [10.06; 5.07]. CofA issued 15.3.08; based North Weald. Regd 24.1.12 to Mid America (UK) Ltd, Tain. Regd 24.5.13 to John Beresford Riversdale Elliot, Great Yarmouth. Regd 30.8.13 (back) to Mid America (UK) Ltd, Tain. Regd 6.5.16 to Thomas Woodstock Harris, Leighton Buzzard (based Holmbeck Farm, Burcott). Regd **G-AZHX** 2.6.16 to same party; now painted as XX625 '45'. Currently regd.

BH100-127 Model 102. To Royal Malaysian AF as **FM1224**. Ff 1.2.72; roaded to London Docks 12.2.72 & shipped to Port Swettenham. Erected at Kuala Lumpur & reflown 3.72. Deld 3.72 to Flying School, Alor Setar. Re-serialled **M25-04** mid 80s. To Kedah Flying Club, Alor Setar .98 (stored as M25-04 [9.04]). To Taunton, UK [11.11] as hulk for sale. Offered at auction 30.5.12; located at Wellington, Somerset. Stored Kemble [1.18; 9.18]. Reportedly sold [11.18].

BH100-128 Model 101. Regd **G-AZHY** (CofR R12524) 4.11.71 to Scottish Aviation (Bulldog) Ltd. Ff 21.12.71. CofA issued 22.12.71 (for 2 months); ferried to Sweden 27.12.71. Regn cld 31.12.71 as sold Sweden. To Swedish AF as Sk61A **Fv61023** 16.2.72 at Ljungbyhed. Later mod to SK61E. Regd **SE-LNG** 19.2.01 to Trafikflyghogskolan (Lund University School of Aviation), Ljungbyhed. Regn cld 23.8.05 as sold USA. Regd **N82696** 31.8.05 to Robert David Garretson, Ipswich (also of Long Beach, CA); ferried to Wick 7.9.05 & on to USA. Sold 12.05 to owner, Phoenix, AZ. Regd 3.06 to Mahmood Tehrani, Playa del Ray, CA; painted in USAF c/s. CofA issued 21.1.11. Regn cld 30.3.18.

BH100-129 Model 101. Regd **G-AZHZ** (CofR R12525) 4.11.71 to Scottish Aviation (Bulldog) Ltd. Ff 24.12.71. CofA issued 1.1.72 (for 2 months); ferried to Sweden 11.1.72. Regn cld 13.1.72 as sold Sweden. To Swedish AF as Sk61A **Fv61024** 16.3.72 at Ljungbyhed. Later mod to SK61D. Regd **SE-LLE** 15.3.01 to Trafikflyghogskolan (Lund University School of Aviation), Ljungbyhed. Sold 19.6.02 to Darryl Snider; ferried to Stapleford 20.6.02. Regn cld 6.9.02 as sold USA. Regd **N129BD** 16.9.02 to Darryl A Snider, Gaithersburg, MD. Sold 3.1.05 & regd 11.3.05 to Scott E Wilson, Erie, PA. Regd **N457FS** 27.6.05 to same owner. CofA issued 1.8.05. Sold 20.1.08 & regd 4.11.08 to Blue Air LLC (James V Barlow), Tucson, AZ. Sold 12.4.10 & regd 21.5.10 to Scott B Meskimen, Fort Walton Beach, FL. Currently regd.

SE-LLE was one of six Bulldogs ferried to the USA in June, 2002. *(PH)*

BH100-130 Model 101. Regd **G-AZIS** (CofR R12546) 25.11.71 to Scottish Aviation (Bulldog) Ltd. Ff 28.12.71. CofA issued 1.1.72 (for 2 months); ferried to Sweden 11.1.72. Regn cld 13.1.72 as sold Sweden. To Swedish AF as Sk61A **Fv61025** 13.3.72 at Ljungbyhed. Wfu & transferred to Swedish AF Museum .01. Regd **SE-FVX** 10.10.08 to Statens Forvarshistoriska Museer/Flygvapenmuseum, Linkoping. Regd 7.9.10 (as operator) to Swedish Air Force Historic Flight, Satenas; to Vanersborg. Currently regd.

BH100-131 Model 102. To Royal Malaysian AF as **FM1225**. Ff 24.2.72; roaded to London Docks 3.3.72 & shipped to Port Swettenham. Erected at Kuala Lumpur & reflown 3.72. Deld 3.72 to Flying School, Alor Setar. Written off 30.1.81.

BH100-132 Model 101. Regd **G-AZIT** (CofR R12547) 25.11.71 to Scottish Aviation (Bulldog) Ltd. Ff 11.1.72. CofA issued 13.1.72 (for 2 months); ferried to Sweden 20.1.72. Regn cld 24.1.72 as sold Sweden. To Swedish AF as Sk61A **Fv61026** 13.3.72 at Ljungbyhed. Regd **SE-LLF** 5.4.01 to Trafikflyghogskolan (Lund University School of Aviation), Ljungbyhed. Deld Southend 24.1.03; North Weald 25.1.03. Regn cld 12.9.03 as sold United Kingdom. Regd **G-RNRS** 12.9.03 to Power Aerobatics Ltd, Emsworth (based Old Sarum; later Kemble, then Goodwood). CofA issued 21.5.04. CofA lapsed 18.8.14 & stored Goodwood. Regn cld 25.4.17 as sold USA. Regd **N114EC** 2.5.17 (21.6.17) to Bulldog 132 LLC/Elliot Crawford, Nederland, CO. CofA issued 26.3.18. Currently regd.

BH100-133 Model 101. Regd **G-AZIU** (CofR R12548) 25.11.71 to Scottish Aviation (Bulldog) Ltd. Ff 14.1.72. CofA issued 19.1.72 (for 2 months); ferried to Sweden 21.1.72. Regn cld 24.1.72 as sold Sweden. To Swedish AF as Sk61A **Fv61027** 13.3.72 at Ljungbyhed. Sold 10.04 to Avia-Rent Kft, Hungary but not regd. On overhaul Kaposujlak [7.18].

BH100-134 Model 101. Regd **G-AZIV** (CofR R12549) 25.11.71 to Scottish Aviation (Bulldog) Ltd. Ff 20.1.72. CofA issued 26.1.72 (for 2 months); ferried to Sweden 27.1.72. Regn cld 4.2.72 as sold Sweden. To Swedish AF as Sk61A **Fv61028** 14.3.72 at Ljungbyhed. Sold 4.01 to Arna Flygklub (Flygklubb F16), Uppsala (but probably not deld). Sold 10.04 to Avia-Rent Kft, Hungary. Regd **HA-TVA** 26.5.12 to Avia-Rent Kft, Budapest. To Aviaticky Klub, Roudnice nad Labem airfield. Currently regd.

20 ex SAF Bulldogs were sold to Hungary, including HA-TVA. *(VK)*

BH100-135 Model 101. Regd **G-AZIW** (CofR R12550) 25.11.71 to Scottish Aviation (Bulldog) Ltd. Ff 25.1.72. CofA issued 26.1.72 (for 2 months); ferried to Sweden 27.1.72. Regn cld 31.1.72 as sold Sweden. To Swedish AF as Sk61A **Fv61029** 22.3.72 at Ljungbyhed. Sold 10.04 to Avia-Rent Kft, Hungary. Regd **HA-VUK** 21.10.14 to Avia-Rent Kft, Budapest. Currently regd; based Kaposujlak.

BH100-136 Model 102. To Royal Malaysian AF as **FM1226**. Ff 7.3.72; roaded to London Docks 6/7.4.72 & shipped to Port Swettenham. Erected at Kuala Lumpur & reflown 4.72. Deld 5.72 to Flying School, Alor Setar. Re-serialled **M25-05** mid 80s. To Kedah Flying Club, Alor Setar; stored as M25-05 [11.99; 3.13].

BH100-137 Model 101. Regd **G-AZJO** (CofR R12569) 8.12.71 to Scottish Aviation (Bulldog) Ltd. Ff 28.1.72. CofA issued 2.2.72 (for 2 months); ferried to Sweden 3.2.72. Regn cld 7.2.72 as sold Sweden. To Swedish AF as Sk61A **Fv61030** 17.3.72 at Ljungbyhed. To Flygvapenmuseum, Linkoping/Malmen .97; stored [8.16].

BH100-138 Model 101. Regd **G-AZJP** (CofR R12570) 8.12.71 to Scottish Aviation (Bulldog) Ltd. Ff 4.2.72. CofA issued 7.2.72 (for 2 months); ferried to Sweden 9.2.72. Regn cld 11.2.72 as sold Sweden. To Swedish AF as Sk61A **Fv61031** 29.3.72 at Ljungbyhed. Regd **SE-LLA** 1.9.01 to Trafikflyghogskolan (Lund University School of Aviation),

Ljungbyhed. Regn cld 8.12.05 as sold USA. Sold 30.5.06 (per Bill of Sale) to Robert D Garretson, Ipswich (also of Long Beach, CA). Sold 18.5.06 (by Garretson) & regd **N7507P** 18.9.06 to Mark Riesterer, Chandler, AZ. Regd **N105MR** 23.6.07 to same owner (based Ryan Field). CofA issued 18.2.08. Sold 3.5.12 & regd 22.6.12 to Stuart G Glenn, Naperville, IL. Sold 26.4.16 & regd 9.11.16 to TDS Logistics LLC (Charles Juneau), Tampa, FL. Currently regd.

BH100-139 Model 101. Regd **G-AZJR** (CofR R12571) 8.12.71 to Scottish Aviation (Bulldog) Ltd. Ff 8.2.72. CofA issued 9.2.72 (for 2 months); ferried to Sweden 17.2.72. Regn cld 28.2.72 as sold Sweden. To Swedish AF as Sk61A **Fv61032** 29.3.72 at Ljungbyhed. Sold 10.04 to Avia-Rent Kft, Hungary. Regd **N19FG** [reserved 31.1.06] 9.3.06 to Fred T Gribble, Fairfax, VT (later Tucson, AZ). CofA issued 29.12.06. Currently regd.

BH100-140 Model 102. To Royal Malaysian AF as **FM1227**. Ff 17.3.72; roaded to London Docks 6/7.4.72 & shipped to Port Swettenham. Erected at Kuala Lumpur & reflown 5.72. Deld 5.72 to Flying School, Alor Setar. Written off 9.3.73.

BH100-141 Model 101. Regd **G-AZJS** (CofR R12572) 8.12.71 to Scottish Aviation (Bulldog) Ltd. Ff 19.2.72. CofA issued 23.2.72 (for 2 months); ferried to Sweden 24-26.2.72. Regn cld 28.2.72 as sold Sweden. To Swedish AF as Sk61A **Fv61033** 29.3.72 at Ljungbyhed. To Ljungbyheds Aeronautiska Sallstap/Ljungbyheds Militarhistoriska Museum, Ljungbyhed 5.01. Stored [8.16] but removed by 2.17; fate unknown.

BH100-142 Model 101. Regd **G-AZJT** (CofR R12573) 8.12.71 to Scottish Aviation (Bulldog) Ltd. Ff 19.2.72. CofA issued 25.2.72 (for 2 months); ferried to Sweden 1-3.3.72. Regn cld 3.3.72. To Swedish AF as Sk61A **Fv61034** 13.4.72 at Ljungbyhed. Later mod to Sk61B. To instructional airframe at Ljungbyhed 4.01; extant 2.17.

BH100-143 Model 101. Regd **G-AZJU** (CofR R12574) 8.12.71 to Scottish Aviation (Bulldog) Ltd. Ff 28.2.72. CofA issued 1.3.72 (for 2 months); ferried to Sweden 3.3.72. Regn cld 6.3.72 as sold Sweden. To Swedish AF as Sk61A **Fv61035** 13.4.72 at Ljungbyhed. Later mod to Sk61D. Regd **SE-LLH** 17.5.01 to Trafikflyghogskolan (Lund University School of Aviation), Ljungbyhed. Current at Lulea [8.16].

BH100-144 Model 103. To Kenya AF as **701**. Ff 25.4.72; airfreighted ex Prestwick 24.7.72 aboard CL-44 TF-LLI. Last reported 4.94.

The first Kenya AF Model 103, serialled 701, was delivered in 1972. *(GJ)*

BH100-145 Model 101. Regd **G-AZMP** (CofR R12660) 1.2.72 to Scottish Aviation (Bulldog) Ltd. Ff 3.3.72. CofA issued 8.3.72 (for 2 months); ferried to Sweden 9-12.3.72. Regn cld 14.3.72 as sold Sweden. To Swedish AF as Sk61A **Fv61036** 28.4.72 at Ljungbyhed. Sold to Hungary 10.04 & regd **HA-TUK** 26.5.12 to Avia-Rent Kft, Budapest. Currently regd; based Kaposujlak [10.16].

BH100-146 Model 101. Regd **G-AZMR** (CofR R12661) 1.2.72 to Scottish Aviation (Bulldog) Ltd. Ff 8.3.72. CofA issued 15.3.72 (for 2 months); ferried to Sweden 16.3.72. Regn cld 20.3.72 as sold Sweden. To Swedish AF as Sk61A **Fv61037** 26.4.72 at Ljungbyhed. Later mod to Sk61D. Regd **SE-LLI** 14.6.01 to Trafikflyghogskolan (Lund University School of Aviation), Ljungbyhed. Deld to UK via Southend 24.1.03; North Weald 25.1.03; to East Winch. Regn cld 12.9.03 as sold United Kingdom. Regd **G-RAIG** 12.9.03 to Craig Stuart Beevers, London SW19 (based North Weald). CofA issued 6.7.04. Regd 30.11.06 to Power Aerobatics Ltd, Emsworth (based Kemble; later Goodwood). Sold 18.4.17 to Elliot Crawford. Regn cld 25.4.17 as sold USA. Regd **N146EC** (appln 25.4.17) 20.6.17 to Bulldog 146 LLC (Elliot Crawford), Nederland, CO. Currently regd (though no CofA yet issued).

The colourful G-RAIG was originally FV61037 with the SAF. *(RS)*

BH100-147 Model 102. To Royal Malaysian AF as **FM1228**. Ff 29.3.72; roaded to London Docks 3.5.72 & shipped to Port Swettenham. Erected at Kuala Lumpur & reflown 5.72. Deld 6.72 to Flying School, Alor Setar. Damaged Alor Setar 14.1.73; repaired. Re-serialled **M25-06** mid 80s. Probably the Bulldog w/off 21.9.95.

BH100-148 Model 101. Regd **G-AZMS** (CofR R12662) 1.2.72 to Scottish Aviation (Bulldog) Ltd. Ff 14.3.72. CofA issued 15.3.72 (for 2 months); ferried to Sweden 16/17.3.72. Regn cld 20.3.72 as sold Sweden. To Swedish AF as Sk61A **Fv61038** 16.5.72 at Ljungbyhed. Later mod to Sk61D. Regd **SE-LLK** 3.9.01 to Trafikflyghogskolan (Lund University School of Aviation), Ljungbyhed. Deld to UK via Southend 24.1.03; North Weald 25.1.03. Regn cld 12.9.03 as sold United Kingdom. Regd **G-OPOD** 12.9.03 to Power Aerobatics Ltd, Chichester (based Old Sarum, later Kemble). Regd **G-ULHI** 30.9.03 to same owner. CofA issued 11.10.04. Regd 4.1.13 to Kryten Systems Ltd, Swindon (based Kemble).

BH100-149 Model 101. Regd **G-AZMT** (CofR R12663) 1.2.72 to Scottish Aviation (Bulldog) Ltd. Ff 17.3.72. CofA issued 22.3.72 (for 2 months); ferried to Sweden 23.3.72. Regn cld 27.3.72 as sold Sweden. To Swedish AF as Sk61A **Fv61039** 5.5.72 at Ljungbyhed. Sold to Avia-Rent Kft, Hungary 10.04. Regd **HA-IHS** 6.11.07 to Avia-Rent Kft, Budapest. Crashed Bicske between Szar & Ujbarok 4.9.11; 2 killed. Remains stored Kaposujlak [10.16].

BH100-150 Model 102. To Royal Malaysian AF as **FM1229**. Ff 21.4.72; roaded to London Docks 3.5.72 & shipped to Port Swettenham. Erected at Kuala Lumpur & reflown 5.72. Deld 6.72 to Flying School, Alor Setar. Later serialled **M25-07** mid 80s. Regd **9M-EEE**. W/off (or regn cld) 5.2.00 but reported as derelict at Sungei Best [11.98].

BH100-151 Model 101. Regd **G-AZMU** (CofR R12664) 1.2.72 to Scottish Aviation (Bulldog) Ltd. Ff 21.3.72. CofA issued 22.3.72 (for 2 months); ferried to Sweden 23.3.72. Regn cld 27.3.72 as sold Sweden. To Swedish AF as Sk61A **Fv61040** 9.5.72 at Ljungbyhed. To Flygteknik Centrum, Vasteras/Hasslo as instructional airframe 8.04. Reportedly transferred to Swedish Air Force Historic Flight, Linkoping (based Satenas) in exchange for Fv61074 25.11.10 [but reported still at Hasslo 6.12].

BH100-152 Model 101. Regd **G-AZPI** (CofR R12723) 13.3.72 to Scottish Aviation (Bulldog) Ltd. Ff 28.3.72. CofA issued 12.4.72 (for 2 months); ferried to Sweden 13.4.72. Regn cld 17.4.72 as sold Sweden. To Swedish AF as Sk61A **Fv61041** 16.5.72 at Ljungbyhed. Sold to Avia-Rent Kft, Hungary 10.04 but not regd. Last reported stored Kaposvar [7.11].

BH100-153 Model 103. To Kenya AF as **702**. Ff 5.5.72; airfreighted ex Prestwick 24.7.72. Last reported [4.94].

BH100-154 Model 101. Regd **G-AZPJ** (CofR R12724) 13.3.72 to Scottish Aviation (Bulldog) Ltd. Ff 31.3.72. CofA issued 12.4.72 (for 2 months); ferried to Sweden 13.4.72. Regn cld 18.4.72 as sold Sweden. To Swedish AF as Sk61A **Fv61042** 18.5.72 at Ljungbyhed. Sold to Avia-Rent Kft, Hungary 10.04 but not regd. Last reported stored Kaposujlak [7.11].

BH100-155 Model 101. Regd **G-AZPK** (CofR R12725) 13.3.72 to Scottish Aviation (Bulldog) Ltd. Ff 18.4.72. CofA issued 19.4.72 (for 2 months); ferried to Sweden 20.4.72. Regn cld 25.4.72 as sold Sweden. To Swedish AF as Sk61A **Fv61043** 19.4.73 at Ljungbyhed. Later mod to Sk61D. Reg **SE-LLL** 3.9.01 to Trafikflyghogskolan (Lund University School of Aviation), Ljungbyhed. Regn cld 6.9.02 as sold USA; ferried via Stapleford 3.7.02. Regd **N5KE** (reserved 28.4.03) 3.6.06 to Edward T Morgan (Wyndham Flyers LLC), Washington, DC. Regd 10.10.09 to Faraway Air LLC, Wilmington, DE. CofA issued 15.6.17. Regd 14.2.18 to Paul Cebeci, Saint Augustine, FL. Currently regd.

BH100-156 Model 101. Regd **G-AZPL** (CofR R12726) 13.3.72 to Scottish Aviation (Bulldog) Ltd. Ff 20.4.72. CofA issued 26.4.72 (for 2 months); ferried to Sweden 27.4.72. Regn cld 1.5.72 as sold Sweden. To Swedish AF as Sk61A **Fv61044** 23.5.72 at Ljungbyhed. To Vannas Motormuseum, Vannas 6.06; on display [7.16].

BH100-157 Model 101. Regd **G-AZPM** (CofR R12727) 13.3.72 to Scottish Aviation (Bulldog) Ltd. Ff 27.4.72. CofA issued 3.5.72 (for 2 months); ferried to Sweden 4.5.72. Regn cld 8.5.72 as sold Sweden. To Swedish AF as Sk61A **Fv61045** 26.5.72 at Ljungbyhed. Later mod to Sk61E. Regd **SE-LNH** 15.3.01 to Trafikflyghogskolan (Lund University School of Aviation), Ljungbyhed. Regn cld 9.12.05 as sold USA. Sold (per Bill of Sale) 6.5.06 to Robert D Garretson, Ipswich (also of Long Beach, CA). Sold 18.5.06 & regd **N713AM** 31.8.06 to Mark J Riesterer, Chandler, AZ (based Ryan Field, Tucson). Regd 3.10.06 to Shelldon Inc (Mark Riesterer). CofA issued 18.1.07. Sold 19.2.07 & regd 28.3.07 to Anthony J Munn, Scottsdale, AZ. Sold 6.12.09 & regd 4.1.10 to William C Hamerstadt, Shelbyville, KY (later Carmel, IN) (based Indianapolis Metropolitan Airport). Sold 19.12.16 (by Estate of WCH) & regd 16.2.17 to Patrick H Apling, Hudson, MI. Currently regd.

The numeral 5 on FV61049 is the base code for Lyungbyhed. (PH)

BH100-158 Model 101. Regd **G-AZPN** (CofR R12728) 13.3.72 to Scottish Aviation (Bulldog) Ltd. Ff 4.5.72. CofA issued 10.5.72 (for 2 months); ferried to Sweden 11.5.72. Regn cld 15.5.72 as sold Sweden. To Swedish AF as Sk61A **Fv61046** 5.6.72 at Ljungbyhed. Regd **SE-LNS** 14.6.01 to Trafikflyghogskolan (Lund University School of Aviation), Ljungbyhed. Sold 12.05 to RD Garretson. Regn cld 9.12.05 as sold USA. Regd **N123SY** 23.6.06 to Robert David Garretson, Ipswich (also of Long Beach, CA); based Compton, CA. CofA issued 19.5.07. Sold 12.7.07 & regd 25.8.07 to Wilhelm A Steinhilber, Killingworth, CT. Sold 12.12.13 & regd 13.2.14 to Wing Waxers of South Florida Inc (Barry Ford), Lakeland, FL. Sold 8.8.17 & regd 3.11.17 to Eric W Bulger, Peachtree City, GA. Currently regd.

BH100-159 Model 102. To Royal Malaysian AF as **FM1230**. Ff 16.5.72; roaded to London Docks 24.5.72 & shipped to Port Swettenham. Erected at Kuala Lumpur & deld 6.72 to Flying School, Alor Setar. Re-serialled **M25-08** mid 80s. To Tentra Udara Diraja Malaysia (TUDM) Museum, Sungai Besi, Kuala Lumpur 12.9.98; on display [3.17].

BH100-160 Model 102. To Royal Malaysian AF as **FM1231**. Ff 8.6.72; roaded to London Docks 1.9.72 & shipped to Port Swettenham. Erected at Kuala Lumpur & deld 10.72 to Flying School, Alor Setar. Reported as re-serialled M25-09 mid 80s (but thought unlikely) To Alor Setar Base Collection, Flying Training Academy [10.93; 9.17]; painted as FM1231 (and on pole outside entrance).

BH100-161 Model 103. To Kenya AF as **703**. Ff 24.5.72; airfreighted ex Prestwick 24.7.72 aboard CL-44 TF-LLI. Last reported [9.09].

BH100-162 Model 101. Regd **G-AZPO** (CofR R12729) 13.3.72 to Scottish Aviation (Bulldog) Ltd. Ff 10.5.72. CofA issued 18.5.72 (for 2 months); ferried to Sweden 19.5.72. Regn cld 22.5.72 as sold Sweden. To Swedish AF as Sk61A **Fv61047** 6.6.72 at Ljungbyhed. Later mod to Sk61E. Regd **SE-LNR** 19.2.01 to Trafikflyghogskolan (Lund University School of Aviation), Ljungbyhed. Sold 12.05 to RD Garretson. Regn cld 9.12.05 as sold USA. Regd **N100MY** (reserved 8.6.06) 1.7.06 to Robert David Garretson, Ipswich (also of Long Beach, CA). Regd 30.9.06 to Mark J Reisterer, Chandler, AZ. Regd 31.3.07 to Thomas D Lee, Phoenix, AZ. CofA issued 26.12.07. Regd **N51TL** 9.11.11 (12.11.11) to same owner. Currently regd.

BH100-163 Model 101. Regd G-AZPP (CofR R12730) 13.3.72 to Scottish Aviation (Bulldog) Ltd. Ff 16.5.72. CofA issued 18.5.72 (for 2 months); ferried to Sweden 19.5.72. Regn cld 22.5.72 as sold Sweden. To Swedish AF as Sk61A **Fv61048** 9.6.72 at Ljungbyhed. Later mod to Sk61E. Regd **SE-LNI** 22.1.01 to Trafikflyghogskolan (Lund University School of Aviation), Ljungbyhed. Sold 17.10.05 to Robert Garretson. Regn cld 26.10.05 as sold USA. Regd **N432BD** 3.1.06 to Robert David Garretson,

Ipswich (also of Long Beach, CA). CofA issued 12.8.06. Sold 21.9.06 & regd 2.11.06 to William F Looke, San Antonio, TX. Sold 13.3.08 & regd 26.6.08 to Edward J & Martha M Hund, Wichita, KS. Forced landed out of fuel & struck fence nr Wichita 22.9.16. Salvage sold 8.5.17 to Dodson International Parts Inc, Rantoul, KS. Regn cld 1.6.18 as destroyed.

BH100-164 Model 101. Regd **G-AZPR** (CofR R12731) 13.3.72 to Scottish Aviation (Bulldog) Ltd. Ff 23.5.72. CofA issued 24.5.72 (for 2 months); ferried to Sweden 6.6.72. Regn cld 8.6.72 as sold Sweden. To Swedish AF as Sk61A **Fv61049** 22.6.72 at Ljungbyhed. Later mod to Sk61E. Regd **SE-LNL** 15.2.01 to Trafikflyghogskolan (Lund University School of Aviation), Ljungbyhed. Sold 17.8.05 to Robert Garretson, Ipswich. Regn cld 23.8.05 as sold USA. Regd **N8272R** 31.8.05 to Robert David Garretson, Ipswich (also of Long Beach, CA); ferried 17.9.05 to USA (ferry permit issued 6.9.05 for flight NE US border to Lebanon, NH). Sold 28.10.05 & regd 29.11.05 to Richard L Ezell, Lawrence, KS. Sold 29.7.09 & regd 4.9.09 to John D Cunningham & Sam Matta, Houston, TX (based West Houston Airport). Regd 29.7.10 to Sam Matta & Christopher Harding, Houston, TX. Regd 26.10.10 to Sam Matta, Christopher Harding & Patrick R Cooper, Houston. Damaged Lakeland-Linder Regional Airport 31.3.11 when DC-3 N839M was blown into it during a storm; repaired. Regd 27.8.15 to Sam Matta, Patrick R Cooper & Michael Bentham, Houston. Sold 11.7.16 & regd 27.1.17 to William E Ellington Jnr, Sam Matta & Patrick R Cooper, Houston, TX. Currently regd.

The Bulldog FV61049 served with Lund University as SE-LNL. (PH)

BH100-165 Model 101. Regd **G-AZPS** (CofR R12732) 13.3.72 to Scottish Aviation (Bulldog) Ltd. Ff 7.6.72. CofA issued 8.6.72 (for 2 months); ferried to Sweden 12.6.72. Regn cld 15.6.72 as sold Sweden. To Swedish AF as Sk61A **Fv61050** 30.6.72 at Ljungbyhed. Later mod to Sk61E. Regd **SE-LND** 15.2.01 to Trafikflyghogskolan (Lund University School of Aviation), Ljungbyhed. Regn cld 8.12.05 as sold USA. Regd **N207MR** (reserved 15.9.06) 9.06 to Mark J Reisterer, Chandler, AZ. Regd **N104MR** (reserved 23.2.07) 3.3.07 to same owner. Regd 3.10.09 to Mark L McCurdy & Matthew B McCurdy, Tucson, AZ. CofA issues 8.8.11. Currently regd.

BH100-166 Model 101. Regd **G-AZTX** (CofR R12803) 28.4.72 to Scottish Aviation (Bulldog) Ltd. Ff 13.6.72. CofA issued 15.6.72 (for 2 months); ferried to Sweden 16.6.72. Regn cld 19.6.72 as sold Sweden. To Swedish AF as Sk61A **Fv61051** 3.7.72 at Ljungbyhed. Later mod to Sk61E. Regd **SE-LNM** 22.1.01 to Trafikflyghogskolan (Lund University School of Aviation), Ljungbyhed. Sold 12.05 to RD Garretson. Regn cld 9.12.05 as sold USA. Regd **N101MY** 23.6.06 to Robert David Garretson, Ipswich (also of Long Beach, CA). Sold 17.7.06 & regd 28.9.06 to Mark J Reisterer, Chandler, AZ. Sold 20.2.07 & regd 28.3.07 to Thomas D Lee, Phoenix, AZ (based Ryan Airport, Tucson). CofA issued 2.6.08. Crashed following engine failure at night nr Chandler, AZ 2.6.11. Sold [8.13] to Sherrill Greene, Fort Myers, FL. Regn cld 13.5.15. Stored for spares Fort Myers, FL [11.18].

BH100-167 Model 101. Regd **G-AZTY** (CofR R12804) 28.4.72 to Scottish Aviation (Bulldog) Ltd. Ff 21.6.72. CofA issued 22.6.72 (for 2 months); ferried to Sweden 23.6.72. Regn cld 26.6.72 as sold Sweden. To Swedish AF as Sk61A **Fv61052** 18.8.72 at Ljungbyhed. Later mod to Sk61E. Regd **SE-LNP** 4.10.01 to Trafikflyghogskolan (Lund University School of Aviation), Ljungbyhed. Sold 10.8.05 to Robert Garretson & ferried to USA via Blackpool & Wick 17.8.05. Regn cld 6.10.05 as sold USA. Regd **N1004N** 6.10.05 to Robert David Garretson, Ipswich (also of Long Beach, CA). CofA issued 25.3.06. Sold 25.9.06 & regd 14.12.06 to Sherrill H Greene, Fort Myers, FL. Sold 30.11.09 & regd 17.12.09 to Antony B Greene, Fort Myers. Sold 12.16 & regd 12.1.17 to David A Stokes, Burton, MI. Currently regd.

BH100-168 Model 102. To Royal Malaysian AF as **FM1232**. Ff 5.7.72; roaded to London Docks 1.9.72 & shipped to Port Swettenham. Erected at

Kuala Lumpur & deld 9.72 to Flying School, Alor Setar. Re-serialled **M25-09** mid 80s. Status uncertain.

BH100-169   Model 102. To Royal Malaysian AF as **FM1233**. Ff 14.7.72; roaded to London Docks 1.9.72 & shipped to Port Swettenham. Erected at Kuala Lumpur & deld 9.72 to Flying School, Alor Setar. Re-serialled **M25-10** mid-80s. Stored Alor Setar [10.88; 1.90]; reportedly still painted as FM1233; stored Sungai Besi [2.96; 4.05] as M25-10 but with former serial showing through paintwork).

BH100-170   Model 103. To Kenya AF as **704**. Ff 26.6.72; airfreighted ex Prestwick 24.7.72 aboard CL-44 TF-LLI. Last reported [4.94].

BH100-171   Model 101. Regd **G-AZTZ** (CofR R12805) 28.4.72 to Scottish Aviation (Bulldog) Ltd. Ff 5.7.72. CofA issued 12.7.72 (for 2 months); ferried to Sweden 16.7.72. Regn cld 17.7.72 as sold Sweden. To Swedish AF as Sk61A **Fv61053** 23.8.72 at Ljungbyhed. Later mod to Sk61E. Regd **SE-LNE** 22.1.01 to Trafikflyghogskolan (Lund University School of Aviation), Ljungbyhed. Regn cld 23.8.05 as sold USA. Regd **N8267E** 31.8.05 to Robert David Garretson, Ipswich (also of Long Beach, CA). CofA issued 14.10.05. Regd 12.05 to Steven P Flippin, Salem, NC; painted in Swedish AF c/s. Currently regd.

The letter E on this fin shows it was changed from a SK61A to SK61E. *(PH)*

BH100-172   Model 101. Regd **G-AZUA** (CofR R12806) 28.4.72 to Scottish Aviation (Bulldog) Ltd. Ff 30.6.72. CofA issued 1.7.72 (for 2 months); ferried to Sweden 7.7.72. Regn cld 10.7.72 as sold Sweden. To Swedish AF as Sk61A **Fv61054** 31.8.72 at Ljungbyhed. Sold 10.04 to Avia-Rent Kft, Hungary but not regd. Stored Kaposujlak [7.18].

BH100-173   Model 101. Regd **G-AZUB** (CofR R12807) 28.4.72 to Scottish Aviation (Bulldog) Ltd. Ff 11.7.72. CofA issued 21.7.72 (for 2 months); ferried to Sweden 23.7.72. Regn cld 1.8.72 as sold Sweden. To Swedish AF as Sk61A **Fv61055** 5.9.72 at Ljungbyhed. To Jamtlands Flyg-och Lottamuseum (Teknikland museum), Ostersund 6.03; stored in nearby barn [8.17].

BH100-174   Model 101. Regd **G-AZUC** (CofR R12808) 28.4.72 to Scottish Aviation (Bulldog) Ltd. Ff 20.7.72. CofA issued 27.7.72 (for 2 months); ferried to Sweden 9.8.72. Regn cld 10.8.72 as sold Sweden. To Swedish AF as Sk61A **Fv61056** 20.11.72 at Ljungbyhed. Sold to Avia-Rent Kft, Hungary 10.04 but not regd. Last reported stored Kaposujlak [7.11].

BH100-175   Model 101. Regd **G-AZUD** (CofR R12809) 28.4.72 to Scottish Aviation (Bulldog) Ltd. Ff 21.7.72. CofA issued 27.7.72 (for 2 months); ferried to Sweden 30.7.72. Regn cld 1.8.72 as sold Sweden. To Swedish AF as Sk61A **Fv61057** 11.9.72 at Ljungbyhed. Sold to Avia-Rent Kft, Hungary 10.04. Regd **HA-TUZ** 6.11.07 to Avia-Rent Kft, Budapest. Crashed Taszar 12.4.14. Stored Kaposujlak [10.16]; repaired?

BH100-176   Model 101. Regd **G-AZUE** (CofR R12810) 28.4.72 to Scottish Aviation (Bulldog) Ltd. Ff 14.8.72. CofA issued 16.8.72 (for 2 months); ferried to Sweden 20-22.8.72. Regn cld 22.8.72 as sold Sweden. To Swedish AF as Sk61A **Fv61058** 23.10.72 at Ljungbyhed. Sold 10.04 to Avia-Rent Kft, Hungary. Regd **HA-TVD** 24.8.15 to Avia-Rent Kft, Budapest. Crashed between Sarvar & Rabapaty 30.11.18; pilot killed.

BH100-177   Model 102. To Royal Malaysian AF as **FM1234**. Ff 20.7.72; roaded to London Docks 1.9.72 & shipped to Port Swettenham. Erected at Kuala Lumpur & deld 9.72 to Flying School, Alor Setar. Re-serialled **M25-11** mid 80s. Reported as stored Sungai Besi 2.96 as M25-11. Regd **9M-EZZ** .98 to Kedah Flying Club, Alor Setar (painted in Northern Warrior c/s). Wfu & stored Alor Setar [3.17].

BH100-178   Model 103. To Kenya AF as **705**. Ff 11.7.72; airfreighted ex Prestwick 24.7.72 aboard CL-44 TF-LLI. Last reported [4.87].

BH100-179   Model 101. Regd **G-AZWH** (CofR R12864) 8.6.72 to Scottish Aviation (Bulldog) Ltd. Ff 16.8.72. CofA issued 24.8.72 (for 2 months); ferried to Sweden 27-28.8.72. Regn cld 29.8.72 as sold Sweden. To Swedish Army as FpL61C **Fv61061** 4.10.72 at Nykoping. To Swedish AF as Sk61C. Wfu .01. To Flygflottij 11 Forbandsmuseum, Nykoping/ Skavsta 11.2.02; on display [8.17].

FV61061 was the first Bulldog for the Swedish Army. *(PH)*

BH100-180   Model 101. Regd **G-AZWI** (CofR R12865) 8.6.72 to Scottish Aviation (Bulldog) Ltd. Ff 22.8.72. CofA issued 29.8.72 (for 2 months); ferried to Sweden 9.9.72. Regn cld 11.9.72 as sold Sweden. To Swedish Army as FpL61C **Fv61062** 22.11.72 at Nykoping. To Swedish AF as Sk61C. Crashed Everod 14.9.76. To instructional airframe at Malmslatt.

BH100-181   Model 101. Regd **G-AZWJ** (CofR R12866) 8.6.72 to Scottish Aviation (Bulldog) Ltd. Ff 25.8.72. CofA issued 29.8.72 (for 2 months); ferried to Sweden 4/6.9.72. Regn cld 12.9.72 as sold Sweden. To Swedish Army as FpL61C **Fv61063** 4.12.72 at Nykoping. Trials with 3-blade Hoffman propeller .74; also with ski u/c. To Swedish AF as Sk61C. Sold to Hungary & regd **HA-TUG** 5.8.04 to Avia-rent Kft, Budaors. To Karoly Gyarmati, Godollo. Deld Munster-Teuge 15.12.12; regd [11.14] to Leo Schoemacher, Teuge. For sale [7.18].

BH100-182   Model 101. Regd **G-AZWK** (CofR R12867) 8.6.72 to Scottish Aviation (Bulldog) Ltd. Ff 30.8.72. CofA issued 5.9.72 (for 2 months); ferried to Sweden 16-18.9.72. Regn cld 19.9.72 as sold Sweden. To Swedish Army as FpL61C **Fv61064** 16.11.72 at Nykoping. To Swedish AF as Sk61C. Crashed nr Almunge, E of Uppsala 23.9.81 when photographer/equipment fouled the controls while flying inverted; pilot Sgt Stig Hennix died of burns.

BH100-183   Model 101. Regd **G-AZWL** (CofR R12868) 8.6.72 to Scottish Aviation (Bulldog) Ltd. Ff 20.9.72. CofA issued 21.9.72 (for 2 months); ferried to Sweden 24.9.72. Regn cld 26.9.72 as sold Sweden. To Swedish Army as FpL61C **Fv61065** 4.12.72 at Nykoping. To Swedish AF as Sk61C. Struck wires & crashed Rinkaby 22.9.78; Sgt Jan Ekblad killed.

BH100-184   Model 101. Regd **G-AZWM** (CofR R12869) 8.6.72 to Scottish Aviation (Bulldog) Ltd. Ff 25.9.72. CofA issued 27.9.72 (for 3 months); ferried to Sweden 1.10.72. Regn cld 3.10.72 as sold Sweden. To Swedish Army as FpL61C **Fv61066**. Regd **G-AZWM** 24.11.72 (back) to Scottish Aviation (Bulldog) Ltd. Regn cld 17.4.73 as sold Sweden. Returned to Swedish Army as **Fv61066** 27.4.73 at Nykoping. To Swedish AF as Sk61C. Stored Ljungbyhed [5.01]. Sold 10.04 to Avia-Rent Kft, Hungary but not regd. Last reported stored Kaposujlak [7.11].

BH100-185   Model 101. Regd **G-AZWN** (CofR R12870) 8.6.72 to Scottish Aviation (Bulldog) Ltd. Ff 10.10.72. CofA issued 11.10.72 (for 3 months); ferried to Sweden 14-16.10.72. Regn cld 17.10.72 as sold Sweden. To Swedish Army as FpL61C **Fv61067**. Regd **G-AZWN** 17.11.72 (back) to Scottish Aviation (Bulldog) Ltd. Regn cld 17.4.73 as sold Sweden. Returned to Swedish Army as **Fv61067** 15.2.73 at Nykoping. To Swedish AF as Sk61C. Dbf at AFS Fattade 19.1.76 during refueling..

BH100-186   Model 101. Regd **G-AZWO** (CofR R12871) 8.6.72 to Scottish Aviation (Bulldog) Ltd. Ff 12.10.72. CofA issued 13.10.72 (for 3 months); ferried to Sweden 14-18.10.72. Regn cld 19.10.72 as sold Sweden. To Swedish Army as FpL61C **Fv61068** 27.4.73 at Nykoping. To Swedish AF as Sk61C. Stored Ljungbyhed [5.01] without wings. To Technical School nr Malmen airfield, Linkoping 5.02; extant [6.12].

BH100-187   Model 101. Regd **G-AZWP** (CofR R12872) 8.6.72 to Scottish Aviation (Bulldog) Ltd. Ff 12.10.72. CofA issued 18.1.73 (for 2 months); ferried to Sweden 26.1.73. Regn cld 17.4.73 as sold Sweden. To Swedish Army as FpL61C **Fv61069** 14.3.73 at Nykoping. To Swedish AF as Sk61C. To Flygteknik Centrum, Kallax 8.01 for ground instruction (extant Lulea 8.17).

BH100-188 Model 101. Regd **G-AZWR** (CofR R12873) 8.6.72 to Scottish Aviation (Bulldog) Ltd. Ff 13.10.72. CofA issued 19.10.72 (for 2 months); ferried to Sweden 15.11.72. Regn cld 17.4.73 as sold Sweden. To Swedish Army as FpL61C **Fv61070** 13.12.72 at Nykoping. To Swedish AF as Sk61C. To Flygteknik Centrum, Linkoping for ground instruction. Made airworthy as student exercise for Air Force Museum. Regd **SE-MEK** (reserved 7.7.10) 4.4.12 to Statens Forsvarshistoriska Museer Flygvapenmuseum, Linkoping; op by Malmens Veteranflygklubb, Norrkoping/Vardsberg Currently regd.

BH100-189 Model 101. Regd **G-BACR** (CofR R13017) 30.8.72 to Scottish Aviation (Bulldog) Ltd. Ff 18.10.72. CofA issued 27.10.72 (for 2 months); ferried to Sweden 17.11.72. Regn cld 17.4.73 as sold Sweden. To Swedish Army as FpL61C **Fv61071** 5.2.73 at Nykoping. To Swedish AF as Sk61C. Sold 10.04 to Avia-Rent Kft, Hungary. Regd **HA-TUH** 21.10.10 to Avia-Rent Kft, Budapest. Currently regd; reportedly based Muhldorf, Germany.

BH100-190 Model 101. Regd **G-BACS** (CofR R13018) 30.8.72 to Scottish Aviation (Bulldog) Ltd. Ff 7.11.72. CofA issued 15.12.72 (for 2 months); ferried to Sweden 9.1.73. Regn cld 17.4.73 as sold Sweden. To Swedish Army as FpL61C **Fv61072** 15.2.73 at Nykoping. To Swedish AF as Sk61C. Sold 10.04 to Avia-Rent Kft, Hungary. Stored Kaposvar [3.08]. Regd **HA-TUV** 27.4.11 to Avia-Rent Kft, Budapest; based Godollo [5.10; 6.17]. Currently regd.

BH100-191 Model 101. Regd **G-BACT** (CofR R13019) 30.8.72 to Scottish Aviation (Bulldog) Ltd. Ff 14.11.72. CofA issued 8.12.72 (for 2 months); ferried to Sweden 14.12.72. Regn cld 17.4.73 as sold Sweden. To Swedish Army as FpL61C **Fv61073** 19.2.73 at Nykoping. To Swedish AF as Sk61C. Sold 10.04 to Avia-Rent Kft, Hungary. Regd **HA-TVC** 8.9.11 to Avia-Rent Kft, Budapest. Currently regd; based in Germany [1.17].

Swedish Army Bulldog FV61073 in typical camouflage. *(PH)*

BH100-192 Model 101. Regd **G-BACU** (CofR R13020) 30.8.72 to Scottish Aviation (Bulldog) Ltd. Ff 8.12.72. CofA issued 18.12.72 (for 2 months); ferried to Sweden 17.1.73. Regn cld 17.4.73 as sold Sweden. To Swedish Army as FpL61C **Fv61074** 27.2.73 at Nykoping. To Swedish AF as Sk61C. To Flygflottilj 07 Gard och Flottiljmuseum, Satenas. To Flygteknik Centrum, Hasslo airfield, Vasteras 24.11.10 as instructional airframe; extant [8.17].

BH100-193 Model 101. Regd **G-BACV** (CofR R13021) 30.8.72 to Scottish Aviation (Bulldog) Ltd. Ff 15.12.72. CofA issued 12.1.73 (for 2 months); ferried to Sweden 22.1.73. Regn cld 17.4.73 as sold Sweden. To Swedish Army as FpL61C **Fv61075** 1.3.73 at Nykoping. To Swedish AF as Sk61C. Sold 10.04 to Avia-Rent Kft, Hungary. Regd **HA-TUM** *26.5.12 to Avia-Rent Kft, Budapest. Currently regd; based on strip at Baja.*

BH100-194 Model 101. Regd **G-BACX** (CofR R13022) 30.8.72 to Scottish Aviation (Bulldog) Ltd. Ff 21.12.72. CofA issued 4.1.73 (for 2 months); ferried to Sweden 17.1.73. Regn cld 17.4.73 as sold Sweden. To Swedish Army as FpL61C **Fv61076** 30.3.73 at Nykoping. To Swedish AF as Sk61C. Sold 10.04 to Avia-Rent Kft, Hungary but not regd. Last reported stored Kaposujlak [7.11].

BH100-195 Model 101. Regd **G-BACY** (CofR R13023) 30.8.72 to Scottish Aviation (Bulldog) Ltd. Ff 4.1.73. CofA issued 12.1.73 (for 2 months); ferried to Sweden 22.1.73. Regn cld 17.4.73 as sold Sweden. To Swedish Army as FpL61C **Fv61077** 1.3.73 at Nykoping. To Swedish AF as Sk61C. Sold 10.04 to Avia-Rent Kft, Hungary but not regd. Last reported stored Kaposujlak [7.11].

BH100-196 Model 101. Regd **G-BACZ** (CofR R13024) 30.8.72 to Scottish Aviation (Bulldog) Ltd. Ff 12.1.73. CofA issued 18.1.73 (for 2 months); ferried to Sweden 26.1.73. Regn cld 17.4.73 as sold Sweden. To Swedish Army as FpL61C **Fv61078** 18.6.73 at Nykoping. To Swedish AF as Sk61C. Sold to Hungary & regd **HA-TUL** 7.1.12 to Avia-Rent Kft,

Budapest/Budaors. Crashed in bad weather nr Zichyujfalu, Zoltan Batki 1.8.18; pilot killed.

BH100-197 Model 101. Regd **G-BADA** (CofR R13025) 30.8.72 to Scottish Aviation (Bulldog) Ltd. Ff 21.2.73. CofA issued 15.3.73 (for 2 months); ferried to Sweden 5.4.73. Regn cld 17.4.73 as sold Sweden. To Swedish Army as FpL61C **Fv61079** 26.6.73 at Nykoping. To Swedish AF as Sk61C. Stalled & crashed Brandholmen 16.6.78 on photographic sortie; pilot Sgt Lars Aspehult & photographer Sgt Christer Gribe killed.

BH100-198 Model 101. Regd **G-BADB** (CofR R13026) 30.8.72 to Scottish Aviation (Bulldog) Ltd. Ff 23.1.73. CofA issued 29.1.73 (for 2 months); ferried to Sweden 31.1.73. Regn cld 17.4.73 as sold Sweden. To Swedish Army as FpL61C **Fv61080** 14.3.73 at Nykoping. To Swedish AF as Sk61C. Regd **SE-LLR** 26.9.05 to Gennart Claesson, Sankt Olof. Regd 7.7.07 to Sven-Olof Lundeborg, Rimbo. Ditched in Lake Limmaren, Norratalje 10.6.11 following engine failure on take-off; crew rescued. Airframe salvaged and rebuilt 2013-2016. Regd 23.1.17 (back) to Gennart Claesson, Rockneby. Regn cld 16.8.18 as sold to USA.

The 100th Bulldog, G-BADB, became FV61080, completing the SAF contract. *(IA)*

BH120-199 Model 121. T.1 **XX513**; ff 30.1.73. Handed over 12.2.73 & ferried to A Sqdn, A&AEE Boscombe Down 20-21.2.73 for trials. Returned to Prestwick 9.7.73. Deld 18.12.73 to Southampton UAS, Hamble; coded '01'. To 5 MU Kemble 4.77; returned to Prestwick 19.5.77 for mods; returned to Southampton UAS 3.6.77. To 6 FTS Finningley 20.10.77; coded '06'. To Royal Navy EFTS, Leeming 4.4.79. To A&AEE Boscombe Down 28.9.79 for BAe flight trials for aerobatics with aft CofG. To 5 MU Kemble 29.2.80. Returned to Royal Navy EFTS 13.8.80; coded '31'; to Linton-on-Ouse/Topcliffe 4.84 & re-coded 'A'. To Central Flying School, Scampton 8.93; coded '10'; to Cranwell 3.95 & unit redesignated 3 FTS. To Shawbury 8.00 for storage/disposal. Regd **G-KKKK** 2.10.01 to Drumforce Ltd (Drum Jones), London W1; deld 16.11.01. CofA issued 17.1.02; painted as XX513 '10'. Regd 10.6.02 to Ivan Harvey Seach-Allen, London W1. Regd 24.1.03 (back) to Drumforce Ltd (based Meppershall). Regd **G-CCMI** 20.11.03 to Just Plane Trading Ltd, Meppershall. Regd 1.4.04 to Edwin Cummings, t/la 617 Syndicate, Sittingbourne (based Biggin Hill). Regd 13.6.05 to Hugh Roderick Moore Tyrrell, t/a XX513 Bulldog Group, Shrewsbury (based Sleap). Regd (back) to **G-KKKK** 17.9.14 to Mark Richard Badminton, Thirsk (based Eshott). Regd 9.12.16 to Michael Cowan, Cambridge. Currently regd.

BH120-200 Model 121. T.1 **XX514**; ff 24.2.73. Deld 6.3.73 to A Sqdn, A&AEE Boscombe Down for handling trials. To 5 MU Kemble 7.3.73; returned 29.3.73 to A&AEE. To Central Flying School, Little Rissington 3.5.73; coded '44' & later named 'Spot'; to Leeming 4.76. To A&AEE 10.6.76 for C(A) release trials for inverted flight. To Royal Navy EFTS, Leeming 28.6.76; coded '25'; to Linton-on-Ouse/Topcliffe 4.84 & re-coded 'B'. Struck tree during simulated forced landing practice Maynooth Farm, Knayton, nr Thirsk 29.9.86. Soc 30.9.86. Wreckage to Topcliffe [12.86] & sold as scrap 3.87.

BH120-201 Model 121. T.1 **XX515**; ff 13.3.73. Deld 23.3.73 to Central Flying School, Little Rissington; coded '40' & later named 'Winston'. Transferred to Royal Navy EFTS, Leeming 12.4.76; coded '7'. Damaged 12.5.83; repaired & deld 20.2.84 to Central Flying School, Leeming (still coded '7'); to Scampton 9.84. To Northumbrian UAS, Leeming [1.91]; coded 'U'. To RAF College Air Sqdn, Cranwell [10.93]; coded 'A2'; unit redesignated 3 FTS 6.95 & recoded '2'. To Manchester & Salford UAS, Woodvale 1.96; coded '4'. To Shawbury 2.01 for storage/disposal. Sold at Phillips auction 24.5.01 for £15,500. Regd **G-CBBC** 8.6.01 to Bulldog Support Ltd, Stratford-upon-Avon; deld Ashbourne, Derby 20.9.01. CofA issued 16.11.01; painted as XX515 '4'. Regd 7.3.02 to Bulldog Flyers Ltd, Wokingham (based Blackbushe). Currently regd.

BH120-202   Model 121. T.1 **XX516**; ff 15.3.73. Deld 25/26.3.73 via Boscombe Down to Central Flying School, Little Rissington; coded '41'. Transferred to Royal Navy EFTS, Leeming 12.4.76; coded '10'; to Linton-on-Ouse/Topcliffe 4.84 & re-coded 'C. To Central Flying School, Scampton [7.93]; coded '1'. To Cambridge UAS, Teversham 10.94; coded 'C'. To RAF Newton 12.8.99. To Bristol UAS, Colerne .99; coded 'A'. Deld Shawbury 21.9.00 for storage/disposal. Sold at Phillips auction 24.5.01 for £12,000 to USA. Regd **N516BG** 8.11.01 to BG Chipmunks Inc (Wilmington, DE). CofA issued 20.11.01. Regd 8.05 to Ronald O'Connor Jnr, Merritt Is, FL. Regd 27.9.08 to Robert L Tomlinson, Richmond, VA; painted as XX516 'A'. Currently regd.

BH120-203   Model 121. T.1 **XX517**; ff 3.4.73. Deld 6.4.73 via Boscombe Down to Central Flying School, Little Rissington; coded '42'. Transferred to Royal Navy EFTS, Leeming 12.4.76; coded '23'. Transferred back to CFS 4.84 & moved to Scampton 9.84; re-coded '8'. Back to Royal Navy EFTS, Linton-on-Ouse/Topcliffe 28.8.86; coded 'S'. Pilot lost control in cloud during aerobatics & abandoned Bulldog; crashed Great Langton, nr Northallerton, North Yorks 25.4.89.

BH120-204   Model 121. T.1 **XX518**; ff 4.4.73. Deld 9.4.73 via Boscombe Down to Central Flying School, Little Rissington; coded '43'. Transferred to Royal Navy EFTS, Leeming 12.4.76; coded '24'. To Blue Goshawk, Cranwell 13.7.82 (for HRH Prince Edward training); to Shawbury 9.8.82 for storage. To Cambridge UAS, Teversham 29.1.87; coded 'Z'; re-coded 'B' [11.96]. To RAF Newton 12.8.99. To Liverpool UAS, Woodvale 9.99; coded 'S'. To Shawbury 14.3.01 for storage/disposal. Sold at Phillips auction 25.10.01 for £17,500. Regd **G-UDOG** 24.1.02 to Gamit Ltd, Stansted; deld 27.3.02; stored Sleap [11.02]. CofA issued 22.4.03; painted as XX518 'S' later based Geneva, North Weald. CofA lapsed 15.8.10. Regd 26.4.12 to Marc van den Broeck, Waasmunster, Belgium; based Ursel, Oost-Vlaandren. CofA renewed 6.6.12. Currently regd.

BH120-205   Model 121. T.1 **XX519**; ff 11.4.73. Deld 18.4.73 to Central Flying School, Little Rissington. To Royal Navy EFTS, Church Fenton 23.5.73; coded '1'; to Leeming 11.74; to Linton-on-Ouse/Topcliffe 4.84 & re-coded 'I'. To RAF College Air Sqdn, Cranwell 1.93; coded 'A1'; unit absorbed into 3 FTS 6.95 & recoded '14'. To Shawbury 11.99 for storage/disposal. Sold 15.9.00 to Robert L Bragg/Bulldog Aircraft Co, Pensacola, FL. Regd **N518BD** allocated 22.3.02 to Robert L Bragg. Regd 2.04 to Bonnie van Schaick, Orange, CA (unconfirmed). Regd 7.12.12 to Collum Aviation LLC, Milton, FL. No CofA issued. Currently regd.

BH120-206   Model 121 T.1 **XX520**; ff 13.4.73. Deld 8.5.73 to Central Flying School, Little Rissington. To Royal Navy EFTS, Church Fenton 31.5.73; coded '2'; to Leeming 11.74. Transferred to CFS 4.84; moved to Scampton 19.9.84; still coded '2'. To 7 AEF, Newton 1.95; coded '78'; transferred to parent East Midlands UAS 11.95 and re-coded 'A'. Damaged in heavy landing Newton 10.98 & stored [3.00]. To Instructional Airframe **9288M** 1.9.00. To 172 ATC Sqdn, Haywards Heath .02; extant .17; painted in EMUAS c/s 'A'.

BH120-207   Model 121. T.1 **XX521**; ff 18.4.73. Deld 8.5.73 to Central Flying School, Little Rissington. To Royal Navy EFTS, Church Fenton 8.6.73; coded '3'; to Leeming 11.74. To East Lowlands UAS, Turnhouse 26.2.75; coded '01'. To Birmingham UAS, Cosford [10.96]; coded 'G'. To Shawbury [2.01] for storage/disposal. Sold at Phillips auction 24.5.01 for £7,200 to Richard James Everett, Sproughton, Ipswich. Regd **G-CBEH** 28.9.01 to Russell Edward Dagless, Dereham; deld 10.9.01. CofA issued 10.9.02; painted as XX521 'H' (based Holly Hill Farm, Guist). Regd 9.12.04 to James Edwin Lewis, Kidlington (based Enstone; later Melhuish Farm, North Moreton). Currently regd.

BH120-208   Model 121. T.1 **XX522**; ff 19.4.73. Deld 8.5.73 to Central Flying School, Little Rissington. To Royal Navy EFTS, Church Fenton 18.6.73; coded '4'; to Leeming 11.74; to Linton-on-Ouse/Topcliffe 4.84 & re-coded 'E'. To RAF College Air Sqdn, Cranwell [6.93]; coded 'B2'; absorbed into 3 FTS 6.95 & re-coded '11'. To East Lowlands UAS, Turnhouse 2.96; coded '06'; absorbed 3.96 into Aberdeen, Dundee & St Andrews UAS, Leuchars. To Shawbury 10.4.00 for storage/disposal. Sold ex Shawbury at Phillips auction 29.11.00 for £13,000. Deld 22.2.01 to RH Goldstone, Manchester. Regd **G-DAWG** 13.3.02 to Robert Harvey Goldstone, Manchester (based Barton). CofA issued 3.10.03; painted as XX522 '06'. CofA lapsed 2.10.06 & stored Barton. Regn cld by CAA 25.2.11. Roaded out of Barton 16.6.12 to Squires Gate. Regd 31.7.12 to Stephen John Wood, Preston (based Squires Gate). CofA renewed 27.11.12. Regd 23.4.18 to High G Bulldog Ltd, Squires Gate. Currently regd.

BH120-209   Model 121 T.1 **XX523**; ff 5.5.73. Deld 31.5/1.6.73 to Central Flying School, Little Rissington. To Royal Navy EFTS, Church Fenton 28.6.73; coded '5'; to Leeming 11.74; to Linton-on-Ouse/Topcliffe 4.84 & re-coded 'F'. To Liverpool UAS, Woodvale [5.93]; coded 'X'. To Oxford UAS, Abingdon 6.99; retained code 'X'. To RAF Newton 22.10.99 for storage/disposal. Sold at Phillips auction 16.3.00 for £10,120. Regd **G-BZFM** 18.4.00 to Towerdrive Ltd (Chris J Perkins), Ashbourne, Derby. Regn cld 27.3.01 as sold USA. Sold 29.11.00 & regd **N523BD** 30.3.01 to Dewey T Rhoades & Robert L Bragg (Bulldog Aircraft Co), Pensacola, FL (based Peter Prince Airport, Milton). CofA issued 5.4.01. Sold 26.4.02 & regd 18.6.02 to John J O'Connor, Mt Dora, FL (based Mid-Florida Airport, Eustis). Sold 31.8.02 to TD Systems, t/a Cordes Aircraft, Leesburg, FL. Sold 16.9.02 & regd 7.5.03 to Daniel A Cherry & John E Thiel Jnr, Folly Beach, SC (based Charleston Executive). Sold 11.5.04 & regd 19.7.04 to Ross V Bunting, Pleasant Ridge, MI (later Franklin, MI); (based Livingston County). Currently regd.

BH120-210   Model 121. T.1 **XX524**; ff 5.9.73 (delayed due to pre-flight engine run damage 5.73). Deld 18/19.9.73 to Central Flying School, Little Rissington. To London UAS, Abingdon 14.11.73; coded '04'; to Benson 6.92; absorbed locally by Oxford UAS late .99. To 3 FTS, Cranwell 2.00; retained code '04'. To Shawbury 30.8.00 for storage/disposal. Sold at Phillips auction 24.5.01 for £11,500. Regd **G-DDOG** 18.6.01 to Gamit Ltd, Stansted (based North Weald). Stored [9.02]. CofA issued 29.5.03; painted as XX524 '04'. Regn cld by CAA 7.6.04. Regd 30.7.04 to Deltaero Ltd, London SW1 (based Malaga, Spain). CofA lapsed 27.7.13. Currently regd.

XX524, coded 04 of London UAS. *(PH)*

BH120-211   Model 121. T.1 **XX525**; ff 8.5.73. To Le Bourget for Paris Air Show 6.73. Deld 14.6.73 to Royal Navy EFTS, Church Fenton; coded '7'; to Leeming 11.74. To East Lowlands UAS, Turnhouse 26.2.75; coded '03'; unit absorbed 3.96 into Aberdeen, Dundee & St Andrews UAS, Leuchars. To Glasgow & Strathclyde UAS, Abbotsinch [6.98]; uncoded. To Southampton UAS, Boscombe Down .00; coded '8'. To Shawbury 31.5.01 for storage/disposal. Regd **G-CBJJ** 3.12.01 to Elite Consultancy Corporation Ltd, Spalding; deld Norwich 5.2.02 & stored. Regd 29.7.05 to Dennis Leonard Thompson & George Victor Crowe, Norwich. CofA issued 5.4.06; painted as XX525 '8'. Regd 23.3.10 to George Victor Crowe, Norwich, Hans Van Snick, Nieuwpoort, Belgium & Tahon Marnix, Veldegem, Belgium. Repainted as XX525 '03'. Regd 6.7.12 (only) to Hans Van Snick & Tahon Marnix (based Koksijde). Regn cld 27.8.13 as sold in USA. Sold 18.4.13 & regd **N525UK** (reserved 12.9.13) 18.4.14 to Rick L Dabney, Santa Rosa, CA. No CofA issued. Currently regd.

BH120-212   Model 121. T.1 **XX526**; ff 10.5.73. Deld 31.5/1.6.73 to Central Flying School, Little Rissington. To Royal Navy EFTS, Church Fenton 4.7.73; coded '8'; to Leeming 11.74. To Oxford UAS, Bicester 5.3.75; coded 'C'; to Abingdon 9.75; to Benson 7.92. To RAF Newton [2.00] for storage; to Shawbury 21.3.00 for storage/disposal. Sold at Phillips auction 25.10.01 for £15,000 to Richard C Slaney; deld ex Shawbury 24.1.02. Regd **N3014T** (allocated 9.4.02) to Richard C Slaney, Eugene, OR. CofA issued 7.2.03. Regd to Phantom Sales Inc, Plantation, FL. Regd 10.5.08 (back) to Richard C Slaney, Eugene, OR.

XX526, coded C, served with Oxford UAS at Abingdon and Bicester. *(PH)*

BH120-213 Model 121. T.1 **XX527**; ff 23.5.73. Deld 7.6.73 to Central Flying School, Little Rissington. To Royal Navy EFTS, Church Fenton 13.7.73; coded '9'; to Leeming 11.74; to Linton-on-Ouse/Topcliffe 4.84 & re-coded 'G'. To Aberdeen, Dundee & St Andrews UAS, Leuchars 11.93; coded 'D'; recoded '05' 3.96 on absorption of East Lowlands UAS. To Shawbury 10.4.00 for storage/disposal. Sold 15.9.00 to Robert L Bragg/Bulldog Aircraft Co, Pensacola, FL. Regd **N527BD** 23.10.00 to Bulldog Inc, Pensacola, FL. Regd 12.03 to Thomas Dent & Lisa Dent, Wichita Falls, TX (later SC/CA and currently Eielson AFB, AK). CofA issued 5.8.08. Currently regd.

BH120-214 Model 121. T.1 **XX528**; ff 24.5.73. Deld 31.5/1.6.73 to Central Flying School, Little Rissington. To Royal Navy EFTS, Church Fenton 9.7.73; coded '10'; to Leeming 11.74. To Oxford UAS, Bicester 20.2.75; coded 'D'; to Abingdon 9.75; to Benson 7.92. To RAF Newton [2.00] for storage. Regd **G-BZON** 19.12.00 to Towerdrive Ltd, Ashbourne, Derbyshire. CofA issued 9.7.01; painted as XX528 'D'. Regd 6.2.02 to Roger Savage Gyroplanes Ltd, Penrith (based Carlisle); re-coded as XX528 'X'. Company name changed 28.7.05 to Roger Savage (Penrith) Ltd. Regd 15.12.06 to David John Critchley, Colchester (based Earls Colne) & reverted to XX528 'D'. Currently regd.

BH120-215 Model 121. T.1 **XX529**; ff 29.5.73. Deld 7.6.73 to Central Flying School, Little Rissington. To Royal Navy EFTS, Church Fenton 13.7.73; coded '11'; to Leeming 11.74; to Linton-on-Ouse/Topcliffe 4.84 & re-coded 'H'. To 6 FTS, Finningley [9.92]; coded 'W'. To 5 AEF, Teversham 9.95; coded 'F'; absorbed into Cambridge UAS 1.96. To RAF Newton 12.8.99. To Aberdeen, Dundee & St Andrews UAS, Leuchars .99; coded '08'. To Shawbury 10.4.00 for storage/disposal. Sold ex Shawbury at Phillips auction 29.11.00 for £10,500. Regd **G-BZOJ** 11.12.00 to Richard James Everett, Sproughton, Ipswich. Regn cld 26.1.01 as sold USA. Sold 7.2.01 & regd **N178BD** 23.3.01 to Wendall W Hall, Cheraw, SC. CofA issued 2.5.01. Sold 6.04 & regd 7.8.04 to Joseph K Newson Snr, Cheraw, SC. Sold 29.12.06 & regd 23.3.07 to BGA-viation Inc (Barry G Avent), Bennettsville, SC. Sold 31.12.11 & regd 10.5.12 to WR White Inc (William D White), Windsor, NC. Currently regd.

BH120-216 Model 121. T.1 **XX530**; ff 30.5.73. Deld 20.6.73 to Central Flying School, Little Rissington. To Royal Navy EFTS, Church Fenton 1.8.73; coded '12'; to Leeming 11.74. Crashed into rising ground at Cockayne Ridge, 10 ml N of Helmsley, Yorks 21.9.78 (Flt Lt JD Piercy/Mid M Simon killed). Soc 22.9.78. Wreckage to Central Training Establishment Fire Training School, Manston [3.79]; scrapped [4.86].
Note: XX637 (c/n 307) has been painted as XX530 as a mobile exhibition airframe.

BH120-217 Model 121. T.1 **XX531**; ff 30.5.73. Deld 20.6.73 to Central Flying School, Little Rissington. To Royal Navy EFTS, Church Fenton 8.8.73; coded '14'; to Leeming 10.74. Transferred to CFS 4.84 & moved to Scampton 9.84 & re-coded '4'. Back to Royal Navy EFTS, Linton-on-Ouse/Topcliffe 16.10.86; coded 'B'; reportedly uncoded 6.93. To Wales UAS, St Athan 7.93; coded '06'; later re-coded '04'; additionally coded 'S' 4.98. To Shawbury 20.4.01 for storage/disposal. To Windmill Aviation, Spanhoe 29.8.01 on sale to J-L Langeard. Regd **F-AZLZ** 10.10.01 to Jean-Luc Langeard, Biscarosse (based Caen/Carpiquet); painted as XX531 'G'. Regd 18.11.02 to Nicolas Intertaglia, Biscarosse. Regd 7.5.12 to Pierre Venec, La Tremblade & Sylvain Geoffriault, St Georges de Rex. Regd 20.2.14 to Anne Desvignes, Niort, Sylvain Geoffriault, St Georges de Rex & Pierre Venec, La Tremblade. Regd 16.1.17 (solely) to Anne Desvignes & Sylvain Geoffriault (based Niort/Marais Poitevin. Currently regd.

BH120-218 Model 121. T.1 **XX532**; ff 30.5.73. Deld 20.6.73 to Central Flying School, Little Rissington. To Royal Navy EFTS, Church Fenton 8.8.73; coded '15'; to Leeming 11.74. Transferred to CFS 26.4.84 & moved to Scampton 9.84; re-coded '5'. To Yorkshire UAS, Finningley 4.86; coded 'J'; re-coded 'D' .93. Returned to CFS Scampton 8.94; coded '7'; to Cranwell 3.95 & re-designated 3 FTS. To Cambridge UAS, Teversham

XX532, is seen here whilst with Cambridge UAS. *(PH)*

1.96; coded 'E'. To RAF Newton 12.8.99. To 3 FTS Cranwell 8.99; coded '1'. To Liverpool/Manchester UAS, Woodvale [.01]; still coded '01'. To Shawbury 19.3.01 for storage/disposal. Ferried 6.9.01 to Windmill Aviation, Spanhoe on sale to J Noyan. Regd **F-AZOB** 14.11.01 to Jean Noyan, Bougival. Regd 27.6.07 to Joaquim Sousa, Davron (based Chavenay/Villepreux); painted as XX532 'E'. Currently regd.

BH120-219 Model 121. T.1 **XX533**; ff 12.6.73. Deld 20.6.73 to Central Flying School, Little Rissington. To Royal Navy EFTS, Church Fenton 10.8.73; coded '16'; to Leeming 11.74; to Linton-on-Ouse/Topcliffe 4.84 & re-coded 'J'. To Northumbrian UAS, Leeming 7.93; coded 'U'. To Shawbury 24.1.01 for storage/disposal. Sold 11.12.01 to Matko, Hungary; deld Shawbury to Budaors 11/12.12.01. Regd **HA-TUI** 28.6.02 to Sabo Fosco. Active at Matkopuszta airfield, Kecskemet [8.13]; but stored Kadarkut [7.17]. Currently regd..

Still with code U of Northumbrian UAS, XX533 became HA-TUI. *(PH)*

BH120-220 Model 121. T.1 **XX534**; ff 9.7.73. Deld 17/18.7.73 to Central Flying School, Little Rissington. To Royal Navy EFTS, Church Fenton 5.9.73; coded '17'; to Leeming 11.74. To East Lowlands UAS, Turnhouse 26.2.75; coded '04'. To Birmingham UAS, Cosford 5.89; coded 'B'. To Shawbury 20.4.01 for storage/disposal. Regd **G-EDAV** 8.8.01 to Edwalton Aviation Ltd, Nottingham (based Tollerton); deld 29.8.01. CofA issued 7.8.02; painted as XX534 'B'. Regd 25.6.05 to Historic Helicopters Ltd, Nottingham (based Tollerton). Regd 12.5.10 (back) to Edwalton Aviation Ltd, Tollerton. CofA lapsed 2.11.17. Currently regd.

BH120-221 Model 121. T.1 **XX535**; ff 11.7.73. Deld 18.7.73 to Central Flying School, Little Rissington. To Royal Navy EFTS, Church Fenton 30.8.73; coded '18'; to Leeming 11.74. To Blue Goshawk, Cranwell/Barkston Heath 13.7.82 (for HRH Prince Edward training); to Shawbury for storage 9.8.82. To London UAS, Abingdon 13.5.85; coded '10'; to Benson 7.92. To East Midlands UAS, Newton 6.93; initially uncoded but coded 'S' .95. Probably briefly to Liverpool/Manchester UAS, Woodvale [.01]. To Shawbury 14.3.01 for storage/disposal. Deld 29.8.01 to Windmill Aviation, Spanhoe following sale to O Lanegeard, France. Regd **F-AZOZ** 10.10.01 to Olivier Lanegeard, Biscarosse (based Caen/Carpiquet). Regd 7.9.06 to Philippe Dhuyvettere, Arques, Marguerite-Marie Genibrel Veuve Demarez, St Martin au Lard & Serge Leclercq, Rang du Fliers. Regd 6.4.07 to Philippe Cornu, Groffliers, Philippe Dhuyvettere, Arques & Serge Leclercq, Rang de Fliers (based Berck sur Mer). Currently regd.

BH120-222 Model 121. T.1 **XX536**; ff 14.7.73. Deld 24.7.73 to Central Flying School, Little Rissington. To Royal Navy EFTS, Church Fenton 5.9.73; coded '19'; to Leeming 11.74. Transferred to CFS 26.4.84 & moved to Scampton 9.84 & re-coded '9'. Back to Royal Navy EFTS, Linton-on-Ouse/Topcliffe 27.6.86; coded 'D'. To Manchester & Salford UAS, Woodvale 6.93; coded '6'. To Shawbury 14.3.01 for storage/disposal. Sold to Everett Aero, Sproughton & deld 10.9.01 to Abbey Oaks, Ipswich for onward shipping to BT Carolina Aviation Corpn, USA. Regd **N433VB** 31.10.01 to Carolina Aviation Corp, Rutherfordton, NC. CofA issued 21.11.01. Regd 15.7.06 to USA Benefits Inc, Uniontown, PA. Currently regd.

BH120-223 Model 121. T.1 **XX537**; ff 15.7.73. Deld 24.7.73 to Central Flying School, Little Rissington. To Royal Navy EFTS, Church Fenton 5.9.73; coded '6'; to Leeming 11.74. To East Lowlands UAS, Turnhouse 21.2.75; coded '02'. Badly damaged when struck object on ground St Athan 10.6.75; to SAL 16/17.7.75 for repairs. Deld 5.2.76 to Leeming; to 5 MU Kemble 11.2.76 & stored. Returned to East Lowlands UAS, Turnhouse 9.7.76; coded '02'; unit absorbed 3.96 into Aberdeen, Dundee & St Andrews UAS, Leuchars. To Yorkshire UAS, Church Fenton 6.99; coded 'C'. To Shawbury 15.8.00 for storage/disposal. Regd **G-CBCB** 25.9.01 to The General Aviation Trading Co Ltd, Ware (based North Weald); deld Sleap 25.9.01. CofA issued 29.11.01; painted as XX537 'C'. Regd 19.2.09 to Mark William Minary, Aylesbury (based RAF Halton, later Turweston). Currently regd.

BH120-224　Model 122. To Ghana AF as **G-100**; ff 13.6.73. Shipped ex Glasgow Docks 27.7.73. Status/fate unknown.

BH120-225　Model 122. To Ghana AF as **G-101**; ff 10.7.73. Shipped ex Glasgow Docks 27.7.73. To Instructional airframe 6.98 at Ghana AF School of Technical Training, Kotaka airport, Accra [extant 3.14].

BH120-226　Model 122. To Ghana AF as **G-102**; ff 11.7.73. Shipped ex Glasgow Docks 27.7.73. Sold to Lawrence Bax, & stored Henstridge [5.95]. To Aerofab Restorations, Bourne Park, Hurstbourne Tarrant [3.98] & stored. To store in Salisbury 4.04 but removed to unknown by mid-06.

BH120-227　Model 122. To Ghana AF as **G-103**; ff 20.7.73. Shipped ex Glasgow Docks 27.7.73. Regd **G-BWIB** 10.10.95 to Lawrence Bax, t/a Direct Equipment Supplies, Salisbury (stored Henstridge). Sold 19.12.98 to Bernard Robertson but regd 18.2.99 to David Joseph Taylor John, t/a Aerofab Restorations, Bourne Park, Hurstbourne Tarrant (as nominee). CofA issued 22.3.00; based Leicester. Regd 28.3.02 to Bernard Ian Robertson, Pontiac, MI; painted in RAF c/s as '514XX'. Regn cld 15.4.13 as sold USA. Regd **N514XX** 9.7.13 to same owner (now Bloomfield Hills, MI); based Carefree Skyranch. CofA issued 8.11.13. Sold 17.6.15 & regd 20.8.15 to Antony B Greene, North Fort Myers, FL. Currently regd.

BH120-228　Model 122. To Ghana AF as **G-104**; ff 23.7.73. Shipped ex Glasgow Docks 27.7.73. Crashed and w/off 11.8.74 as a result of fuel starvation.

BH120-229　Model 122. To Ghana AF as **G-105**; ff 24.7.73. Shipped ex Glasgow Docks 27.7.73. To Lawrence Bax, Henstridge [5.95]. Regd **G-BXGU** 15.5.97 to Lawrence Bax, t/a Direct Equipment Services, Salisbury (stored Bourne Park, Hurstbourne Tarrant). Regd **G-GRRR** 19.10.98 to same owner. CofA issued 26.5.99. Regd 25.5.00 to Horizons Europe Ltd, Frome (based Old Sarum, later Compton Abbas). Currently regd.

BH120-230　Model 121. T.1 **XX538**; ff 16.7.73. Deld 26.7.73 to Central Flying School, Little Rissington; coded '45'. Transferred to Royal Navy EFTS, Leeming 12.4.76. To East Midlands UAS, Newton 29.6.76; coded 'E'. Damaged in heavy landing; ferried to Prestwick 20.11.79 for repairs; to 5 MU Kemble 7.12.79 & returned to EMUAS 23.1.80. To Shawbury 17.2.83 for storage. To Royal Navy EFTS, Linton-on-Ouse/Topcliffe 7.1.88; coded 'P'. To 6 FTS, Finningley 30.6.93; coded 'V'; later re-coded 'X'. To 3 FTS, Cranwell 10.95; coded '18'. To Aberdeen, Dundee & St Andrews UAS, Leuchars 4.98; coded '03'. To Liverpool UAS, Woodvale c3.00; still coded '03'. To Shawbury 14.3.01 for storage/disposal. Regd **G-TDOG** 17.9.01 to Geoffrey Stephen Taylor, Kidderminster; deld 4.10.01. CofA issued 26.4.02; painted as XX538 'O' (based Shobdon). Currently regd.

BH120-231　Model 121. T.1 **XX539**; ff 18.7.73. Deld 26.7.73 to Central Flying School, Little Rissington; coded '46'. Transferred to Royal Navy EFTS, Leeming 4.76. Damaged in heavy landing prior to 16.2.78; to SAL for repairs 13.6.78; reflown 30.3.79. To East Lowlands UAS, Turnhouse 1.6.79; still coded '46'. To Glasgow & Strathclyde UAS, Perth 28.1.80; still coded '46'. To Royal Navy EFTS, Leeming 8.5.80; coded '12'. Transferred to Central Flying School 4.84; moved to Scampton 19.9.84 and re-coded '1'. To Liverpool UAS, Woodvale 10.93; coded 'L'. To Shawbury 1.9.00 for storage/disposal. Sold 8.01 to Military Aircraft Spares Ltd, Poole; roaded 13.8.01 to (associate) Mercia Aviation Spares, Wellesbourne Mountford. To Derbyshire [8.07] for storage. Status uncertain.

BH120-232　Model 121. T.1 **XX540**; ff 14.8.73. Deld 22.8.73 via Shawbury to Central Flying School, Little Rissington; coded '47'; later named 'Lassie'. Transferred to Royal Navy EFTS, Leeming 12.4.76; coded '28'; to Linton-on-Ouse/Topcliffe 4.84 & re-coded 'K'. To RAF College Air Sqdn, Cranwell 10.93; coded 'C2'; unit absorbed into 3 FTS 6.95 & re-coded '15'. To RAF Newton 26.1.00 for storage; to Shawbury 20.3.00 for storage/disposal. Sold 15.9.00 to Robert L Bragg/Bulldog Aircraft Co,

Seen here is XX540, coded C2 with the RAF College Air Squadron, Cranwell. *(PH)*

Pensacola, FL. Regn **N540BD** applied for 20.10.00 by Bulldog Aircraft but cld 11.01 as NTU. Refreshed appln made 22.3.02. Regd 1.04 to Philip V Kingry, Gulf Breeze, FL. CofA issued 7.9.04. Regd 10.6.06 to Eclipse Enterprises Inc, Pensacola, FL. Regd 7.11.09 to Jennifer S Ferguson, Pensacola. Regd 25.9.10 to Gordon S Bell, Burbank, CA; painted as XX540 '15'. Currently regd.

BH120-233　Model 121. T.1 **XX541**; ff 16.8.73. Deld 22.8.73 via Shawbury to Central Flying School, Little Rissington; coded '48'; later named 'Prince'. Transferred to Royal Navy EFTS, Leeming 22.4.76; coded '29'; to Linton-on-Ouse/Topcliffe 4.84 & re-coded 'L'. To Bristol UAS, Colerne 8.93; coded 'F'. To Shawbury 31.3.00 for storage/disposal. Sold ex Shawbury at Phillips auction 29.11.00 for £9,000. Sold 21.1.01 to Bulldog Inc, Pensacola, FL & shipped 21.1.01 to California. Regd **N9179C** 10.5.01 to James F Moody, Atascadero, CA. CofA issued 7.8.01. Sold 27.3.03 & regd 16.5.03 to Nigel R Ellis, Pleasant Hill, CA (based Concord). Sold 6.2.06 & regd 2.3.06 to William Lux & Becky Lux, Statesboro, GA. Sold 6.12.06 to Flyforfun LLC, Fort Atkinson, WI (not regd). Sold 5.1.07 to David Wise, Michell, SD (not regd). Sold 16.12.10 & regd 7.5.11 to Timothy M Liewer, Hershey, NE (based North Platte). Currently regd.

BH120-234　Model 121. T.1 **XX542**; ff 17.8.73. Deld 29/30.8.73 to Central Flying School, Little Rissington; coded '49'. Transferred to Royal Navy EFTS, Leeming 4.3.76; coded '13'. Abandoned in turbulence & crashed nr Skipton-on-Swale, Yorks 16.11.79. Wreckage to Leeming & stored [3.80]; later scrapped.

BH120-235　Model 121. T.1 **XX543**; ff 20.8.73. Deld 29/30.8.73 to Central Flying School, Little Rissington. To Royal Navy EFTS Church Fenton 6.12.73; coded '20'; to Leeming 11.74. To Yorkshire UAS, Finningley 29.7.76; coded 'F'; to Church Fenton 10.95. To Shawbury 15.8.00 for storage/disposal. Sold at Phillips auction 24.5.01 for £9,800. Regd **G-CBAB** 14.6.01 to Propshop Ltd (J Romain), Duxford; deld 25.7.01. CofA issued 15.3.02; painted as XX543 'F'. Regd 5.3.08 to Laurence Christopher Tyacke George, Cambridge; John Nicholas Robert Davidson, Hay Moon Bay, CA & Peter John Richardson-Hill, Newmarket (based Duxford). Repainted [.12] as XX543 'U' in East Midlands UAS c/s. Regd 12.11.15 to Thomas Woodstock Harris, Leighton Buzzard (based Holmbeck Farm, Burcott). Regd 2.6.16 to Mid-America (UK) Ltd, Dornoch. Regd **G-UWAS** 13.9.17 to same owner. Painted as XX625 '45'. CofA lapsed 26.7.17. Currently regd.

XX543 is coded F with the Yorkshire UAS at Finningley. *(PH)*

BH120-236　Model 121. T.1 **XX544**; ff 23.8.73. Deld 4.9.73 to Central Flying School, Little Rissington. To London UAS, Abingdon 26.10.73; coded '01'; to Benson 7.92. To RAF Newton .99 and stored. Regd **G-BZLR** 16.8.00 to Lawrence Bax, Salisbury. Sold (by Bax) 7.7.00 to Robert L Bragg/The Bulldog Aircraft Co, Pensacola, FL. To Shawbury 8.9.00; crated/shipped 14.9.00 to Mobile, Alabama; then roaded to Milton Airport, Milton, FL. Regn cld 7.11.00 as sold USA. Regn **N544BD** requested 20.10.00 by Bulldog Aircraft but NTU. Stored Milton Airport; moved 11.01 to Bob Kapa's hangar, Pace, FL. Refreshed appln made 22.3.02; regd 4.4.02 to Robert L Bragg, Pensacola. Sold 5.3.02 & regd 2.5.02 to Airplanet Productions Inc, (Angela Masson), Miami Beach, FL. CofA issued 16.4.02 (based North Perry Field, FL). Currently regd.

BH120-237　Model 121. T.1 **XX545**; ff 28.8.73. Deld 11/12.9.73 to Central Flying School, Little Rissington. To London UAS, Abingdon 18.10.73; coded '02'. Loaned to RAE Farnborough 11.77 to test fly European astronaut candidates for Institute of Aviation Medicine; named 'Enterprise'. Returned to London UAS, Abingdon [12.78] (still coded '02'). Stalled and crashed on practice engine failure on take-off Abingdon 18.9.80. Soc 30.12.80. Wreck (or cockpit) to Turnhouse 2.81 for GI; scrapped c9.95.

BH120-238　Model 121. T.1 **XX546**; ff 30.8.73. Deld 11/12.9.73 to Central Flying School, Little Rissington. To London UAS, Abingdon

1.11.73; coded '03'; to Benson 7.92; absorbed locally by Oxford UAS late .99. To RAF Newton [2.00] for storage; to Shawbury 23.3.00 for storage/disposal. Sold at Phillips auction 24.5.01 for £12,000. Regd **G-CBCO** 9.8.01 to Paul Stephenson, Great Oakley, Clacton; deld 25.9.01. Regd 19.5.03 to Bernard Peter Robinson, Aldershot (based Blackbushe). CofA issued 16.6.03; painted as XX546 '03'. Regd **G-WINI** 23.9.03 to same owner. Regd 16.6.05 to Alexander (Sandy) Bole, Huntingdon (based Conington). Currently regd.

BH120-239   Model 124. Ff 27.8.73 as **G-31-17**. Regn **G-BBHF** initially allocated but NTU. Regd **G-ASAL** (CofR R13766) 5.9.73 to Scottish Aviation (Bulldog) Ltd. Ff (as G-ASAL) 29.10.73; used as demonstrator. CofA issued 7.5.74; to Jordan same day for demonstrations. Regd 2.4.75 to British Aerospace plc, Scottish Division. To Baldonnel for Irish Air Corps demos 22.9.75. CofA lapsed 30.11.89; stored Prestwick. Regn cld 5.12.94 as pwfu. Regd 17.10.95 to Pioneer Flying Co Ltd, Troon (based Prestwick). PtoF issued 8.2.96. Currently regd.

SAL's Model 124 demonstrator G-ASAL wearing G-31-17. *(DC)*

BH120-240   Model 121. T.1 **XX547**; ff 25.9.73. Deld 2/3.10.73 to Central Flying School, Little Rissington. To London UAS, Abingdon 29.11.73; coded '05'; to Benson 7.92; absorbed locally by Oxford UAS late .99. To Yorkshire UAS, Church Fenton 2.00; coded 'A'. Briefly to Liverpool/Manchester UAS, Woodvale late .00. To Shawbury 19.3.01 for storage/disposal. Deld to Armed Forces of Malta 30.7.01 with serial **AS0124**. Stored Luqa [12.16].

BH120-241   Model 121. T.1 **XX548**; ff 25.9.73. Deld 10/11.10.73 to Central Flying School, Little Rissington. To London UAS, Abingdon 29.11.73; coded '06'; to Benson 7.92. To RAF Newton [2.00] for storage; to Shawbury 21.3.00 for storage/disposal. Sold to J Brun, Canada; deld ex Shawbury 24.1.02. Regd **C-FLBD** 5.9.02 to Joel Brun, Sainte Foy, PQ. Currently regd

BH120-242   Model 121. T.1 **XX549**; ff 4.10.73. Deld 1/4.3.74 to Central Flying School, Little Rissington. Deld 16.5.74 to Manchester & Salford UAS, Woodvale; coded '5'. To Royal Navy EFTS, Linton-on-Ouse/Topcliffe 26.3.87; coded 'T'. To Central Flying School, Scampton 5.93; coded '14'. To Southampton UAS, Boscombe Down 11.93; coded '06'. To Shawbury 30/31.5.01 for storage/disposal. Sold at Phillips auction 25.10.01 for £14,500. Regd **G-CBID** 14.12.01 to Douglas Alexander Steven, Wokingham; t/a Red Dog Group/Bulldog Group; deld White Waltham 12.3.02. CofA issued 23.8.02; painted as XX549 '06'. CofA lapsed 22.8.05; renewed 26.1.07. Regd 23.5.14 to Colin Robert Arkle, Ascot; t/a The Red Dog Group, White Waltham. Currently regd.

BH120-243   Model 121. T.1 **XX550**; ff 5.10.73. Deld 17.10.73 to Central Flying School, Little Rissington. To London UAS (6 AEF), Abingdon 10.12.73; coded '08'. To Royal Navy EFTS, Leeming 29.9.75; coded '8'. Loaned to Procurement Executive and to SAL 16.12.75 for trials of various mods; returned to RNEFTS 8.4.76. To Blue Goshawk, Cranwell/Barkston Heath 25.6.82 (training Prince Edward); to Shawbury 9.8.82 for storage. To Northumbrian UAS, Leeming 25.9.86; coded 'Z'. To Shawbury 25.1.01 for storage/disposal. Regd **G-CBBL** 8.8.01 to Ian Russell Bates, Spalding (based Fenland). CofA issued 17.10.01; painted as XX550 'Z'. Regd 15.2.08 to Andrew Cunningham, Swords, Co Dublin (based Abbeyshrule). Currently regd.

BH120-244   Model 121. T.1 **XX551**; ff 9.10.73. To Central Flying School, Little Rissington 14.1.74. To Southampton UAS, Hamble 26.2.74; coded '03'. To 6 FTS, Finningley 12.9.77; coded '51'. To Royal Navy EFTS, Leeming 30.3.79; coded '32'; to Linton-on-Ouse/Topcliffe 4.84 & re-coded 'M'. To Oxford UAS, Benson 7.93; coded 'E'. To RAF Newton 29.9.99 for storage. Sold at Phillips auction 16.3.00 for £18,400. Regd **G-BZDP** 31.3.00 to Derek Murray Squires, Stratford-upon-Avon (based Wellesbourne Mountford). CofA issued 9.7.01; painted as XX551 'E'. Regd 20.3.03 to David James Rae, Chippenham (based RAF Colerne; later Boscombe Down). Currently regd.

BH120-245   Model 121. T.1 **XX552**; ff 25.10.73. To Central Flying School, Little Rissington 1.1.74 (6.12.73?). To Southampton UAS, Hamble 29.1.74; coded '02'. To London UAS, Abingdon 29.6.77; coded '08'; to Benson 7.92. (Loaned to RAE Farnborough 11.77 to test fly European astronaut candidates for Institute of Aviation Medicine; named 'Orbiter'; returned to London UAS 9.78). Absorbed locally by Oxford UAS late .99. To RAF Newton [2.00] for storage; to Shawbury 22.3.00 for storage/disposal. Sold at Phillips auction 25.10.01 for £16,500 to Larry H Mehelic, La Habra, CA; shipped ex Shawbury 13.12.01. *Regd **N415BD** 14.11.01 to Jerry Lee Polson, Cheran, SC; this probably a clerical error for c/n 246*. Sold 3.3.02 & regd **N1080V** 28.6.02 to Biggles Aviation Inc (George V Crowe), La Habra, CA (based Chino). CofA issued 29.6.02. Sold 19.11.04 & regd 17.5.05 to Luke S Sollitt, Pasadena, CA (based El Monte). Regn cld 23.10.13 as expired. Regd 31.5.16 to same owner, (now, Mount Pleasant, SC). Currently regd.

XX552 was loaned to Farnborough to screen potential astronauts. *(PH)*

BH120-246   Model 121. T.1 **XX553**; ff 14.11.73. To Central Flying School, Little Rissington 1.1.74. To London UAS, Abingdon 18.1.74; coded '07'; to Benson 7.92; absorbed locally by Oxford UAS late .99. To Northumbrian UAS, Leeming 3.00; retained code '07'. To Shawbury 9.8.00 for storage/disposal. Deld ex Shawbury 10.9.01 to Everett Aero, Sproughton, Ipswich. Regd **N415BD** 6.02 (see c/n 245). Regd [6.06] to Dwayne Woods, Taylorsville, GA. Regd 22.3.08 to Richard L Stefanick, Morgantown, WV. CofA issued 24.11.08. Regd 6.6.14 to Ian W Whiting, Coto de Caza, CA. Regn **N553X** reportedly reserved; NTU 3.17. Currently regd (as **N415BD**).

BH120-247   Model 121. T.1 **XX554**; ff 15.11.73. To Central Flying School, Little Rissington 1.1.74. To London UAS, Abingdon 15.1.74; coded '09'; to Benson 7.92. To RAF Newton 11.99 for storage/disposal. Sold 9.6.00. Regd **G-BZMD** 18.8.00 to Witham (Specialist Vehicles) Ltd, Grantham (based Spanhoe). Regd 18.1.01 to John Cooper, Moreton-in-Marsh. CofA issued 14.11.01; painted as XX554 '09'. Regd 2.8.02 to Derek Murray Squires, Stratford-upon-Avon (based Wellesbourne Mountford; later Green Farm, Cornbrook). Regd 20.6.06 to Christopher Hunter, Salisbury. Regd 30.3.07 to David Ridley, Burgess Hill, t/a Mad Dog Flying Group, Shoreham. Regd 20.5.11 to Douglas Clarke, Arundel, t/a Mad Dog Flying Group (based Goodwood). Regd 12.12.13 to Alexander Potiatynyk, Pulborough, t/a Mad Dog Flying Group, Goodwood. Damaged when struck hedge on take-off Slinfold 22.3.18. Regn cld 14.11.18 as destroyed.

BH120-248   Model 121. T.1 **XX555**; ff 6.12.73. Deld 14.1.74 to Central Flying School, Little Rissington. To Southampton UAS, Hamble 1.3.74; coded '04'. To Royal Navy EFTS, Leeming 12.9.77; coded '20'; transferred to CFS 4.84; to Scampton 9.84 & re-coded '10'. To Liverpool UAS, Woodvale 12.93; coded 'U'. To Shawbury 1.9.00 for storage/disposal. Sold at Phillips auction 24.5.01 for £8,200 to J Valla, France. Regd **F-AZKJ** 4.10.01 to Jean-Jacques Valla, Peage de Roussillon (based St Rambert d'Albon). Regd 1.6.04 to Francois Franceschetti, Chanas (based St Rambert d'Albon). Currently regd.

BH120-249   Model 121. T.1 **XX556**; ff 16.12.73 (or 18.12.73). Deld 14.1.74 to Central Flying School, Little Rissington. To Southampton UAS, Hamble 14.3.74; coded '05'. To Royal Navy EFTS, Leeming 11.10.77; coded '17'. To London UAS, Abingdon 12.5.80; coded '10'. To East Midlands UAS, Newton 1.3.82; coded 'S'. Transferred to 7 AEF, Newton 28.1.95; coded '76'; transferred (back) to East Midlands UAS 11.95; now coded 'M'. To Shawbury 31.8.00 for storage/disposal. Sold at Phillips auction 24.5.01 for £12,000 to USA; shipped 16.8.01 via Everett Aero, Sproughton. Regd **N556WH** 24.9.01 to Willie W Hilton, Chesterfield, SC. CofA issued 27.8.01. Regd to George Crowe, Fullerton. Regd 30.7.02 to Steven A Sanders & Martha W Sanders, Knoxville, TN. Currently regd.

BH120-250   Model 123. Regd **G-BBJJ** (CofR R13823) 18.9.73 to Scottish Aviation Ltd. Ff 22.11.73. CofA issued 4.1.74 (3 months); ferried to Nigeria via Gatwick 24.1.74. Regn cld 13.2.74 as sold Nigeria. To Nigerian AF **NAF221**. Wfu 5.90 & stored Kaduna [2.06]; offered for sale 6.12. Open storage at Palmerston North, New Zealand (6.14).

BH120-251   Model 123. Regd **G-BBJK** (CofR R13824) 18.9.73 to Scottish Aviation Ltd. Ff 30.11.73. CofA issued 13.1.74 (3 months); ferried to Nigeria via Gatwick 24.1.74. Regn cld 13.2.74 as sold Nigeria. To Nigerian AF **NAF222**. Wfu 7.90 & stored Kaduna [2.06]; offered for sale 6.12. Open storage at Palmerston North, New Zealand (6.14).

G-BBJK en route to Nigeria where it became NAF222. *(GJ)*

BH120-252   Model 123. Regd **G-BBJL** (CofR R13825) 18.9.73 to Scottish Aviation Ltd. Ff 10.12.73. CofA issued 13.1.74 (3 months); ferried to Nigeria via Gatwick 24.1.74. Regn cld 13.2.74 as sold Nigeria. To Nigerian AF **NAF223**. Wfu Kaduna [6.02].

BH120-253   Model 121. T.1 **XX557**; ff 17.12.73. To Central Flying School, Little Rissington 21.1.74. Deld 5.4.74 to Glasgow & Strathclyde UAS, Perth; coded '03'. Crashed into trees in Torres Forest, Callander, Perthshire 11.9.75 while low-flying. Soc 15.9.75. To Leeming for spares recovery [4.77]; to St Athan for conversion to PAX trainer; to RAF Topcliffe [12.79]. Scrapped c.85.

BH120-254   Model 121. T.1 **XX558**; ff 20.12.73. Deld 19/21.1.74 (via Abingdon) to Central Flying School, Little Rissington. To Southampton UAS, Hamble 20.3.74; coded '06'. To Birmingham UAS, Shawbury 28.10.77; coded 'A'; to Cosford 3.78. To Shawbury 25.4.01 for storage/disposal. Deld 6.9.01 to Windmill Aviation, Spanhoe on sale to M Hermaine (sic), France. Regd **F-AZOG** 10.10.01 to Olivier Germain, Palaiseau (based Les Mureaux). Regd 26.9.16 to Marc Scheffler, Cognac (based Cognac/Chateaubernard). Currently regd.

BH120-255   Model 121. T.1 **XX559**; ff 18.12.73. Deld 19/21.1.74 (via Abingdon) to Central Flying School, Little Rissington. Deld 22.3.74 to Glasgow & Strathclyde UAS, Perth (later Abbotsinch); coded '01'; uncoded wef [89]. To Birmingham UAS, Cosford 15.3.00; coded 'F'. To Shawbury 20.4.01 for storage/disposal. Sold to B Russ & deld to Windmill Aviation, Spanhoe 29.8.01 for onward delivery to France. Regd **F-AZOD** 14.11.01 to John Dubouchet, Geneva (based Lons). Regd 19.3.03 to Jean Cherpin, Lyon & Rene Regis, Fontaines St Martin. Regd 5.6.15 to Melanie Bockemuhl & Frederic Loock, Camphin en Pevele (based Lille/Marcq) Currently regd.

BH120-256   Model 121. T.1 **XX560**; ff 19.12.73. Deld 19/21.1.74 (via Abingdon) to Central Flying School, Little Rissington. Deld 28.3.74 to Glasgow & Strathclyde UAS, Perth (later Abbotsinch); coded '02'; uncoded wef [89]. To RAF Newton 15.3.00 for storage. To Bristol UAS, Colerne 5.00; coded 'F'. To Shawbury 21.9.00 for storage/disposal. Sold at Phillips auction 24.5.01 for £12,000 & deld 21.6.01 to M Swick, USA. Regd **N560XX** 6.7.01 to Michael M Swick, Acworth, GA. CofA issued 28.8.01. Currently regd.

XX560 of Glasgow & Strathclyde UAS based at Abbotsinch. *(PH)*

BH120-257   Model 121. T.1 **XX561**; ff 25.1.74. Deld 7/8.2.74 to Central Flying School, Little Rissington. To Queen's UAS, Sydenham 24.4.74; coded 'Q'. To BAe Prestwick 9.11.81 for tests of canopy jettison on ground.

To Aberdeen, Dundee & St Andrews UAS, Leuchars 18.3.82; coded 'A' (replacing XX662). To 3 FTS, Cranwell 1.96; coded '7'. To RAF Newton 29.9.99 for storage/disposal. Sold at Phillips auction 16.3.00 for £10,925 to AJ Amato, Biggin Hill. Regd **G-BZEP** 4.4.00 to Iain David McClelland, London SW3 (based Biggin Hill). CofA issued 26.5.02; painted as XX561 '7'. Regd 25.3.03 to Anthony John Amato, Orpington (based Biggin Hill). CofA lapsed 25.5.05. Regd 29.1.13 to Robert Clive Skinner, Trenchard Farm, Eggesford; stored [8.14]. Currently regd (without CofA).

BH120-258   Model 121. T.1 **XX562**; ff 24.1.74. Deld 13/14.2.74 to Central Flying School, Little Rissington. To Queen's UAS, Sydenham 8.5.74; coded 'S'. To (associated) 13 AEF, Sydenham 10.86; coded 'E'; to Aldergrove 1.92; reverted to Queen's UAS 6.94, still coded 'E'. To 3 FTS, Cranwell 6.96; coded '19'; re-coded '18' .98. Reported to Northumbrian UAS, Leeming [11.99]; still coded '18'. To Shawbury 24.1.01 for storage/disposal. Sold at Phillips auction 25.10.01 for £14,000 to Mr Dougherty, USA; shipped ex Shawbury 13.12.01. Regd **N427VC** (reserved 27.3.02). CofA issued 22.7.02. Regd 10.05 to John G Gililand, Chandler, AZ. Sold – regn pending 28.10.06 to Delaware corporation. Sold – regn pending 29.9.07 to owner, Corvallis, MT. Regn cld 23.8.12.

BH120-259   Model 121. T.1 **XX611**; ff 1.2.74. Deld 13/14.2.74 to Central Flying School, Little Rissington. Deld 5.4.74 to Glasgow & Strathclyde UAS, Perth; coded '04'; uncoded wef [89]; to Abbotsinch 1.93. To East Midlands UAS, Newton 15.2.00; later coded 'U'. To Southampton UAS, Boscombe Down late .00; coded '07'. To Shawbury 23.5.01 for storage/disposal. Regd **G-CBDK** 26.9.01 to James Neville Randle, t/a Randle Engineering, Stratford-upon-Avon; deld Baginton 10.9.01. CofA issued 21.10.02; painted as XX611 '7'. Currently regd.

BH120-260   Model 121. T.1 **XX612**; ff 31.1.74. Deld 13/14.2.74 to Central Flying School, Little Rissington. To Queen's UAS, Sydenham 3.5.74; coded 'U'. Damaged in forced landing nr Groomsport, NI 3.3.76; airlifted to Sydenham 4.3.76 and roaded to Prestwick for rebuild 24/25.4.76. To 5 MU Kemble 16.11.76. To Royal Navy EFTS, Leeming 2.6.77; coded '17'. To Southampton UAS, Hamble 19.9.77; coded '05'; to Hurn 12.78. To Wales UAS, St Athan 14.10.81; coded '05'; later re-coded '03'; additionally coded 'A' 4.98. To Shawbury 30.8.00 for storage/disposal. Sold at Phillips auction 24.5.01 for £12,000. Regd **G-BZXC** 8.6.01 to Gareth Jones, New Malden. Regd 7.11.02 to Peter James Murray Squires & Christopher Charles Murray Squires, Stratford-upon-Avon (based Wellesbourne Mountford). CofA issued 18.12.02; painted as XX612 'A03'. Regd 23.9.03 to Anthony Reginald Oliver, Saffron Walden (based Duxford). Regn cld 5.3.08 as pwfu prior to CofA lapse & stored Prestwick. To instructional airframe [10.09] at Carnegie College, Dunfermline. To Prestwick 14.10.10 for storage. Roaded 23.11.11 to Ayr College, Dam Park, Ayr as instructional airframe (extant 9.13).

BH120-261   Model 121. T.1 **XX613**; ff 14.2.74. Deld 1/4.3.74 to Central Flying School, Little Rissington. To Queen's UAS, Sydenham 24.4.74; coded 'A'; to Aldergrove 1.92. Forced landed with engine failure and crashed into wall Comber, Co Down 16.10.92; pilot killed & student injured. Soc.

BH120-262   Model 123. Regd **G-BBJM** (CofR R13828) 18.9.73 to Scottish Aviation Ltd. Ff 5.2.74. CofA issued 15.2.74 (3 months); ferried to Nigeria via Gatwick 22.2.74. Regn cld 26.7.74 as sold Nigeria. To Nigerian AF **NAF224**. Fate unknown.

BH120-263   Model 123. Regd **G-BBJN** (CofR R13829) 18.9.73 to Scottish Aviation Ltd. Ff 8.2.74. CofA issued 15.2.74 (3 months); ferried to Nigeria via Gatwick 22.2.74. Regn cld 11.4.74 as sold Nigeria. To Nigerian AF **NAF225**. Wfu 5.87 & stored Kaduna [2.06]; offered for sale 6.12. Open storage at Palmerston North, New Zealand (6.14).

BH120-264   Model 123. Regd **G-BBJO** (CofR R13832) 18.9.73 to Scottish Aviation Ltd. Ff 9.2.74. CofA issued 15.2.74 (3 months); ferried to Nigeria via Gatwick 22.2.74. Regn cld 11.4.74 as sold Nigeria. To Nigerian AF **NAF226**. Wfu 12.87 & stored Kaduna [6.02].

BH120-265   Model 123. Regd **G-BBJP** (CofR R13830) 18.9.73 to Scottish Aviation Ltd. Ff 18.2.74. CofA issued 4.3.74 (3 months); ferried to Nigeria via Shoreham 2.5.74. Regn cld 20.5.74 as sold Nigeria. To Nigerian AF **NAF227**. Fate unknown.

BH120-266   Model 123. Regd **G-BBJR** (CofR R13831) 18.9.73 to Scottish Aviation Ltd. Ff 25.2.74. CofA issued 4.3.74 (3 months); ferried to Nigeria via Shoreham 2.5.74. Regn cld 20.5.74 as sold Nigeria. To Nigerian AF **NAF228**. Wfu Kaduna; noted on dump [2.06].

BH120-267   Model 123. Regd **G-BBOU** (CofR R13965) 30.10.73 to Scottish Aviation Ltd. Ff 26.2.74. CofA issued 4.3.74 (3 months); ferried to Nigeria via Shoreham 2.5.74. Regn cld 20.5.74 as sold Nigeria. To Nigerian AF **NAF229**. Wfu 9.88. On display on gate of HQ Training Command, Kaduna [1.10].

BH120-268   Model 123. Regd **G-BBOV** (CofR R13966) 30.10.73 to Scottish Aviation Ltd. Ff 7.3.74. CofA issued 26.3.74 (3 months); ferried to Nigeria via Shoreham 17.5.74. Regn cld 5.6.74 as sold Nigeria. To Nigerian AF **NAF230**. Instructional airframe [2.06] at 301 Flying Training School, Kaduna.

BH120-269   Model 123. Regd **G-BBOW** (CofR R13967) 30.10.73 to Scottish Aviation Ltd. Ff 12.3.74. CofA issued 2.5.74 (3 months); ferried to Nigeria via Shoreham 17.5.74. Regn cld 5.6.74 as sold Nigeria. To Nigerian AF **NAF231**. Wfu 1.89 & stored Kaduna [2.06]; offered for sale 6.12. Open storage at Palmerston North, New Zealand (6.14).

BH120-270   Model 123. Regd **G-BBOZ** (CofR R13968) 30.10.73 to Scottish Aviation Ltd. Ff 9.5.74. CofA issued 25.4.74 (3 months); ferried to Nigeria via Shoreham 17.5.74. Regn cld 5.6.74 as sold Nigeria. To Nigerian AF **NAF232**. Wfu 4.89 & stored Kaduna [2.06]; reportedly sold to New Zealand (as spares?).

BH120-271   Model 123. Regd **G-BBPA** (CofR R13969) 30.10.73 to Scottish Aviation Ltd. Ff 17.5.74. CofA issued 27.5.74 (3 months); ferried to Nigeria via Gatwick 3.6.74. Regn cld 26.7.74. To Nigerian AF **NAF233**. Wfu 5.90. Preserved [6.02; 12.12] at 301 Flying Training School, Kaduna Air Force Base Collection.

BH120-272   Model 121. T.1 **XX614**; ff 28.3.74. Deld 24.4.74 to Central Flying School, Little Rissington. Deld 4.6.74 to Manchester & Salford UAS, Woodvale; coded '1'. To Shawbury 1.9.84 for storage. To Central Flying School, Scampton 1.89; coded '11'; re-coded '6' [4.93]; to Cranwell 3.95 & unit redesignated 3 FTS. To Oxford UAS, Benson 1.96; coded 'B'. To Northumbrian UAS 13.1.00; coded 'V'. To Shawbury 21.9.00 for storage/disposal. Sold at Phillips auction 24.5.01 for £12,000. Regd **G-CBAM** 6.7.01 to Francis Patrick Corbett, London SW3 (based White Waltham). Regd **G-GGRR** 11.7.01 to same owner. CofA issued 3.9.01; painted as XX614 'V'. Regd 21.7.05 to Mark Litherland, Banbury (based Enstone). CofA lapsed 15.10.08. Regd 6.9.11 to Christopher George Sims, Henley-on-Thames (based Enstone). CofA renewed 20.10.11. Regd 29.1.13 to Derek John Sharp, Swindon (based Turweston, later Staverton). Later painted as XX614 '1'. Currently regd.

BH120-273   Model 121. T.1 **XX615**; ff 29.3.74. Deld 24.4.74 to Central Flying School, Little Rissington. Deld 4.6.74 to Manchester & Salford UAS, Woodvale; coded '2'. To Shawbury 6.9.00 for storage/disposal. Sold at Phillips auction 24.5.01 for £7,300 to French buyer. Regd **F-AZKI** 30.8.01 to Christian Martin, Maclas. Regd 5.2.16 to Alain Flotard, Bourg Charente (based Cognac/Chateaubernard). Currently regd.

XX615 of Manchester UAS based at Woodvale. *(PH)*

BH120-274   Model 121. T.1 **XX616**; ff 29.3.74. Deld 6.5.74 to Central Flying School, Little Rissington. Deld 11.7.74 to Manchester & Salford UAS, Woodvale; coded '3'. To Cambridge UAS, Teversham 4.12.98; coded 'U'. To RAF Newton 12.8.99 for storage/disposal. Sold at Phillips auction 16.3.00 for £10,925; ferried to Spanhoe Lodge. Regd **F-AZRM** 28.7.00 to Maurice Rabattet, Seyssins. Regd 10.4.14 to GBI SAS, Lyon (based Lyon/Bron). Currently regd.

BH120-275   Model 121. T.1 **XX617**; ff 31.3.74. Deld 24.4.74 to Central Flying School, Little Rissington. Deld 4.6.74 to Manchester & Salford UAS, Woodvale; coded '4'. To 3 FTS, Cranwell 1.96; coded '2'. To RAF Newton [2.00] for storage; to Shawbury 31.8.00 for storage/disposal; declared surplus 12.10.00 & soc 30.5.01. Sold at Phillips auction 24.5.01 (as Lot 5 for £11,985+VAT) to William B Pope; shipped out to USA 21.6.01. Regd **N25GA** 18.9.01 to William B Pope, Farmington, MI. CofA issued 27.9.01. Sold 28.2.02 & regd 22.5.02 to William M McCabe & Paul

Joseph Rhodes, Charleston, SC (later Scottsdale, AZ). Sold 19.9.06 to William H Bigelow, Houston; amended by revised Bill of Sale 9.7.07 to Bulldog Aviation (Bigelow was simply the manager there) & finally regd 26.3.09 to Bulldog Aviation LLC, Houston. Currently regd.

BH120-276   Model 121. T.1 **XX618**; ff 31.3.74. Deld 24.4.74 to Central Flying School, Little Rissington. To Yorkshire UAS, Church Fenton 14.6.74; coded 'A'; to Finninghley 8.75. Spun in and crashed Southport Sands, Birkdale, Lancs 22.7.76. Soc same date. Wreckage to Prestwick [10.76].

BH120-277   Model 121. T.1 **XX619**; ff 10.4.74 (or 9.4.74). Deld 6.5.74 to Central Flying School, Little Rissington. To Yorkshire UAS, Church Fenton 14.6.74; coded 'B'; to Finninghley 8.75; back to Church Fenton 10.95. To Northumbrian UAS, Leeming 1.96; coded 'T'. To Shawbury 23.1.01 for storage/disposal. Regd **G-CBBW** 1.8.01 to Stuart Edward Robottom-Scott, Solihull (based Baginton). CofA issued 18.10.01; painted as XX619 'T'. CofA lapsed 27.8.03 & stored; CofA renewed 18.8.14. CofA lapsed 15.9.16. Currently regd.

XX619 of Yorkshire UAS based at Church Fenton. *(PH)*

BH120-278   Model 123. Regd **G-BBPB** (CofR R13970) 30.10.73 to Scottish Aviation Ltd. Ff 30.5.74. CofA issued 18.7.74; ferried to Nigeria via Shoreham 7.8.74. Regn cld 28.8.74 as sold Nigeria. To Nigerian AF **NAF234**. Wfu 8.89 & stored Kaduna [2.06]; offered for sale 6.12. Open storage at Palmerston North, New Zealand (6.14).

BH120-279   Model 123. Regd **G-BBPR** (CofR R13971) 30.10.73 to Scottish Aviation Ltd. Ff 25.5.74. CofA issued 27.5.74 (3 months); ferried to Nigeria via Shoreham 3.6.74. Regn cld 26.7.74 as sold Nigeria. To Nigerian AF **NAF235**. Reported as written-off 1.4.78 but also as crashed nr Kaduna 4.82. To instructional airframe at Kaduna [4.82; 2.06].

BH120-280   Model 123. Regd **G-BBPD** (CofR R13972) 30.10.73 to Scottish Aviation Ltd. Ff 18.7.74. CofA issued 29.7.74; ferried to Nigeria via Shoreham 7.8.74. Regn cld 28.8.74 as sold Nigeria. To Nigerian AF **NAF236**. Wfu Kaduna [2.06]; for sale. Noted stored [9.11].

BH120-281   Model 123. Regd **G-BBPE** (CofR R13973) 30.10.73 to Scottish Aviation Ltd. Ff 30.7.74. CofA issued 26.9.74 (3 months); ferried to Nigeria via Shoreham 23.10.74. Regn cld 12.11.74 as sold Nigeria. To Nigerian AF **NAF237**. Written-off 22.6.84.

BH120-282   Model 123. Regd **G-BBPF** (CofR R13974) 30.10.73 to Scottish Aviation Ltd. Ff 5.8.74 & displayed Farnborough static 8.74. CofA issued 29.9.74 (3 months); ferried to Nigeria via Shoreham 23.10.74. Regn cld 12.11.74 as sold Nigeria. To Nigerian AF **NAF238**. Wfu 7.90 & stored Kaduna [6.02; 2.06].

BH120-283   Model 123. Regd **G-BBPG** (CofR R13975) 30.10.73 to Scottish Aviation Ltd. Ff 2.12.74. CofA issued 11.12.74 (3 months); shipped via Liverpool Docks 20.12.74. Regn cld 30.12.74 as sold Nigeria. To Nigerian AF **NAF239**. Wfu 11.87 & stored Kaduna [2.06]; offered for sale 6.12. Open storage at Palmerston North, New Zealand (6.14).

BH120-284   Model 123. Regd **G-BBPI** (CofR R13976) 30.10.73 to Scottish Aviation Ltd. Ff 29.11.74. CofA issued 11.12.74 (3 months); shipped via Liverpool Docks 18.12.74. Regn cld 30.12.74 as sold Nigeria. To Nigerian AF **NAF240**. Noted on dump [2.06] at Kaduna.

BH120-285   Model 121. T.1 **XX620**; ff 25.4.74. Deld 26/27.6.74 to Church Fenton. To Yorkshire UAS, Church Fenton 25.7.74; coded 'C'; to Finninghley 8.75; back to Church Fenton 10.95. To Aberdeen, Dundee & St Andrews UAS, Leuchars .99; coded '02'. To Shawbury 31.8.00 for storage/disposal & soc 4.12.00. Sold ex Shawbury at Phillips auction 29.11.00 for £11,000 to Stephen Fisher; sold 8.12.00 to Robert L Bragg, USA; shipped ex UK 15.1.01 to Pensacola. Regd **N621BD** 23.3.01 to Robert L Bragg, Pensacola, FL (based Peter Prince Airport, Milton, FL). CofA issued 5.4.01. Sold 14.2.02 & regd 19.3.02 to Mark Sarkowsky, Van Nuys, CA. Sold 10.6.05 & regd 30.6.05 to Jack Shamgar Douglas, Hurricane, UT. Sold

27.9.09 & regd 12.8.10 to John Fulton Davis III, Englewood, CO. Sold 2.1.13 (but not regd) to Bulldawg LLC (Brandon Jewett), Brighton, CO (based Van Aire Airport). Sold 15.3.13 & regd 29.3.13 James A Yeagle, Atlanta, GA. Currently regd; painted as XX620 '02'.

BH120-286 Model 121. T.1 **XX621**; ff 30.5.74. Deld 13.6.74 to Church Fenton. To Yorkshire UAS, Church Fenton 16.7.74; coded 'D'; to Finningley 8.75. To 6 FTS, Finningley 8.92; coded 'X'. Transferred to 9 AEF, Finningley 2.95; coded '87'; absorbed into Yorkshire UAS, Church Fenton 12.95; coded 'G'. To Birmingham UAS, Cosford; coded 'H'. To Shawbury 20.4.01 for storage/disposal. Sold & ferried ex Shawbury 6.9.01 to Geddington, Northants. Regd **G-CBEF** 3.10.01 to Mark Ashby Wilkinson, Kettering (based Sywell; later Spanhoe Lodge). CofA issued 1.2.02; painted as XX621 'H'. Regd 22.8.06 to James Alexander Ingram, Nottingham (based Tollerton, later Leicester). Regd 18.10.10 to James Alexander Ingram, Nottingham & Anthony Michael Farmer, Oakham. Regd 21.2.12 to Francis William Sandwell & Andrew Lawrence Butcher, Cambridge (based Little Gransden). Currently regd.

BH120-287 Model 121. T.1 **XX622**; ff 31.5.74. Deld 13.6.74 to Royal Navy EFTS, Church Fenton. To Yorkshire UAS, Church Fenton 16.7.74; coded 'E'; to Finningley 8.75. Transferred to 9 AEF, Finningley 2.95; coded '88'; transferred back into parent Yorkshire UAS, Church Fenton 12.95; re-coded 'B'. To Shawbury 15.8.00 for storage/disposal. Regd **G-CBGX** 26.11.01 to Robert Bernard Black, Guildford; deld ex Shawbury 14.12.01. Regd 1.8.02 to Gordon Bramwell Edward Pearce, Worthing, t/a Golf Xray Group, Washington. CofA issued 8.10.02; painted as XX622 'B'. Regd 19.10.06 to Henfield Lodge Aviation Ltd, Shoreham. CofN 12.5.09 to Henfield Lodge Ltd, Shoreham. Regd 25.3.14 to Phoenix Flyers Ltd, Pulborough (based Shoreham). Regd 8.4.17 to Andrew David Reohorn, Pulborough, t/a Bulldog GX Group, Shoreham. Currently regd.

BH120-288 Model 121. T.1 **XX623**; ff 2.6.74. Deld 27/28.6.74 to Royal Navy EFTS, Church Fenton. To Yorkshire UAS, Church Fenton 25.7.74; coded 'F'; to Finningley 8.75. Damaged when overturned Southport beach, Birkdale, Lancs 22.7.76 (investigating accident to XX618). To Prestwick 24.9.76 for repairs (including new fuselage). To East Midlands UAS, Newton 16.10.77; coded 'M'. Badly damaged in forced landing with engine failure 2 ml NW of Folkestone 26.7.95. Roaded to RAF Newton 16.8.95 & stored on pallet. Sold 15.9.00 (or at auction 9.6.00) to Robert L Bragg/Bulldog Aircraft Co, Pensacola, FL for spares. Airframe sold on to Lawrence Bax/Aerofab Restorations, Bourne Park, Hurstbourne Tarrant for spares [3.01]; last reported 5.05 and presumed scrapped (also reported as sold as spares to USA).

XX623 had two major incidents before sale for spares. *(PH)*

BH120-289 Model 121. T.1 **XX624**; ff 7.6.74. Deld 27/28.6.74 to Royal Navy EFTS, Church Fenton. To Yorkshire UAS, Church Fenton 6.8.74; coded 'G'; to Finningley 8.75. To 6 FTS, Finningley 8.92; coded 'Y'. To Northumbrian UAS, Leeming 9.95; coded 'T'. To Cambridge UAS, Teversham 1.96; coded 'D'. To RAF Newton 12.8.99. To Bristol UAS, Colerne 9.99; coded 'E'. To Shawbury 21.9.00 for storage/disposal. Sold at Phillips auction 24.5.01 for £13,000. Regd **G-KDOG** 18.6.01 to Gamit Ltd, Stansted (based North Weald). CofA issued 7.7.03; painted as XX624 'E'. CofA lapsed 6.7.06; renewed 7.9.07. Regd 3.4.12 to Marc Van den Broeck, Waasmunster, Belgium (based Ursel, Oost-Vlaanderen). Regd 21.10.15 to Simon Robert Tilling, Andover (based Thruxton). Currently regd.

BH120-290 Model 121. T.1 **XX625**; ff 11.6.74. Deld 27/28.6.74 to Royal Navy EFTS, Church Fenton; on to 5 MU Kemble for spraying. To Wales UAS, St Athan 29.8.74; coded '45'; re-coded '01' 9.82; additionally coded 'U' 4.98. Reportedly to Northumbrian UAS, Leeming late .00; still coded '01'. To Shawbury 24.1.01 for storage/disposal. Regd **G-CBBR**

8.8.01 to Elite Consultancy Corporation Ltd, Spalding; deld 5.2.02 ex Shawbury to Norwich & stored; painted as XX625 '01'. No CofA issued. Regd 29.7.05 to George Victor Crowe & Dennis Leonard Thompson, Norwich; still stored Norwich [5.06]. Regd 19.2.09 to George Victor Crowe, Norwich & David Peckham, Malaga. To USA 5.09; presumed to George Crowe/Biggles Aviation Inc, La Habra Heights, CA. Regn cld 7.9.09 as sold USA (but not regd there). Status uncertain.
Note: G-UWAS [c/n 235] has been repainted as XX625.

XX625 of Wales UAS based at St Athan. *(PH)*

BH120-291 Model 121. T.1 **XX626**; ff 25.6.74. Deld 1.8.74 to Royal Navy EFTS, Church Fenton. To Wales UAS, St Athan 17.9.74; coded '46'; re-coded '02' 9.82; additionally coded 'W' 4.98. To Instructional Airframe **9290M** 14.11.00 with 4 SofTT/Civilian Technical Training School, St Athan. Sold by tender 22.11.05. Regd **G-CDVV** 27.1.06 to Derek Murray Squires, Stratford-upon-Avon (based Wellesbourne Mountford). CofA issued 14.7.06; painted as XX626 'W02' (& 9290M). Regd 28.7.10 to William Henry Moberley Mott, Macclesfield (based Yeatsall Farm, Abbots Bromley). Currently regd.

BH120-292 Model 121. T.1 **XX627**; ff 22.7.74. Deld 1.8.74 to Royal Navy EFTS, Church Fenton. To Wales UAS, St Athan 12.9.74; coded '47'; re-coded '03' 9.82. To Southampton UAS, Boscombe Down .96; coded '07'. To Shawbury 25.9.00 for storage/disposal. Sold at Phillips auction 24.5.01 for £9,000 to George Crowe, USA. Deld ex Shawbury to Richard Everett, Sproughton, Ipswich & shipped to USA 29.7.01 ; erected & reflown Chino 9.01. Regd **N321BD** 5.11.01 to Biggles Aviation Inc (George Crowe), La Habra Heights, CA (based Fullerton). CofA issued 15.11.01. Sold 10.2.02 & regd 15.4.02 to Aero Enterprises Inc, Carson City, NV. Sold 26.2.05 & regd 16.6.05 to Arreed Franz Barabasz, Palouse, WA. Currently regd.

BH120-293 Model 121. T.1 **XX628**; ff 23.7.74. Deld 1.8.74 to Royal Navy EFTS, Church Fenton. To Wales UAS, St Athan 12.9.74; coded '48'; re-coded '04' 9.82. To Bristol UAS, Colerne 1.96; coded 'J'. To Southampton UAS, Boscombe Down late .00; coded '9'. To Shawbury 30/31.5.01 for storage/disposal. Sold at Phillips auction 25.10.01 for £13,200 to Chunnel Hire Dover. Regd **G-CBFU** 12.11.01 to John Ronald Huggins, Dover & Simon John Huggins, Folkestone (based Lamberhurst Farm, Faversham, later Greenwood Farm, Alkham, Dover); deld 23.1.02. CofA issued 16.4.02; painted as XX628 '9'. Currently regd.

BH120-294 Model 121. T.1 **XX629**; ff 27.7.74. Deld 22.8.74 to Royal Navy EFTS, Church Fenton. To Northumbrian UAS, Leeming 1.10.74; coded 'V'. Loaned to A Sqdn A&AEE Boscombe Down 1.10.76 for spinning characteristic trials; returned to NUAS 3.12.76. To Liverpool UAS, Woodvale .98; still coded 'V'. To Shawbury 25.7.00 for storage/disposal. Sold at Phillips auction 24.5.01 for £9,000. Regd **G-BZXZ** 21.6.01 to Air & Ground Aviation Ltd, Stafford (based Sleap). CofA issued 12.9.01; painted as XX629 'V'. Regd 23.5.03 to Clive Ralph Tilley, Wolverhampton (based Sleap). Regd 31.1.05 to Alan George Fowles, Shrewsbury (based Sleap). Regd 7.4.05 to John Arthur Douglas Richardson, Rugby (based Wellesbourne Mountford). Regd 10.6.08 to Richard Ian Kelly & Edward James Burford, Leamington Spa (based Wellesbourne Mountford). Regd 17.9.10 to David Haworth, Abingdon. Regd 10.1.12 to Richard Bray, Oxford (based Enstone). Regd 4.3.13 to Christopher Michael Fopp, Aylesbury (based RAF Halton). Regd 7.9.15 to Colin Nicholas Wright, Princes Risborough (based Turweston). Currently regd.

BH120-295 Model 121. T.1 **XX630**; ff 1.8.74. Deld 21.11.74 to Leeming. To East Midlands UAS, Newton 19.12.74; coded 'gamma'. To Liverpool UAS, Woodvale 26.10.77; coded 'A'. Forced landed with engine failure on Pakefield Beach, S of Lowestoft 19.7.88; To Marshalls, Cambridge 20.7.88 for repair & returned to unit 14.9.88. To 3 FTS, Cranwell 3.96; coded '5'. To RAF Newton 9.99 for storage/disposal. Sold at Phillips auction 16.3.00 for £12,650. Regd **G-SIJW** 31.3.00 to Barry Whitworth, Sheffield (based Sleap). CofA issued 3.9.01; painted as XX630 '5'. Regd

1.11.01 to Michael Miles, Haverhill (based Shenington; later Audley End). Currently regd.

BH120-296 Model 121. T.1 **XX631**; ff 2.8.74. Deld 22.8.74 to Royal Navy EFTS, Church Fenton. To Northumbrian UAS, Leeming 18.10.74; coded 'W'. To 9 AEF, Finningley 3.95; coded '89' but reverted to Northumbrian UAS 9.95; retaining code 'W'. To Shawbury 10.8.00 for storage/disposal. Sold at Phillips auction 24.5.01 for £10,500. Regd **G-BZXS** 21.6.01 to Kieran Joseph Thompson, Newport, Co Mayo (based Newtownards, later Strandhill, Co Sligo). CofA issued 9.5.03; painted as XX631 'W'. CofA lapsed 7.5.10; stored Strandhill [4.14]. Currently regd.

BH120-297 Model 121. T.1 **XX632**; ff 6.11.74. Deld 20/22.11.74 to Leeming. Deld 5.2.75 to Bristol UAS, Filton; coded 'D'; to Hullavington 3.92; to Colerne 11.92. To Yorkshire UAS, Church Fenton 2.96; coded 'A'. To RAF Newton 4.2.00 for storage; to Shawbury 22.3.00 for storage/ disposal. Sold 15.9.00 to Robert L Bragg/Bulldog Aircraft Co, Pensacola, FL. Regd **N632BD** 15.11.00 to Robert L Bragg, Pensacola, FL (based Peter Prince, Milton). CofA issued 16.11.00. Sold 20.11.00 & regd 8.2.01 to Charles W McCoy, Prescott, AZ (based Ernest A Love Field). Regd 19.11.07 to Charles W McCoy & Joseph L Matheny & Margaret R Matheny, Prescott, AZ. Sold 6.3.12 & regd 6.4.12 to Charles W McCoy & Lynn A McCoy, Prescott. Sold 4.2.18 & regd 22.5.18 to Rudolph de Wit Steenkamp, Jupiter, FL. Currently regd.

BH120-298 Model 125. Regd **G-BCAA** (CofR R14212) 4.3.74 to Scottish Aviation Ltd. Ff 15.6.74. CofA issued 28.6.74; ferried to Kidlington 6.7.74 and deld Amman 14.7.74. Regn cld 29.8.74 as sold Amman. Regd **JY-ADW** to Royal Jordanian Academy of Aeronautics. Regn cld 1.1.78. To **RJAF 400**. Reportedly w/off nr Shabab 15.8.74 but, if so, presumably repaired.. Sold 21.7.03 to Vision Engineering Group, Amman. Regd **N9206F** (reserved 9.2.06 for Vision Engineering Group). Regd [6.06] to Skymasters Flying Club Inc, South Lyon, MI. CofA issued 23.6.07. Regd 26.9.08 to Karl W Mickelson, Colorado Springs, CO. Regd N575KM 21.10.08 to same owner. Currently regd.

BH120-299 Model 125. Regd **G-BCAU** (CofR R14213) 4.3.74 to Scottish Aviation Ltd. Ff 19.6.74. CofA issued 28.6.74; ferried to Kidlington 6.7.74 and deld Amman 14.7.74. Regn cld 29.8.74 as sold Amman. Regd **JY-ADX** to Royal Jordanian Academy of Aeronautics Regn cld 1.1.78. To **RJAF 401**. Last reported [7.98].

BH120-300 Model 125. Regd **G-BCAV** (CofR R14214) 4.3.74 to Scottish Aviation Ltd. Ff 19.6.74. CofA issued 28.6.74; ferried to Kidlington 6.7.74 and deld Amman 14.7.74. Regn cld 29.8.74 as sold Amman. Regd **JY-ADY** to Royal Jordanian Academy of Aeronautics. Regn cld 1.1.78. To **RJAF 402**. Sold 21.7.03 to Vision Engineering Group, Amman. Sold 30.12.04 to Gesoco Industries Inc, Franklin County Airport, Swanton, VT. Regd **N402JA** (reserved 24.8.05) 9.05 to Kevin Lyons, Incline Village, NV. CofA issued 20.9.05. Regd 11.11.06 to Francis T Lyons, Sudbury, MA. Regn cld 13.2.18.

BH120-301 Model 125. Regd **G-BCAW** (CofR R14215) 4.3.74 to Scottish Aviation Ltd. Ff 25.6.74. CofA issued 28.6.74; ferried to Kidlington 6.7.74 and deld Amman 14.7.74. Regn cld 29.8.74 as sold Amman. Regd **JY-ADZ** to Royal Jordanian Academy of Aeronautics. Regn cld 1.1.78. To **RJAF 403**. Preserved at King Hussein Air College Collection, Mafraq [4.00].

RJAF 403 was part of the initial RJAF Bulldog order. *(PH)*

BH120-302 Model 125. Regd **G-BCAX** (CofR R14216) 4.3.74 to Scottish Aviation Ltd. Ff 26.6.74. CofA issued 28.6.74; ferried to Kidlington 6.7.74 and deld Amman 14.7.74. Regn cld 29.8.74 as sold Amman. Regd **JY-AEA** to Royal Jordanian Academy of Aeronautics. Regn cld 1.1.78. To **RJAF 404**. Sold 21.7.03 to Vision Engineering Group, Amman. Sold 30.12.04 to Gesoco Industries Inc, Franklin County Airport,

Swanton, VT. Sold 20.6.05 to Don & Monica Selby, Turlock, CA. Sold 20.4.13 & regd **N9043A** 15.9.15 to Zack S Hylton, Boise, ID. CofA issued 24.2.16. Sold 15.2.17 & regd 10.4.17 to David T Taylor, Greenleaf, ID. Currently regd.

BH120-303 Model 121. T.1 **XX633**; ff 12.8.74. Deld 9/12.9.74 to Royal Navy EFTS, Church Fenton. To Northumbrian UAS, Leeming 25.10.74; coded 'X'. To Shawbury 4.9.00 for storage/disposal. Roaded out 7.9.01 to J Kelsall, Mansfield, Notts. Stored [12.07; 9.12] with Joe Goy, Diseworth, Leics. Shipped to Sweden 4.16; probably for spares.

BH120-304 Model 121. T.1 **XX634**; ff 5.11.74. Deld 10.12.74 to Leeming. To Cambridge UAS, Teversham 14.2.75; coded 'C'. To Central Flying School, Scampton 10.94; coded '1'; to Cranwell 3.95 and absorbed into 3 FTS. To East Midlands UAS, Newton 11.98; coded 'A'. To Liverpool UAS, Woodvale 10.00; coded 'T'. To Shawbury 7.2.01 for storage/disposal. Sold 8.01 to Military Aircraft Spares Ltd, Poole; roaded 10.8.01 to (associate) Mercia Aviation Spares, Wellesbourne Mountford & stored. Roaded to Newark Air Museum, Winthorpe 9.1.06 & on display.

BH120-305 Model 121. T.1 **XX635**; ff 26.8.74. Deld 21.11.74 to Leeming. To East Midlands UAS, Newton 19.12.74; coded 'delta'. Nosewheel collapsed on landing Bicester 17.7.75; repaired & returned to unit 23.7.75; re-coded 'S' 9.77. Damaged 3.12.81; to Shawbury [7.82]. To Instructional Airframe **8767M** 25.8.82 & to 4 SofTT/Civilian Technical Training School, St Athan 1.83; unit later renamed DARA Training School. Sold by tender 22.11.05 to USA. Regd **N635XX** (reserved 22.5.07) 25.8.07 to Velox Aviation Inc, Stuart, FL. CofA issued 1.11.07. Currently regd.

BH120-306 Model 121. T.1 **XX636**; ff 6.9.74. Deld 9.10.74 to Royal Navy EFTS, Church Fenton. To Northumbrian UAS, Leeming 21.11.74; coded 'Y'. To Shawbury 25.1.01 for storage/disposal. Regd **G-CBFP** 29.10.01 to Iain David McClelland, London SW3; deld Biggin Hill 16.11.01. CofA issued 24.1.02; painted as XX636 'Y'. Regd 4.10.04 to Taylor Aviation Ltd, Cranfield. Regd 7.9.06 to David John Scott, Milton Keynes (based Cranfield). Regn cld by CAA 26.6.08. Regd 3.7.08 to Robert Nisbet & Andrew Robert Dix, Stamford (based Shacklewell Farm, Empingham). Regd 24.5.17 to Robert Nisbet, Stamford; t/a Shacklewell Bulldog Group, Empingham. Currently regd.

Northumbrian UAS had a blue cross marking as seen on XX636. *(PH)*

BH120-307 Model 121. T.1 **XX637**; ff 23.9.74. Deld 10.10.74 to Royal Navy EFTS, Church Fenton. To Northumbrian UAS, Leeming 21.11.74; coded 'Z'; reportedly re-coded 'U' [1.88]. Overstressed during aerobatics Tees-side Airport 12.87; roaded to Shawbury 25.2.88 for repairs. Reported to Yorkshire UAS, Finningley 7.91; coded 'U' [9.92]. To Instructional Airframe **9197M** 7.6.93 at RAF Exhibition Production & Transportation Unit, St Athan; coded 'U' (as travelling exhibit); repainted as 'XX530/F' [5.96]; to Barkston Heath [.99]. Allocated to 2175 ATC Sqdn, Hillington, Glasgow .00, but deld instead to RAF Kinloss for damage repairs (also reported to 446 Sqdn ATC, Kinloss); still present [11.08] but current status unknown.

BH120-308 Model 121. T.1 **XX638**; ff 25.9.74. Deld 10.10.74 to Royal Navy EFTS, Church Fenton. To East Midlands UAS, Newton 15.11.74; coded 'alpha'. To Royal Navy EFTS, Leeming 9.12.77; coded '21'; to Linton-on-Ouse/Topcliffe 4.84 & re-coded 'N'. To Yorkshire UAS, Finningley 30.6.93; coded 'H'. To Central Flying School, Cranwell 6.94; coded '12' (repainted in special black/yellow c/s); unit absorbed into 3 FTS 3.95. To Shawbury 25.1.01 for storage/disposal. Regd **G-DOGG** 3.10.01 to Paul Sengupta, Guildford; deld Bourne Park, Hurstbourne Tarrant 10.9.01. CofA issued 27.3.02; painted as XX638. CofA lapsed 16.1.11; renewed 10.12.14. CofA lapsed 27.4.17. Currently regd.

BH120-309 Model 121. T.1 **XX639**; ff 26.9.74. Deld 10.10.74 to Royal Navy EFTS, Church Fenton. To East Midlands UAS, Newton 24.11.74; coded 'beta'. To 5 MU Kemble for storage 27.10.77. To London UAS,

XX638 was one of the few Bulldogs with the black and yellow scheme. *(PH)*

Abingdon 2.12.80; coded '02' (replacing XX545); to Benson 7.92. To Yorkshire UAS, Church Fenton 12.99; coded 'D'. To Northumbrian UAS, Leeming late .00; still coded 'D'. To Shawbury 24.1.01 for storage/disposal. Sold & deld 25.9.01 to Spanhoe Lodge on sale to WT Froggatt, France. Regd **F-AZTF** 1.2.02 to William Froggatt, La Baule; operated by Association Ailes Anciennes La Baule. Currently regd.

BH120-310   Model 121. T.1 **XX640**; ff 28.10.74. To Leeming 21.11.74. To Bristol UAS, Filton 19.12.74 (on loan?). To East Midlands UAS, Newton 31.1.75; coded 'epsilon'. To Queen's UAS, Sydenham 29.10.77; coded 'U'; to Aldergrove 1.92; re-coded 'B' .93; re-coded 'Q' 4.96. To Bristol UAS, Colerne 6.96; coded 'K'. To Shawbury 19.10.00 for storage/disposal. Sold at Phillips auction 24.5.01 for £8,200. Ferried 16.8.01 to Richard Everett, Sproughton, Ipswich. Sold 18.9.01 & regd **N640RH** 24.9.01 to Willie W Hilton, Chesterfield, SC. CofA issued 25.10.01. Sold 26.10.01 & regd 19.12.01 to Everett E Demby, Chesterfield, SC. Damaged in ground-loop on crosswind landing Greeley, CO 11.11.01; repaired. Sold 12.10.10 (following Demby's death) & regd 26.10.10 to Dragon Balloons Inc, Malibu, CA. Sold 22.11.11 & regd 4.1.12 to Beegles Aircraft Service Inc, Greeley, CO. Sold 15.12.11 (to dealer) & regd 29.4.14 to American Aircraft Sales Inc, Lincolnshire, IL (later Wonewec, WI). Sold 25.9.16 & regd 8.12.16 to Brendan P Carmody, Sequim, WA. Currently regd.

BH120-311   Model 121. T.1 **XX653**; ff 29.10.74. Deld 20/22.11.74 to Leeming. Deld 14.2.75 to Bristol UAS, Filton; coded 'E' to Hullavington 3.92; to Colerne 11.92. To RAF Newton 9.99 for storage/disposal. To Instructional Airframe at DERA, Boscombe Down late .00. To Parkway Transport Technology Centre, Stoke Gifford, Glos.

BH120-312   Model 121. T.1 **XX654**; ff 16.10.74. To Leeming 21.11.74. Deld 21.1.75 to Bristol UAS, Filton; coded 'A'; to Hullavington 3.92; to Colerne 11.92. To 3 FTS, Cranwell 1.96; coded '3'. To Shawbury 11.5.00 for storage/disposal; earmarked for RAF Museum. To RAF Museum, Cosford 14.1.04 & on display.

BH120-313   Model 121. T.1 **XX655**; ff 15.10.74. To Leeming 21.11.74. Deld 21.1.75 to Bristol UAS, Filton; coded 'B'; to Hullavington 3.92; to Colerne 11.92. To Shawbury 11.5.00 for storage/disposal. To Cosford 7.00 as In-service Training Aircraft (IPT). Allocated **9294M** 15.3.01 and issued to Defence Fire Services Central Training Establishment, Manston [8.01]. Reduced to poor state [by 9.03]. Hulk (mainly cockpit section) to AeroVenture/South Yorkshire Aircraft Museum, Doncaster 11.09 as spares for rebuild of XX669; stored [1.12] & while reportedly scrapped, the cockpit was reported to have moved to Stockport area; then Evesham [details unknown].

BH120-314   Model 121. T.1 **XX656**; ff 28.10.74. To Leeming 21.11.74. Deld 21.1.75 to Bristol UAS, Filton; coded 'C'; to Hullavington 3.92; to Colerne 11.92. To Shawbury 15.3.01 for storage/disposal. Sold 10.8.01 to Military Aircraft Spares Ltd, Poole; roaded 13.8.01 to (associate) Mercia Aviation Spares, Wellesbourne Mountford. Stored [8.07] in Derbyshire.

BH120-315   Model 121. T.1 **XX657**; ff 26.11.74. Deld 16.12.74 to Leeming. To Cambridge UAS, Teversham 21.2.75; coded 'U'. Wfu after over-stressed 22.11.98; roaded to RAF Newton 18.2.99 & stored on pallet. Sold 15.9.00 to Robert L Bragg/Bulldog Aircraft Co, Pensacola, FL; sold & deld [3.01] to Lawrence Bax/Aerofab Restorations, Bourne Park, Hurstbourne Tarrant; stored [4.02]. To Colerne [7.02] for rebuild; later airfreighted from Lyneham to New Zealand. Regd **ZK-WUF** 27.4.04 to Colin Howcroft, North Shore City (based Whenuapai); painted as XX657. Regd 11.6.07 to MH Wills, Havelock North (based Hastings). For sale from Ardmore [5.18].

BH120-316   Model 121. T.1 **XX658**; ff 26.11.74. Deld 16.12.74 to Leeming. To Oxford UAS, Bicester 13.3.75. To Cambridge UAS, Teversham 26.3.75; coded 'A'. To RAF Newton 12.8.99. To Aberdeen, Dundee & St Andrews UAS, Leuchars 9.99; coded '07'. To Shawbury 10.4.00 for storage/disposal. Sold ex Shawbury at Phillips auction 29.11.00 for £8,800. Regd **G-BZPS** 8.1.01 to Derek Murray Squires, Stratford-upon-Avon (based Wellesbourne Mountford). No CofA issued & stored [1.03]; painted as XX658 '03'. Regd 23.1.09 to Andrew John Robinson, Cambridge & Mark John Miller, Royston (still stored near Audley End). Currently regd.

BH120-317   Model 121. T.1 **XX659**; ff 20.11.74. Deld 18.12.74 to Leeming. To Cambridge UAS, Teversham 19/20.2.75; coded 'S'. To RAF Newton 12.8.99. To Yorkshire UAS, Church Fenton 8.99; coded 'E'. To Shawbury 15.8.00 for storage/disposal. Sold at Phillips auction 24.5.01 for £7,000. Deld 14.8.01 to Air & Ground Aviation, Hixon. Stored [8.07] in Derbyshire.

BH120-318   Model 121. T.1 **XX660**; ff 20.11.74. Deld 18.12.74 to Leeming. To Oxford UAS, Bicester 13.3.75; coded 'A'; to Abingdon 9.75. Damaged in heavy landing at Binbrook 7.79; to Shawbury 23.7.79 for repairs & returned to Oxford UAS 13.11.79. Aircraft abandoned in spin & crashed Ducklington, nr Witney, Oxon 25.3.85; instructor killed when separated from parachute. Soc 28.3.85 as scrap. Airframe deld 5.7.85 to BAe Prestwick; sectioned airframe stored [2.92]; scrapped by 10.92.

BH120-319   Model 121. T.1 **XX661**; ff 25.11.74. Deld 18.12.74 to Leeming. To Oxford UAS, Bicester 7.2.75; coded 'B'; to Abingdon 9.75; to Benson 7.92. To 3 FTS, Cranwell 1.96; coded '6'. Stored at RAF Newton [3.00]; to Shawbury 22.11.00 for storage/disposal. Sold at Phillips auction 24.5.01 for £13,000 to USA. Regd **N661BD** 18.12.01 to Donald A Shoop, Chambersburg, PA. CofA issued 15.5.02. Regd 25.10.17 to Antony B Greene, Fort Myers, FL. Currently regd.

BH120-320   Model 121. T.1 **XX662**; ff 19.12.74. Deld 13.1.75 to Leeming. To London UAS, Abingdon 18.3.75. Deld 9.4.75 to Aberdeen UAS, Dyce; coded 'A'; to Leuchars 12.80; unit renamed Aberdeen, Dundee & St Andrews UAS 10.81. Abandoned in spin and crashed nr Radernie Primary School, Peat Inn, Neacham, Fife 20.2.82. Soc 26.7.82 as scrap. Airframe deld 6.8.82 to Prestwick; scrapped by .87.

BH120-321   Model 121. T.1 **XX663**; ff 13.12.74. Deld 13.1.75 to Leeming. To London UAS, Abingdon 18.3.75. Deld 9.4.75 to Aberdeen UAS, Dyce; coded 'B'; to Leuchars 12.80; unit renamed Aberdeen, Dundee & St Andrews UAS 10.81; re-coded '01' 3.96 on absorption of East Lowlands UAS. To RAF Newton for storage; to Shawbury 8.6.00 for storage/disposal. Sold ex Shawbury at Phillips auction 29.11.00 for £11,000. Regd **F-AZLK** 26.1.01 to Jean-Luc Langeard, Biscarrosse, Claude Langeard, Creuilly & Thierry Lemale, St Aubin d'Arquenay (based Biscarrosse Parentis). Currently regd.

XX663, coded B wears the squadron badge of Aberdeen UAS on the rear fuselage. *(PH)*

BH120-322   Model 121. T.1 **XX664**; ff 19.12.74. Deld 13.1.75 to Leeming. To East Lowlands UAS, Turnhouse 8/11.4.75; coded '05'; re-coded '04' 7.90; unit absorbed 3.96 into Aberdeen, Dundee & St Andrews UAS, Leuchars. To Northumbrian UAS, Leeming 10.00; retaining code '04'. To Shawbury 23/24.1.01 for storage/disposal. Regd **G-CBCT** 23.8.01 to Thierry Brun, Paris (based Cergy-Pontoise). Stored by Loctudy Air, Sleap [9.01]. No CofA issued. Regn cld 8.9.06 as sold France. Regd **F-AZTV** 26.4.07 to Thierry Brun, Paris (based Pontoise/Cormeilles en Vexin). Currently regd.

BH120-323   Model 121. T.1 **XX665**; ff 20.12.74. Deld 13.1.75 to Leeming. To East Lowlands UAS, Turnhouse 19.3.75; coded '06'. To Aberdeen, Dundee & St Andrews UAS, Leuchars 16.10.81; coded 'E'. To Glasgow UAS, Abbotsinch [96]; uncoded. Damaged in forced landing following power loss nr Balloch, Strathclyde 20.9.97. Not repaired & to RAF Newton 15.12.98 (stored on pallet 3.00). To Instructional airframe **9289M** 1.9.00 & fuselage to No.2409 ATC Sqdn, RAF Halton 11.00;

repaired with parts from XX669. Roaded [4.15] to Wellesbourne Mountford and converted to cockpit simulator.

BH120-324   Model 121. T.1 **XX666**; ff 9.1.75. Deld 5.2.75 to Leeming. Deld 24/25.4.75 to Aberdeen UAS, Dyce; coded 'C'; to Leuchars 12.80; unit renamed Aberdeen, Dundee & St Andrews UAS 10.81. To Royal Navy EFTS, Linton-on-Ouse/Topcliffe 1.6.87; coded 'V'. To Queen's UAS, Aldergrove [6.94]; coded 'A'. To Aberdeen, Dundee & St Andrews UAS, Leuchars 7.96; coded '08'. Damaged in heavy landing during 'engine failure on take-off' training Leuchars 5.3.99; not repaired. To RAF Newton; stored on pallet [3.00]. Soc 8.8.00. Sold ex Shawbury at Phillips auction 24.5.01 for £7,200 to USA (but reportedly sold 15.9.00 to Robert L Bragg/Bulldog Aircraft Co, Pensacola, FL for spares). Regn **N524SB** reserved 27.4.10 by Stewart Carsten, Lincoln, NE. Sold 6.6.10 to Timothy M Liewer, Hershey, NB (and regn appln made 11.6.10). Not followed up & regn cld 9.5.11 as NTU. Status unknown.

BH120-325   Model 121. T.1 **XX667**; ff 10.1.75. Deld 5.2.75 to Leeming. Deld 24/25.4.75 to Aberdeen UAS, Dyce; coded 'D'; to Leuchars 12.80; unit renamed Aberdeen, Dundee & St Andrews UAS 10.81. To RAF College Air Sqdn, Cranwell 9.93; coded 'C1'; absorbed into 3 FTS 6.95 & re-coded '16'. To RAF Newton 26.6.99 for storage/disposal. Sold at Phillips auction 16.3.00 for £12,075. Regd **G-BZFN** 18.4.00 to Towerdrive Ltd, Ashbourne, Derby. CofA issued 8.10.01; painted as XX667 '16'. Regd 30.8.02 to Thomas Aviation Ltd, Cheltenham (based Ashbourne). Regd 7.10.05 to Risk Logical Ltd, Ronaldsway. Currently regd.

XX667 was operated by the RAF College and is seen here after civilianisation as G-BZFN. *(RS)*

BH120-326   Model 121. T.1 **XX668**; ff 21.1.75. Deld 5.2.75 to Leeming. To Birmingham UAS, Shawbury 29.4.75; coded 'A'. Damaged on landing Benson 27/28.7.76; to Prestwick for repairs 14.9.76. To Central Flying School, Leeming 20.6.77; coded '45'; transferred to Royal Navy EFTS, Leeming [5.82]; coded '26'; to Linton-on-Ouse/Topcliffe 4.84 & re-coded 'P'. To Manchester & Salford UAS, Woodvale 18.12.87; coded '1'. To Shawbury 13.12.00 for storage/disposal. Regd **G-CBAN** 26.7.01 to Carl John David Howcroft & Clifford Hilliker, Bristol (based RAF Colerne). CofA issued 5.10.01; painted as XX668 '1'. Regd 28.7.03 to Clifford Hilliker, Bristol (based RAF Colerne). CofA lapsed 4.10.04; renewed 22.5.07. CofA lapsed 21.5.10; stored St Athan [3.13]. CofA renewed 12.5.14. Regd 29.7.15 to Adam Christopher Scott Reynolds, Martock, Devon (based RNAS Yeovilton). Currently regd.

BH120-327   Model 121. T.1 **XX669**; ff 29.1.75. Deld 5.2.75 to Leeming. To Birmingham UAS, Shawbury 29.4.75; coded 'B'; to Cosford 3.78. Crashed on landing Cosford 6.9.88; to Instructional Airframe **8997M** 19.5.89 with Birmingham UAS, Cosford. Sold [11.91] [possibly sold 8.90] to Phoenix Aviation [Nevill Martin], Bruntingthorpe. Deld 30.6.98 to Mr/Mrs J Little, Llantrisant, Wales for static rebuild; extant [1.00]. To Aerofab Restorations, Bourne Park, Hurstbourne Tarrant as hulk [3.01]; stored 10.01. Fuselage hulk to No.2409 ATC Sqdn, RAF Halton [8.03] for composite rebuild of XX665. To AeroVenture, Doncaster Leisure Park [4.06]; coded 'B'. Renamed South Yorkshire Aircraft Museum & fuselage on display [3.16].

BH120-328   Model 121. T.1 **XX670**; ff 28.1.75. Deld 26.2.75 to Leeming. To Birmingham UAS, Shawbury 13.5.75; coded 'C'; to Cosford 3.78. To Shawbury 20.4.01 for storage/disposal. Sold at Phillips auction 25.10.01 for £12,000 to USA; departed Shawbury 13.12.01 for Falconer, California. Regd **N50UP** reserved 28.3.02 to Todd Falconer, CA. Regd 6.04 to Steven C Pistole, Fresno, CA (later Bend, OR). Regd 7.11.09 to Kevin L Ford, Peachtree City, GA. Regd 27.3.10 to Richard L Stefanick, Morgantown, WV. CofA issued 19.10.17. Currently regd.

BH120-329   Model 121. T.1 **XX671**; ff 14.2.75. Deld 26.2.75 to Leeming. To Birmingham UAS, Shawbury 16.5.75; coded 'D'; to Cosford 3.78. To Shawbury 1.3.01 for storage/disposal. Sold 8.01 to Military Aircraft Spares Ltd, Poole; roaded 10.8.01 to (associate) Mercia Aviation Spares, Wellesbourne Mountford & stored. Roaded 12.07 to Joe Goy, Diseworth, Leics; stored [9.12]. Shipped to Sweden 4.16; probably for spares.

BH120-330   Model 121. T.1 **XX672**; ff 14.2.75. Deld 10.3.75 to Leeming. To Birmingham UAS, Shawbury 23.5.75; coded 'E'; to Cosford 3.78. To Shawbury 20.4.01 for storage/disposal. Deld 12.7.01 to International Centre for Aerospace Training/Barry Technical College, Cardiff. Sold [4.05] to Witham Specialist Vehicles (Paul Southerington), Colsterworth, Grantham. Roaded to Windmill Aviation, Spanhoe 31.3.07 & sold by auction 12.7.07 to Dorothy Boyd-Bragg, USA. Regd **N3672** 1.6.09 to Dorothy A Boyd-Bragg, McGaheysville, VA. No CofA Issued. Regn cld 31.5.17 by FAA.

BH120-331   Model 121. T.1 **XX685**; ff 3.3.75. Deld 18/20.3.75 to Leeming. To Liverpool UAS, Woodvale 16.5.75; coded 'L'. To Aberdeen, Dundee & St Andrews UAS, Leuchars 9.93; coded 'C'. To 3 FTS Cranwell 1.96; coded '11'. To RAF Newton 1.97 for storage due to high airframe hours; but returned to 3 FTS by 5.98. To RAF Newton 9.99 for storage/disposal. Sold at auction 9.6.00. Regd **G-BZLB** 15.8.00 to Lawrence Bax, Salisbury (stored Bourne Park, Hurstbourne Tarrant 10.01). Regn cld 19.11.02 as sold USA. Regd **N709AB** 3.12.02 to William B Pope, Farmington, MI. Regd 25.2.04 to David P Lohmann, Edwards, CO. CofA issued 9.11.07. Currently regd.

XX685 of Liverpool UAS based at Woodvale. *(PH)*

BH120-332   Model 121. T.1 **XX686**; ff 3.3.75. Deld 10.3.75 to Leeming. To Liverpool UAS, Woodvale 16.5.75; coded 'U'. To Glasgow & Strathclyde UAS, Abbotsinch 9.93; uncoded. To 3 FTS Cranwell 1.96; coded '4'. To RAF Newton 2.00 for storage (though reported still with 3 FTS [5.00] ; re-coded '5'). To Instructional Airframe **9291M** 14.11.00 at 4 SofTT/ Civilian Technical Training School, St Athan; unit renamed to Defence Aviation Repair Agency (DARA) Training School; still coded '5'. Sold by tender 22.11.05. Regd **N686XX** 30.8.06 to Fly One LLC, Chandler, AZ. CofA issued 3.1.07. Regd 28.7.12 to Daniel F Herbert, Chandler, AZ. Regd 10.1.14 to Terry L Herbert, Chandler, AZ. Currently regd.

BH120-333   Model 121. T.1 **XX687**; ff 6.3.75. Deld 18/20.3.75 to Leeming. To Liverpool UAS, Woodvale 10.6.75; coded 'A'. To East Midlands UAS, Newton 28.10.77; coded 'A'. To 3 FTS, Cranwell 1.96; coded '13'. To Bristol UAS, Colerne .00; coded 'B'. To Northumbrian UAS, Leeming 21.9.00; still coded 'B'. To Shawbury 24.1.01 for storage/disposal. Deld 18/19.7.01 to International Centre for Aerospace Training/Barry Technical College, Cardiff (extant 3.14).

BH120-334   Model 121. T.1 **XX688**; ff 11.3.75. Deld 7/11.4.75 to Leeming. To Liverpool UAS, Woodvale 10.6.75; coded 'S'. To 3 FTS, Cranwell 1.96; coded '8'. To Shawbury 19.4.01 for storage/disposal. Deld 8.01 to Windmill Aviation, Spanhoe on sale to France. Regd **F-AZOA** 14.11.01 to Martial Roux, Frebauns (based Lons le Saulnier/Courlaoux). Currently regd.

BH120-335   Model 121. T.1 **XX689**; ff 24.3.75. Deld 9/11.4.75 to Leeming; to Royal Navy EFTS 11.6.75; coded '3' (replacing XX521). To MoD/PE & returned to Prestwick 24.8.76 for propeller overspeed tests; returned after mods to RNEFTS, Leeming 7.2.77 (still coded '3'). Transferred to Central Flying School 4.84 & moved to Scampton 9.84; still coded '3'; unit to Cranwell 3.95 & redesignated 3 FTS. To Bristol UAS, Colerne 2.96; coded 'D'. To Shawbury 21.9.00 for storage/disposal. Sold at Phillips auction 24.5.01 for £11,500 to USA (Mr Emanuel, Sullivan County, NY). Regn **N689BD** reserved 8.4.02 to Windham Flyers LLC. Regd 31.12.03 to Thomas J Smith, Phillipsport, NY. No CofA issued. Currently regd.

XX689 was another Bulldog painted in black and yellow. *(P.H)*

BH120-336 Model 121. T.1 **XX690**; ff 28.3.75. Deld 10/11.4.75 to Leeming; to Royal Navy EFTS 12.6.75; coded '6'. To Yorkshire UAS, Finningley 22.7.76; coded 'A' (replacement for XX618). To Central Flying School, Scampton 8.94; coded '5'; unit to Cranwell 3.95 & redesignated 3 FTS. To Liverpool UAS, Woodvale 2.96; coded 'A'. To Shawbury 6.9.00 for storage/disposal. Sold at Phillips auction 25.10.01 for £12,000 and roaded 21.3.02 to James Watt College, Greenock, Port Glasgow. Roaded 14.9.11 to [unknown]; then on 14.9.12 to VT10 Aero Company, Archerfield, Dirleton, East Lothian (stored 10.17).

BH120-337 Model 121. T.1 **XX691**; ff 28.3.75. To AT&DF Leeming 18/24.4.75; to 5 MU Kemble 3.6.75 for storage. Roaded to Shawbury 13.12.82 for storage. Finally issued to Yorkshire UAS, Finningley 6.12.85; coded 'H'; re-coded 'G' 9.92; to Church Fenton 10.95. To London UAS, Benson 1.96; initially uncoded; later coded '10'. To RAF Newton 10.99 for disposal. Sold 12.99 to Armed Forces of Malta. Regd **9H-ADQ** 13.2.00; deld ex RAF Newton 13.2.00; arr Luqa 19.2.00. To **AS0020** 5.00 (reportedly to be named 'Hope'). Crashed Santu Pietru, nr Dwejra, Gozo 5.8.07. Remains stored Luqa [7.14] but removed by [12.16].

BH120-338 Model 125. Regd **G-BCSN** (CofR R14652) 27.11.74 to Scottish Aviation Ltd. Ff 12.3.75. CofA issued 11.4.75 (4 months); ferried to Amman via Shoreham 6.5.75-13.5.75. Regn cld 9.6.75 as sold Jordan. Regd **JY-AEL** to Royal Jordanian Academy of Aeronautics. Regn cld 1.1.78. To **RJAF 405**. Sold 21.7.03 to Vision Engineering Group, Amman. Sold 12.04 to Gesoco Industries, USA. Regd **N8804P** 16.3.05 to Steven M Riley, Bucyrus, KS. CofA issued 3.6.05. Regd 9.2.06 to Sherrill H Greene, Fort Myers, FL. Stored for spares Fort Myers [11.18]. Currently regd.

BH120-339 Model 125. Regd **G-BCSO** (CofR R14653) 27.11.74 to Scottish Aviation Ltd. Ff 17.3.75. CofA issued 23.4.75 (4 months); ferried to Amman via Shoreham 6.5.75-13.5.75. Regn cld 9.6.75 as sold Jordan. Regd **JY-AEM** to Royal Jordanian Academy of Aeronautics. Crashed Amman 22.7.75 prior to delivery to RJAF.

BH120-340 Model 125. Regd **G-BCSP** (CofR R14654) 27.11.74 to Scottish Aviation Ltd. Ff 20.3.75. CofA issued 23.4.75 (4 months); ferried to Amman via Biggin Hill 17.5.75-21.5.75. Regn cld 9.6.75 as sold Jordan. Regd **JY-AEN** to Royal Jordanian Academy of Aeronautics. Regn cld 1.1.78. To **RJAF 406**. Sold 21.7.03 to Vision Engineering Group, Amman. Sold to UK .05. Regd **F-AZOI** 6.2.09 to Gilles Beda, Paris (based Le Plessis Belleville). Currently regd.

BH120-341 Model 121. T.1 **XX692**; ff 15.4.75. To AT&DF Leeming 13/14.5.75; to 5 MU Kemble 3.6.75 for storage; roaded to Shawbury 20.12.82 for storage. To Central Flying School, Scampton 19.5.86; coded '5'. To Yorkshire UAS, Finningley 6.94; coded 'A'; to Church Fenton 10.95. To Bristol UAS, Colerne 2.96; still coded 'A'. To RAF Newton 9.99 for storage/disposal. Sold at auction 9.6.00. Regd **G-BZMH** 21.8.00 to MEJ Hingley & Co Ltd, Birmingham (based Wellesbourne Mountford). CofA issued 18.10.01; painted as XX692 'A'. Regd 13.2.09 to Michael Ernest James Hingley, Birmingham (based Wellesbourne Mountford). Currently regd.

BH120-342 Model 121. T.1 **XX693**; ff 23.4.75. To AT&DF Leeming 13/14.5.75; to 5 MU Kemble 4.6.75 for storage; roaded to Shawbury 10.1.83 for storage. Roaded back to 5 MU Kemble 7/8.1.86. To Central Flying School, Scampton 2.7.86; coded '11'; but re-coded '4' [6.89]; to Cranwell 3.95 & redesignated 3 FTS. To Glasgow UAS, Abbotsinch 1.96; uncoded. To East Lowlands UAS, Turnhouse .96; coded '07'; absorbed 3.96 into Aberdeen, Dundee & St Andrews UAS, Leuchars. To RAF Newton 9.99 for storage/disposal. Sold at auction 9.6.00. Regd **G-BZML** 1.9.00 to Ian Douglas Anderson, Colchester (based Poplar Hall Farm, Elmsett). CofA issued 15.11.01; painted as XX693 '07'. Currently regd.

BH120-343 Model 121. T.1 **XX694**; ff 24.4.75. To AT&DF Leeming 20/21.5.75; to 5 MU Kemble 17.7.75 for storage & use as hack. To East Midlands UAS, Newton 4.2.82; coded 'E'. To Shawbury 31.8.00 for storage/disposal. Regd **G-CBBS** 8.8.01 to Elite Consultancy Corporation Ltd (T Thompson), Spalding; deld 2.11.01. Stored Egginton [1.03]. CofA issued 14.4.03; painted as XX694 'E'. Regd 4.7.03 to European Light Aviation Ltd, Newcastle. Regd 6.9.07 to Newcastle Aerobatic Academy Ltd, Newcastle. Regd 28.7.14 to David Raymond Keene, Oxford (based Turweston; later Slay Barn Farm, Cuddesdon). Currently regd.

BH120-344 Model 121. T.1 **XX695**; ff 30.4.75. To AT&DF Leeming 20/21.5.75; to 5 MU Kemble 27.6.75 for storage. To 13 AEF, Sydenham 21.9.82. To London UAS, Abingdon 24.1.83; coded '10'. To Oxford UAS, Abingdon 29.3.85; coded 'A'; to Benson 7.92. To Manchester UAS, Woodvale 11.99; coded '3'. To Shawbury 14.3.01 for storage/disposal. Regd **G-CBBT** 8.8.01 to Elite Consultancy Corporation Ltd (T Thompson), Spalding; deld 2.11.01. Regd 14.8.03 to CM Aviation Ltd, Billingham (based Morgansfield, Fishburn). CofA issued 26.1.04; painted as XX695 '3'. Regd 7.1.13 to Kerr Allen Johnston, Pitlochry (based Perth). Repainted as XX695 'C' & 'M'. Currently regd.

BH120-345 Model 121. T.1 **XX696**; ff 5.5.75. To AT&DF Leeming 20/21.5.75; to 5 MU Kemble 27.6.75 for storage. Roaded to Shawbury 5.1.83 for storage; returned by road to 5 MU 8/9.1.86. To Central Flying School, Scampton 17.9.86; coded '8'; to Cranwell 3.95 & unit redesignated 3 FTS. To Liverpool UAS, Woodvale 1.96; coded 'S'. To RAF Newton 9.99 for disposal. Sold 12.99 to Armed Forces of Malta. Regd **9H-ADR** 13.2.00; deld ex Newton 13.2.00; arr Luqa 19.2.00. To **AS0021** 5.00 (reportedly to be named 'Faith'). Stored Luqa [7.14; 12.16].

XX696 was one of four Bulldogs sold to the Malta DF. *(PH)*

BH120-346 Model 121. T.1 **XX697**; ff 6.5.75. To AT&DF Leeming 20/21.5.75; to 5 MU Kemble 27.6.75 for storage. To Queen's UAS, Sydenham 29.1.81; coded 'Q'; to Aldergrove 1.92; re-coded 'C' .93. To Bristol UAS, Colerne 1.96; coded 'H'. To Shawbury 22.9.00 for storage/disposal. Sold at Phillips auction 24.5.01 for £12,000 to USA; shipped ex Shawbury 21.6.01. Regd **N697BD** 24.7.01 to Timothy J Blofeld, Novato, CA (based Marin County). CofA issued 28.8.01. Regd 2.5.06 to Blue Horizon Ltd, Novato, CA. Currently regd.

BH120-347 Model 121. T.1 **XX698**; ff 12.5.75. To AT&DF Leeming 10.6.75; to 5 MU Kemble 11.8.75 for storage. To BAe Prestwick 21.7.81 for trial installation of Sylvania 067A UHF radio; to A&AEE Boscombe Down 7.7.82; returned to Prestwick 9.3.83. To Shawbury 29.6/1.7.83 for storage. To Royal Navy EFTS, Linton-on-Ouse/Topcliffe 10.4.85; coded 'D'. To Central Flying School, Scampton 27.6.86; coded '9'; to Cranwell 3.95 & unit redesignated 3 FTS. To RAF Newton 8.99 for storage/disposal. Sold at auction 9.6.00. Regd **G-BZME** 18.8.00 to Witham (Specialist Vehicles) Ltd, Grantham (based Spanhoe). Regd 22.5.01 to Barry Whitworth, Sheffield (based Breighton). CofA issued 3.9.01; painted as XX698 '9'. [Coded 'Q' 3.93?] Regd 24.9.07 to Simon Jeremy Whitworth, Sheffield (based Breighton). Regd 27.8.14 to Hugh Roderick Moore Tyrell, Shrewsbury, t/a XX698 Bulldog Group, Sleap. Currently regd.

BH120-348 Model 121. T.1 **XX699**; ff 10.6.75. To AT&DF Leeming 26.6.75; to 5 MU Kemble 19.8.75 for storage/station hack. Op 1.79 by RNAS Culdrose (possibly unofficially). To Royal Navy EFTS, Leeming 3.5.79; coded '30'; to Linton-on-Ouse/Topcliffe 4.84 & re-coded 'Q'. To Birmingham UAS, Cosford 15.7.93; coded 'F'. To Shawbury 21.3.00 for storage/disposal. Sold to K Ward, Bangor-on-Dee & regd **G-CBCV** 30.8.01 to Cheshire Aviators Ltd, Wrexham; deld Speke 25.9.01. CofA issued 9.7.02; painted as XX699 'F'. Regd 22.6.04 to Charles Ainsley Patter, Newark (based North Coates). Regn cld 21.6.12 as sold Australia. Regd **VH-XVE** 29.11.12 to Stephen J Lovegrove, Angle Vale, SA; still painted as XX699 'F'.

BH120-349 Model 121. T.1 **XX700**; ff 28.5.75. To AT&DF Leeming 26.6.75; to 5 MU Kemble 19.8.75 for storage. To Royal Navy EFTS, Leeming 11.10.78; coded '27'; to Linton-on-Ouse/Topcliffe 4.84 & re-coded 'R'. To RAF College Air Sqdn, Cranwell [6.93]; coded 'B1'; absorbed into 3 FTS 6.95 & re-coded '17'. To Southampton UAS, Boscombe Down 18.12.00; still coded '17'. To Shawbury 23.5.01 for storage/disposal. Regd **G-CBEK** 26.9.01 to Stuart Landregan, Basingstoke; deld Blackbushe 1.10.01. CofA issued 16.11.01; painted as XX700 '17'. Regd 17.5.08 to Bernard Peter Robinson, Aldershot (based Blackbushe). Regd 4.9.17 to Benjamin Clive Faulkner, Warminster & Timothy Wakeman, Woking (based Thruxton). Currently regd.

BH120-350 Model 121. T.1 **XX701**; ff 29.5.75. To AT&DF Leeming 26.6.75; to 5 MU Kemble 11.8.75 for storage. To Royal Navy EFTS, Linton-on-Ouse/Topcliffe 6.10.75. To London UAS, Abingdon 12.3.76; coded '08'. To Southampton UAS, Hamble 29.6.77; coded '02'; to Hurn 12.78; Lee-on-Solent 4.88; Boscombe Down 4.93. To Shawbury 22.9.00 for storage/disposal; declared surplus 30.1.01 & soc 30.5.01. Sold at Phillips auction 24.5.01 (as Lot 18 for £14,687+VAT) to William B Pope, Farmington, MI; shipped ex Shawbury 21.6.01. Regd **N701AB** (reserved 15.8.01). Regd [6.06] to William Dale Sollenberger, Carmel, IN. Regd 29.11.13 to Nicholas E Vonalven, Beecher, IL. Regd 12.12.14 to Richard D Ezell, Port Orange, FL. CofA issued 2.3.15. Regd 14.9.18 to Stervet A Haktanir, Houston, TX. Currently regd.

BH120-351 Model 121. T.1 **XX702**; ff 12.6.75. To AT&DF Leeming 26.6.75; to 5 MU Kemble 11.8.75 for storage. To Glasgow & Strathclyde UAS, Perth 1.10.75; coded '03'; (replacement for XX557); uncoded [89]; to Abbotsinch 1.93. To Central Flying School, Leeming [8.93]; coded '11'; to Scampton 9.84. To 7 AEF, Newton 1.95; coded '77'; to joint op with East Midlands UAS [12.95] now coded 'pi'. To Liverpool/Manchester UAS, Woodvale 30.8.00; still coded 'pi'. To Shawbury 15.3.01 for storage/disposal. Regd **G-CBCR** 5.9.01 to Simon Clarence Smith, Spalding; deld Fenland 10.9.01. CofA issued 2.7.02; painted as XX702 'P'. Regd 31.1.06 to Donald Wells, Nottingham (based Tollerton; later Egginton). Currently regd.

BH120-352 Model 121. T.1 **XX703**; ff 20.6.75. Deld 26.6.75 to AT&DF Leeming. To East Lowlands UAS, Turnhouse 23.9.75; coded '02'. Forced landed with engine failure nr Glenrothes 3/4.6.76. Soc 10.6.76.

BH120-353 Model 121. T.1 **XX704**; ff 17.6.75. Deld 26.6.75 to AT&DF Leeming; to 5 MU Kemble 11.8.75 for storage. To Royal Navy EFTS, Leeming 29.9.75. To Queen's UAS, Sydenham 18.3.76; coded 'U' (replacement for XX612). To East Midlands UAS, Newton 4.11.77; coded 'U'. To Shawbury 13.3.00 for storage/disposal. Sold 15.9.00 to Robert L Bragg/Bulldog Aircraft Co, Pensacola, FL. Regd **N706BD** 22.3.01 to Robert L Bragg, Pensacola, FL. CofA issued 18.10.02. Regd [6.06] to David E Olsen, Fremont, CA. Sale reported 26.5.17 to Sherrill Greene, Fort Myers, FL. Regn cld 31.5.18. Stored for spares Fort Myers [11.18].
Note: G-BCUV (c/n 376) is painted as XX704.

BH120-354 Model 121. T.1 **XX705**; ff 23.7.75. Deld 10.10.75 to AT&DF Leeming; to 5 MU Kemble 10.11.75 for storage. To Birmingham UAS, Shawbury 16.9.76; coded 'A' (replacing XX668). To Southampton UAS, Hamble 28.10.77; coded '06'; to Hurn 12.78; re-coded '05' [2.83]; to Lee-on-Solent 4.88; Boscombe Down 4.93. Wfu & to Instructional Airframe 4.01 with Boscombe Down Apprentices School. Roaded 4.15 to Jet Art Aviation Ltd, Selby.

BH120-355 Model 121. T.1 **XX706**; ff 30.7.75. Deld 10.10.75 to AT&DF, Leeming; to 5 MU Kemble 25.11.75 for storage. To 6 FTS, Finningley 8.1.76; coded '06'. To Southampton UAS, Hamble 28.10.77; coded '01'; to Hurn 12.78; Lee-on-Solent 4.88; Boscombe Down 4.93. To Shawbury 23.5.01 for storage/disposal. Sold at Phillips auction 25.10.01 for £12,000 to USA; departed Shawbury 13.12.01 to Mr Mehelic, CA. Regn **N3043A** reserved 11.3.02 by Larry F Mehelic; NTU. Regd **N706X** 5.9.02 to Arnon Matityahu, Half Moon Bay, CA; later Palo Alto, CA. Regd 2.04 to Biggles Aviation, Los Angeles (unconfirmed). Struck tree & crashed nr South Lake Tahoe, CA 7.4.07; pilot killed. Regn cld 7.11.13.

BH120-356 Model 121. T.1 **XX707** ff 5.9.75. Deld 10.10.75 to AT&DF Leeming; to 5 MU Kemble 10.11.75 for storage/hack. To Royal Navy EFTS, Leeming 3.6.77; coded '20'. To Southampton UAS, Hamble 13.9.77; coded '04'; to Hurn 12.78; Lee-on-Solent 4.88; Boscombe Down 4.93. To Shawbury 14.2.01 for storage/disposal. Sold to Dennis Squires, Wellesbourne Mountford. Regd **G-CBDS** 27.7.01 to Bulldog Support Ltd, Stratford-upon-Avon (based Wellesbourne Mountford); deld 21.9.01.

CofA issued 7.12.01; painted as XX707 '4'. Regd 9.1.02 to Hugh Roderick Moore Tyrrell, Shrewsbury (based Sleap). Regd 9.6.05 to John Rodney Parry, Bangor (based Caernarfon). CofA lapsed 27.5.11. Regn cld by CAA 13.5.14. Stored Caernarfon [8.15].

BH120-357 Model 121. T.1 **XX708** ff 30.9.75. Deld 4/5.11.75 to Leeming. To 6 FTS, Finningley 17.1.76; coded '08'. To Southampton UAS, Hamble 13.9.77; coded '03'; to Hurn 12.78; Lee-on-Solent 4.88; Boscombe Down 4.93. To Shawbury 30/31.5.01 for storage/disposal. Sold at Phillips auction 25.10.01 for £22,000 to George Crowe & departed Shawbury 8.11.01 to Long Beach, CA.. Soc 5.11.01. Regd **N708BD** 2.4.02 to Bulldog Aircraft USA Inc (George V Crowe), La Habra, CA (based Chino). CofA issued 13.4.02. Sold 23.12.04 & regd 10.2.05 to Steven D Ritzi, San Diego, CA (to Tampa, FL 6.07). Currently regd.

XX708 served with 6FTS at RAF Finningley. *(PH)*

BH120-358 Model 121. T.1 **XX709** ff 1.10.75. Deld 4/5.11.75 to Leeming; to 5 MU Kemble 14.1.76 for storage. To Royal Navy EFTS, Leeming 12.11.79; coded '33'. To 5 MU Kemble 8.7.81 for storage. Removed from storage 21.4.82; returned to RNEFTS 14.6.82 & to Blue Goshawk, Cranwell 15.7.82 for Prince Andrew's refresher training. To Shawbury for storage 9.8.82. To Aberdeen, Dundee & St Andrews UAS, Leuchars 8.4.87; coded 'C'. To Central Flying School, Cranwell [8.93]; coded '12'. To Yorkshire UAS, Finningley 6.94; coded 'H'; re-coded 'E' 2.95; to Church Fenton 10.95. To RAF Newton 9.99 for disposal. Sold to 12.99 to Armed Forces of Malta. Regd **9H-ADS** 13.2.00; deld ex RAF Newton 13.2.00; arr Luqa 19.2.00. To **AS0022** 5.00 (reportedly to be named 'Desperation'). Stored Luqa [7.14; 12.16].

In July 1982 XX709 was used for Prince Andrew's refresher training. *(PH)*

BH120-359 Model 121. T.1 **XX710** ff 28.10.75. Deld 4/5.11.75 to Leeming; to 5 MU Kemble 14.1.76 for storage. To Royal Navy EFTS, Leeming 19.11.79; coded '34'. To 5 MU Kemble 8.7.81 for storage; removed from storage 21.4.82; returned to RNEFTS 14.6.82 & to Blue Goshawk, Cranwell 15.7.82 for Prince Andrew's refresher training. To Shawbury for storage 9.8.82. To Manchester & Salford UAS, Woodvale 23.3.87; coded '5'. While operated by (locally-based) Liverpool UAS, it stalled following engine failure on 'touch and go' and crashed Woodvale 21.7.97; 2 killed. Wreckage to RAF Newton; stored [3.00] & reportedly scrapped 8.00 (also reported being scrapped at Benson 4.98!). *However also reportedly deld 20.3.01 to '4 SofTT/Central Technical Training School, St Athan for scrapping (unlikely).*

BH120-360 Model 121. T.1 **XX711** ff 7.11.75. Deld 9.12.75 to Leeming; to 5 MU Kemble 14.1.76 for storage. To Central Flying School, Leeming 23.6.77; coded '40'. To 13 AEF, Sydenham 4.10.78; coded 'E'. To [associated] Queen's UAS, Sydenham 10.86; coded 'S'; to Aldergrove 1.92; re-coded 'D' 10.93 (for use by 13 AEF); reverted to QUAS & re-coded back to 'S' 4.96. To Oxford UAS, Benson .86; allocated code 'F' (but retained 'S'). To Liverpool UAS, Woodvale 6.99; coded 'X'. To Shawbury 14.12.00 for storage/disposal. Sold to T Thompson. Regd **G-CBBU** 6.8.01 to Elite Consultancy Corporation Ltd, Spalding; deld 20.9.01. Stored Egginton

[1.03]; still painted as XX711 'X'. Regd 1.9.05 to Newcastle Bulldog Group Ltd, Newcastle (stored Egginton). No CofA issued. Regn cld 16.12.10 as pwfu. Stored dismantled [10.11; 6.12] at Fishburn (Morgansfield). To Perth 10.14 but removed [by 9.16].

BH120-361   Model 121. T.1 **XX712** ff 20.11.75. Deld 16/18.12.75 to Leeming; to 5 MU Kemble 8.3.76 for storage. To Royal Navy EFTS, Leeming 12.8.76; coded '6'; to Linton-on-Ouse/Topcliffe 4.84 & re-coded 'D'. To Manchester & Salford UAS, Woodvale 6.3.85; coded '1'. Crashed/dbf during low-level manoeuvre Southport beach 2.3.88; P/O MF Davies killed.

BH120-362   Model 121. T.1 **XX713** ff 2.2.76. To Leeming 19.3.76; to 5 MU Kemble 22.4.76 for storage. To Central Flying School, Leeming 23.6.77; coded '41'. To Royal Navy EFTS, Leeming [7.81]; coded '22'. Transferred to CFS 4.84 & moved to Scampton 9.84 & re-coded '6'. To 6 FTS, Finningley 14.5.92; coded 'Z'. To Bristol UAS, Colerne 11.95; coded 'G'. To Southampton UAS, Boscombe Down 21.9.00; coded '2'. To Shawbury 31.5.01 for storage/disposal. Regd **G-CBJK** 3.12.01 to Elite Consultancy Corporation Ltd. Spalding; deld Norwich 29.1.02. Regd 29.7.05 to George Victor Crowe & Dennis Leonard Thompson, Norwich; stored [5.06]; still painted as XX713 '2'. No CofA issued. Sold 1.9.08 to CD Zimmer/Zimmer Performance Motorsports, WA. Regn cld 12.11.08 as sold USA. Stored Mukilteo, WA until regd **N713Z** 23.5.11 to Christopher David Zimmer/Zimmer Performance Motorsports LLC, Mukilteo, WA. CofA issued 22.7.11. Sold 15.10.13 & regd 19.11.13 to Bulldog Aviation LLC, Poulsbo, WA. Currently regd.

BH120-363   Model 121. T.1 **XX714** ff 21.6.76. To Leeming 22.6.76. Returned to Prestwick 28.7.76 for mods & transferred to MoD/PE fleet as test aircraft for measurement of loads imposed on tailplane during aerobatics. To A&AEE Boscombe Down [8.82]; returned to BAe Prestwick 13.10.82. To Central Flying School, Scampton 16.8.89; coded '12'; re-coded '7' .93. To Yorkshire UAS, Finningley 6.94; coded 'D'; to Church Fenton 10.95. To RAF Newton 11.99 & sold 12.99 to Armed Forces of Malta. Regd **9H-ADT** 13.2.00 and deld ex Newton 13.2.00; arr Luqa 19.2.00. To **AS0023** 5.00 (reportedly to be named 'Charity'). Stored Luqa [5.13; 12.16].

BH120-364   Model 126. Regd **G-BCTL** (CofR R14674) 23.12.74 to Scottish Aviation Ltd. Ff 29.7.75. CofA issued 22.8.75 (4 months); ferried via Fairoaks 17.9.75 to Beirut. Regn cld 30.9.75 as sold Lebanon. To Lebanese Air Force as **L-141**. Fate unknown.

BH120-365   Model 126. Regd **G-BCTM** (CofR R14675) 23.12.74 to Scottish Aviation Ltd. Ff 7.8.75. CofA issued 3.9.75 (4 months); ferried via Fairoaks 17.9.75 to Beirut. Regn cld 30.9.75. To Lebanese Air Force as **L-142**. Stored Rayak AB [06-.10]; on display [10.10] in Lebanese Air Force Museum, Rayak. Overhauled & returned to service with 1 Sqdn Aviation School at Beirut [6.18].

BH120-366   Model 126. Regd **G-BCTN** (CofR R14676) 23.12.74 to Scottish Aviation Ltd. Ff 12.8.75. CofA issued 11.9.75 (4 months); ferried via Fairoaks 17.9.75 to Beirut. Regn cld 30.9.75 as sold Lebanon To Lebanese Air Force as **L-143**. Fate unknown.

BH120-367   Model 126. Regd **G-BCTO** (CofR R14677) 23.12.74 to Scottish Aviation Ltd. Ff 15.8.75. CofA issued 10.10.75 (4 months); ferried via Luton 16.10.75 to Beirut. Regn cld 30.10.75 as sold Lebanon. To Lebanese Air Force as **L-144**. Stored Rayak AB [06-.11]; preserved [10.11] in Lebanese Air Force Museum, Rayak. Overhauled & returned to service with 1 Sqdn Aviation School at Beirut [6.18].

BH120-368   Model 126. Regd **G-BCTP** (CofR R14678) 23.12.74 to Scottish Aviation Ltd. Ff 25.8.75. CofA issued 10.10.75 (4 months); ferried via Luton 16.10.75 to Beirut. Regn cld 30.10.75 as sold Lebanon. To Lebanese Air Force as **L-145**. Stored Rayak AB [06-.11]; preserved [10.10] in Lebanese Air Force Museum, Rayak. Overhauled & returned to service with 1 Sqdn Aviation School at Beirut [6.18].

BH120-369   Model 126. Regd **G-BCTS** (CofR R14679) 23.12.74 to Scottish Aviation Ltd. Ff 2.9.75. CofA issued 10.10.75 (4 months); ferried via Luton 16.10.75 to Beirut. Regn cld 30.10.75 as sold Lebanon. To Lebanese Air Force as **L-146**. Fate unknown; last reported Rayak AB [3.93].

BH120-370   Model 122A. Regd **G-BCUN** (CofR R14700) 9.1.75 to Scottish Aviation Ltd. Ff 13.10.75. CofA issued 6.11.75 (4 months); ferried via Gatwick 11.12.75 to Takoradi. Regd cld 22.1.76 as sold Ghana. To Ghana Air Force as **G-106**. W/off in Ghana prior to 8.82.

G-BCUN at Gatwick en route to Takoradi, Ghana. *(KB)*

BH120-371   Model 122A. Regd **G-BCUO** (CofR R14701) 9.1.75 to Scottish Aviation Ltd. Ff 17.10.75. CofA issued 6.11.75 (4 months); ferried via Gatwick 11.12.75 to Takoradi. Regd cld 22.1.76 as sold Ghana. To Ghana Air Force as **G-107**. To Lawrence Bax & stored Henstridge [5.95]. Regd **G-BCUO** 14.2.97 to Lawrence Bax, t/a Direct Equipment Services, Amesbury (based Bourne Park, Hurstbourne Tarrant, Hants). CofA renewed 17.10.97. Regd 1.10.98 to Cranfield University, Cranfield (Cranfield College of Aeronautics). Currently regd.

BH120-372   Model 122A. Regd **G-BCUP** (CofR R14702) 9.1.75 to Scottish Aviation Ltd. Ff 24.10.75 (29.10.75?). CofA issued 19.11.75 (4 months) but then stored. Ferried via Halfpenny Green 24.5.76; Shoreham 25.5.76; arr Takoradi 31.5.76. Regd cld 9.6.76 as sold Ghana. To Ghana Air Force as **G-108**. Sold [5.95] to Lawrence Bax, stored Henstridge. To Aerofab Restorations, Bourne Park, Hurstbourne Tarrant nr Andover [3.98] & stored. To store in Salisbury 4.04 but removed to [unknown] mid-06.

BH120-373   Model 122A. Regd **G-BCUS** (CofR R14703) 9.1.75 to Scottish Aviation Ltd. Ff 30.10.75. CofA issued 14.11.75 (4 months) but then stored. Ferried via Halfpenny Green 24.5.76; Shoreham 25.5.76; arr Takoradi 31.5.76. Regd cld 9.6.76 as sold Ghana. To Ghana Air Force as **G-109**. Regd **G-BCUS** 1.5.95 to Stephen Joseph Ollier & Julia Jane Ollier, Derby (based Egginton; later Tatenhill). CofA renewed 3.4.96. Regd 2.12.04 to Charles David Hill, London E14 (based North Weald). Regd 2.6.08 to Roger George Hayes, Cirencester, t/a Falcon Group, Kemble. Currently regd.

G-BCUS served with the Ghana Air Force as G-109. *(RS)*

BH120-374   Model 122A. Regd **G-BCUT** (CofR R14704) 9.1.75 to Scottish Aviation Ltd. Ff 20.11.75. CofA issued 24.12.75 (4 months) but then stored. Ferried via Halfpenny Green 24.5.76; Shoreham 25.5.76; arr Takoradi 31.5.76. Regd cld 9.6.76 as sold Ghana. To Ghana Air Force as **G-110**. W/off in Ghana prior to 8.82.

BH120-375   Model 122A. Regd **G-BCUU** (CofR R14705) 9.1.75 to Scottish Aviation Ltd. Ff 2.12.75. CofA issued 24.12.75 (4 months) but then stored. Ferried via Shoreham 7.6.76 to Takoradi. Regd cld 24.6.76 as sold Ghana. To Ghana Air Force as **G-111**. To Lawrence Bax [5.95] & stored Henstridge [4.96]. Regd **G-CCOA** 4.9.96 to Cranfield University, Cranfield. CofA issued 24.2.97. Damaged in heavy landing Cranfield 22.8.01 during practice engine failure on take-off. Regd cld 11.6.02 to pwfu. Sold to [owner] in Yarmouth, IoW [5.04] & fuselage painted as 'G-AXEH' for proposed museum exhibit; stored [12.13].

BH120-376   Model 122A. Regd **G-BCUV** (CofR R14706) 9.1.75 to Scottish Aviation Ltd. Ff 8.12.75. CofA issued 7.1.76 (4 months) but then stored. Ferried via Shoreham 7.6.76 to Takoradi. Regd cld 24.6.76 as sold Ghana. To Ghana Air Force as **G-112**. To Lawrence Bax & stored Henstridge [5.95]; later to Aerofab Restorations, Bourne Park, Hurstbourne Tarrant. Regd **G-BCUV** 18.10.96 to Dolphin Property Management Ltd, Salisbury (based Old Sarum). CofA renewed 14.4.97; painted in RAF c/s as 'CB733' (in honour of Sir Christopher Benson); repainted as XX704 '12' [.05]. Regd 7.12.09 to Flew LLP, op by Bournemouth Flying Club, Hurn. CofA lapsed 5.8.14; stored Hurn [6.17]. Currently regd.

G-BCUV was flown for some while with the markings "CB733". *(RS)*

BH120-377 Model 125. Regd **G-BDIN** 20.8.75 to Scottish Aviation Ltd. Ff 10.2.76. CofA issued 5.3.76 (4 months); ferried via Hurn/Jersey 11.3.76 to Jordan. Regn cld 13.4.76 as sold Jordan. Regd **JY-BAI** to Royal Jordanian Academy of Aeronautics. Regn cld 1.1.78. To **RJAF 408**. Gifted by Prince Feisal to the British Disabled Flying Club & airfreighted 11.03 to RAF Wittering & stored locally. Regd **G-BDIN** 25.8.04 to Roger David Dickson, t/a British Disabled Flying Association, Lasham. CofA not renewed; to spares for G-DISA. Regn cld 1.8.07 as pwfu. Remains to Popham [12.12]. To Yorkshire Aircraft Museum store, Doncaster 12.12 as spares for XX669; stored [3.16].

BH120-378 Model 125. Regd **G-BDIO** 20.8.75 to Scottish Aviation Ltd. Ff 13.2.76. CofA issued 5.3.76 (4 months); ferried via Hurn 12.3.76 to Jordan. Regn cld 13.4.76 as sold Jordan. Regd **JY-BAH** to Royal Jordanian Academy of Aeronautics. Regn cld 1.1.78. To **RJAF 407**. Sold 21.7.03 to Vision Engineering Group, Amman. Sold 30.12.04 to Gesoco Industries Inc, Franklin County Airport, Swanton, VT. Regd **N9151R** 2.06 to Gary Vos, Commerce TWP, MI. Sale reported 7.4.07 to [owner], Waterford, MI. Regn cld 29.8.13.
Note: N416JA (c/n 416) was originally regd as c/n 378 due to paperwork error.

BH120-379 Model 125. Regd **G-BDIP** 20.8.75 to Scottish Aviation Ltd. Ff 24.2.76. CofA issued 30.3.76 (4 months); ferried via Shoreham 9.4.76 to Jordan; arr Amman 17.4.76. Regn cld 28.4.76 as sold Jordan. Regd **JY-BAJ** to Royal Jordanian Academy of Aeronautics. Regn cld 1.1.78. To **RJAF 409**. Sold 21.7.03 to Vision Engineering Group, Amman. Sold 30.12.04 to Gesoco Industries Inc, Franklin County Airport, Swanton, VT. Regd **N9875N** 8.9.05 to Arthur E Casares, Merced, CA. CofA issued 14.10.05. Regd 5.06 to Robert B Carpenter, Big Pine Key, FL. Regd 24.5.08 to Bulldog Pilots Association LLC, Daniel Island, SC; to Dallas, TX 3.12, later Altus, OK then Woodward, IA. Currently regd.

BH120-380 Model 125. Regd **G-BDIR** 20.8.75 to Scottish Aviation Ltd. Ff 8.3.76. CofA issued 30.3.76 (4 months); ferried via Shoreham 15.4.76 to Jordan; arr Amman 17.4.76. Regn cld 28.4.76 as sold Jordan. Regd **JY-BAK** to Royal Jordanian Academy of Aeronautics. Regn cld 1.1.78. To **RJAF 410**. Fate not known.

BH200-381 Model 200 Prototype. Regd **G-BDOG** 18.12.75 to Scottish Aviation Ltd. Rolled out 16.8.76 & ff 20.8.76 & type named as Bullfinch. To SBAC show at Farnborough 3.9.76. No CofA issued & stored Prestwick wef 12.76. Cld 9.6.80 & regd 14.8.80 to Dukeries Aviation Ltd, Netherthorpe; deld 26.5.80. PtoF issued 2.7.80 (and regd as Dukeries Bulldog 200). Regd 9.2.83 to Ian Drake, Worksop (based Netherthorpe). Regd 6.7.89 to David Colin Bonsall (Phoenix Flying Group), Sutton-in-Ashfield (based Netherthorpe). Currently regd.

BH120-382 Model 125. Regd **G-BDIS** 20.8.75 to Scottish Aviation Ltd. Ff 1.4.76. CofA issued 6.4.76 (4 months); ferried via Shoreham 9.4.76 to Jordan; arr Amman 17.4.76. Regn cld 28.4.76 as sold Jordan. Regd **JY-BAL** to Royal Jordanian Academy of Aeronautics. Regn cld 1.1.78. To **RJAF 411**. Stored Amman/Marka AB [10.03]; later to gate guard [6.14].

BH120-383 Model 127. Regd **G-BDTY** 19.3.76 to Scottish Aviation Ltd. Ff 13.5.76. CofA issued 4.6.76 (4 months); ferried via Shoreham 22.7.76 to Kenya. Regn cld 13.8.76 as sold Kenya. To Kenya Air Force as **706**. Last reported [10.93].

BH120-384 Model 127. Regd **G-BDTZ** 19.3.76 to Scottish Aviation Ltd. Ff 18.5.76. CofA issued 4.6.76 (4 months); ferried via Shoreham 22.7.76 to Kenya. Regn cld 13.8.76 as sold Kenya. To Kenya Air Force as **707**. Written off 3.85.

BH120-385 Model 127. Regd **G-BDUA** 19.3.76 to Scottish Aviation Ltd. Ff 9.6.76 (25.6.76?). CofA issued 29.6.76 (4 months); ferried via Shoreham 22.7.76 to Kenya. Regn cld 13.8.76 as sold Kenya. To Kenya Air Force as **708**. Fuselage noted at Nairobi/Wilson [3.98].

BH120-386 Model 127. Regd **G-BDUB** 19.3.76 to Scottish Aviation Ltd. Ff 23.6.76 (24.6.76?). CofA issued 24.8.76 (4 months); ferried via Shoreham 7.9.76 to Kenya. Regn cld 28.9.76 as sold Kenya. To Kenya Air Force as **709**. Status not known.

BH120-387 Model 127. Regd **G-BDUC** 19.3.76 to Scottish Aviation Ltd. Ff 5.8.76. CofA issued 24.8.76 (4 months); ferried via Shoreham 7.9.76 to Kenya. Regn cld 28.9.76 as sold Kenya. To Kenya Air Force as **710**. Crashed 20.3.84; 2 killed.

BH120-388 Model 127. Regd **G-BDUE** 19.3.76 to Scottish Aviation Ltd. Ff 12.8.76. CofA issued 24.8.76 (4 months); ferried via Shoreham 7.9.76 to Kenya. Regn cld 28.9.76 as sold Kenya. To Kenya Air Force as **711**. Last reported [9.09].

BH120-389 Model 127. Regd **G-BDUF** 19.3.76 to Scottish Aviation Ltd. Ff 15.8.76. CofA issued 20.10.76 (4 months); ferried via Shoreham 23.11.76 to Kenya (incl demos to Hellenic Air Force en route). Regn cld 20.12.76 as sold Kenya. To Kenya Air Force as **712**. Reported as damaged 19.3.87; status not known.

BH120-390 Model 127. Regd **G-BDUG** 19.3.76 to Scottish Aviation Ltd. Ff 16.8.76. CofA issued 20.10.76 (4 months); ferried via Shoreham 23.11.76 to Kenya. Regn cld 20.12.76 as sold Kenya. To Kenya Air Force as **713**. Status not known.

BH120-391 Model 127. Regd **G-BDUH** 19.3.76 to Scottish Aviation Ltd. Ff 4.10.76. CofA issued 20.10.76 (4 months); ferried via Shoreham 23.11.76 to Kenya. Regn cld 20.12.76 as sold Kenya. To Kenya Air Force as **714**. Status not known.

BH120-392 Model 128. Ff 16.9.77 as **G-31-18**. Shipped to Hong Kong Auxiliary Air Force with serial **HKG-5**. Regd **G-BULL** 20.9.88 to Jacqueline Denise Richardson, Southend. CofA renewed 1.6.89; later based Wellcross Grange, Slinfold [95]; painted in HKAAF c/s as HKG-5. Regd 29.10.96 to Cyril David Weiswall, London W1 (based White Waltham, later Elstree). Regd 20.4.00 to Solo Leisure Ltd, Old Sarum. Regd 16.11.07 to Nicholas Victor Sills, Malmesbury (based Old Sarum; to Oaksey Park [7.12]). Regd 25.10.13 to Bulldog Aeros Ltd, Calne (based Kemble). Currently regd.

BH120-393 Model 128. Ff 23.9.77 as **G-31-19**. Shipped to Hong Kong Auxiliary Air Force with serial **HKG-6**. Regd **G-BPCL** 20.9.88 to Jacqueline Denise Richardson, Southend. CofA renewed 1.6.89. Regd 13.11.89 to Isohigh Ltd, Maldon, t/a 121 Group, Elstree (later North Weald); painted in HKAAF c/s as HKG-6. Currently regd.

HKG-6 was one of two Bulldogs operated by the RHKAF. *(GJ)*

BH120-394 Model 123 Ff 6.3.78 as **NAF241** & dismantled for shipment by sea to Nigeria. Re-erected and regd **G-BFUW** 9.6.78 to British Aerospace Aircraft Group, Scottish Division; reflown 20.6.78. CofA issued 27.6.78; ferried via Shoreham 30.6.78 to Nigeria. Regn cld 11.12.78 as sold Nigeria. To Nigerian AF as **NAF241**. Fate unknown.

BH120-395 Model 123 Ff 15.3.78 as **NAF242** & dismantled for shipment by sea to Nigeria. Re-erected and regd **G-BFUX** 9.6.78 to British Aerospace Aircraft Group, Scottish Division; reflown 22.6.78. CofA issued 27.6.78; ferried via Shoreham 30.6.78 to Nigeria. Regn cld 11.12.78 as sold Nigeria. To Nigerian AF as **NAF242**. Fate unknown.

BH120-396 Model 123 Ff 21.3.78 as **NAF243** & dismantled for shipment by sea to Nigeria. Re-erected and regd **G-BFUY** 9.6.78 to British Aerospace Aircraft Group, Scottish Division; reflown 23.6.78. CofA issued 27.6.78; ferried via Shoreham 30.6.78 to Nigeria. Regn cld 11.12.78 as sold Nigeria. To Nigerian AF as **NAF243**. Wfu 3.90 and stored Kaduna [2.06]; offered for sale 6.12. Open storage at Palmerston North, New Zealand (6.14).

BH120-397 Model 123 Ff 7.4.78 as **NAF244** & dismantled for shipment by sea to Nigeria. Re-erected and regd **G-BFVJ** 9.6.78 to British Aerospace Aircraft Group, Scottish Division; reflown 17.7.78. CofA issued 18.7.78; ferried via Shoreham 20.7.78 to Nigeria. Regn cld 11.12.78 as sold Nigeria. To Nigerian AF as **NAF244**. Wfu 9.88 and stored Kaduna [6.02; 2.06].

BH120-398 Model 123 Ff 25.4.78 as **NAF245**. Regd **G-BFVK** 9.6.78 to British Aerospace Aircraft Group, Scottish Division. CofA issued 27.6.78; ferried via Shoreham 20.7.78 to Nigeria. Regn cld 11.12.78 as sold Nigeria. To Nigerian AF as **NAF245**. Wfu 5.90 & stored Kaduna [6.02; 2.06].

Nigerian Air Force Bulldog NAF245 in poor condition at Kaduna. *(AM)*

BH120-399 Model 123 Ff 24.4.78 as **NAF246**. Regd **G-BFVL** 9.6.78 to British Aerospace Aircraft Group, Scottish Division. CofA issued 27.6.78; ferried via Shoreham 20.7.78 to Nigeria. Regn cld 11.12.78 as sold Nigeria. To Nigerian AF as **NAF246**. Wfu 9.86 & stored Kaduna [2.06]; offered for sale 6.12. Open storage at Palmerston North, New Zealand (6.14).

BH120-400 Model 123 Ff 5.5.78 as **NAF247**. Regd **G-BFWO** 3.7.78 to British Aerospace Aircraft Group, Scottish Division. CofA issued 2.7.78; ferried via Shoreham 15.8.78 to Nigeria. Regn cld 11.12.78 as sold Nigeria. To Nigerian AF as **NAF247**. Wfu 4.89 & stored Kaduna [6.02]; noted stored for sale [9.11].

BH120-401 Model 123 Ff 16.5.78 as **NAF248**. Regd **G-BFWP** 3.7.78 to British Aerospace Aircraft Group, Scottish Division. CofA issued 2.7.78; ferried via Shoreham 15.8.78 to Nigeria. Regn cld 11.12.78 as sold Nigeria. To Nigerian AF as **NAF248**. Wfu 6.89 & stored Kaduna [6.02; 2.06].

BH120-402 Model 123 Ff 23.5.78 as **NAF249**. Regd **G-BFWR** 3.7.78 to British Aerospace Aircraft Group, Scottish Division. CofA issued 2.7.78; ferried via Shoreham 15.8.78 to Nigeria. Regn cld 11.12.78 as sold Nigeria. To Nigerian AF as **NAF249**. Written off 16.4.84. Noted on Kaduna dump [2.06].

BH120-403 Model 123 Regd **G-BFWS** 3.7.78 to British Aerospace Aircraft Group, Scottish Division. Ff 17.8.78. CofA issued 29.8.78 (2 months); ferried via Shoreham 14.9.78 to Nigeria. Regn cld 11.12.78 as sold Nigeria. To Nigerian AF as **NAF250**. Written off 16.2.83; pilot killed.

BH120-404 Model 123 Regd **G-BFWT** 3.7.78 to British Aerospace Aircraft Group, Scottish Division. Ff 25.7.78. CofA issued 29.8.78 (2 months); ferried via Shoreham 14.9.78 to Nigeria. Regn cld 11.12.78 as sold Nigeria. To Nigerian AF as **NAF251**. Fate unknown.

BH120-405 Model 123 Regd **G-BFWU** 3.7.78 to British Aerospace Aircraft Group, Scottish Division. Ff 2.8.78. CofA issued 29.8.78 (2 months); ferried via Shoreham 14.9.78 to Nigeria. Regn cld 11.12.78 as sold Nigeria. To Nigerian AF as **NAF252**. Fate unknown.

BH120-406 Model 129. Ff 28.11.79 as **G-31-32**. Shipped to BAe Representative in Venezuela, Sir Raymond Smith, 8.2.80 as **YV-375-CP**. Regd **YV-2037P** to Dorothy Hart Pocaterra de Smith, Caracas. Regd to Jusito Evaristo Saavedra, Maracay. Regd **YV-2019** to same owner. Regn expired 23.1.06.

BH120-407 Model 130. Regd **G-BHXA** 9.6.80 to British Aerospace Aircraft Group, Scottish Division. Ff 17.6.80. CofA issued 30.6.80 (2

months); ferried via Shoreham 2.7.80 to Botswana. Regn cld 8.10.80 as sold Botswana. To Z1 Unit, Thebephatshwa AB, Botswana Defence Force as **OD-1**. Regd **G-BHXA** 4.3.91 to AW Aviation Ltd, Sandown; ferried ex Botswana to Luqa, Malta & stored. Regd 14.9.92 to Sayf Aviation Ltd, Yarmouth, IoW; stored Luqa. Ferried to Speke late .94 & regd 9.12.94 to David Alan Williams, Chester; stored Speke [1.97]; to Hawarden [2.99]. Regd 22.3.00 to Airplan Flight Equipment Ltd, Manchester (based Barton, later Eggington; then Stapleford). CofA renewed 26.7.00. CofA lapsed 28.4.17. Currently regd & stored Eggington.

BH120-408 Model 130. Regd **G-BHXB** 9.6.80 to British Aerospace Aircraft Group, Scottish Division. Ff 25.6.80. CofA issued 30.6.80 (two months); ferried via Shoreham 2.7.80 to Botswana. Regn cld 8.10.80 as sold Botswana. To Z1 Unit, Thebephatshwa AB, Botswana Defence Force as **OD-2**. Regd **G-BHXB** 4.3.91 to AW Aviation Ltd, Sandown; ferried ex Botswana to Luqa, Malta & stored. Regd 14.9.92 to Sayf Aviation Ltd, Yarmouth, IoW; stored Luqa. Ferried to Speke late .94 & regd 9.12.94 to David Alan Williams, Chester (based Speke). CofA renewed 24.4.95; op by Deltair, Speke; to Hawarden [2.99]. Regd **G-JWCM** 19.10.99 to Michael Lee Johnson Goff, Dereham (based Old Buckenham). Regd 16.4.08 to Goon Aviation Ltd, London SW6 (based North Weald). Regd 18.10.13 to Neil Cooper, London SW18 (based North Weald). Regd 30.3.15 to Mark William Meynell, Darlington (based Morgansfield, Fishburn). Regd 7.11.16 to Derek Christopher Wright, Morpeth (based Eshott). Regd **G-BHXB** 25.7.17 to Sylvia Dawn Wright, Morpeth, t/a XB Group, Eshott. Damaged in forced landing nr Station Road, Embleton 24.9.17. Currently regd.

G-JWCM was one of the ex-Botswana Bulldogs. *(RS)*

BH120-409 Model 130. Ff 15.7.80 as **G-31-33**. Regd **G-BHZP** 23.7.80 to British Aerospace Aircraft Group, Scottish Division. CofA issued 8.8.80 (2 months); ferried via Shoreham 12.8.80 to Botswana. Regn cld 8.10.80 as sold Botswana. To Z1 Unit, Thebephatshwa AB, Botswana Defence Force as **OD-3**. Written off in fatal crash 19.11.82.

BH120-410 Model 130. Regd **G-BHZR** 23.7.80 to British Aerospace Aircraft Group, Scottish Division. Ff 4.8.80. CofA issued 8.8.80 (2 months); ferried via Shoreham 12.8.80 to Botswana. Regn cld 8.10.80 as sold Botswana. To Z1 Unit, Thebephatshwa AB, Botswana Defence Force as **OD-4**. Regd **G-BHZR** 4.3.91 to AW Aviation Ltd, Sandown; ferried ex Botswana to Malta but suffered minor accident en route and stored Paphos, Cyprus (erroneously painted as G-BHZS). Regd 14.9.92 to Sayf Aviation Ltd, Yarmouth, IoW (still stored Paphos). Regd 6.7.95 to Mohamed Ahmed Elobeid, Ryde, IoW (stored Henstridge 7.95; 8.97). CofA renewed 30.6.00; based Withybush. Regd 22.1.02 to Raymond Burgess, Haverfordwest (based Withybush). Regd 26.8.04 to White Knuckle Air Ltd, Haverfordwest (based Withybush/Pembrey); named 'Winston'. CofA lapsed 9.7.12; stored Withybush [6.16]. Regd 14.9.17 to James Gerard McTaggart, t/a VT10 Aero Company, Dirleton, North Berwick. Regd 18.12.17 to Michael Robbie Hunter, Oswestry. Regd 30.1.18 (back) to James Gerard McTaggart, Dirleton. PtoF issued 15.2.18. Currently regd.

BH120-411 Model 130. Regd **G-BHZS** 23.7.80 to British Aerospace Aircraft Group, Scottish Division. Ff 15.8.80. CofA issued 12.9.80 (2 months); ferried via Shoreham 18.9.80 to Botswana. Regn cld 8.10.80 as sold Botswana. To Z1 Unit, Thebephatshwa AB, Botswana Defence Force as **OD-5**. Regd **G-BHZS** 4.3.91 to AW Aviation Ltd, Sandown; ferried ex Botswana to Luqa, Malta & stored. Regd 14.9.92 to Sayf Aviation Ltd, Yarmouth, IoW (still stored Luqa). Ferried to Speke late .94 & regd 9.12.94 to David Alan Williams, Chester. CofA renewed 9.2.96 & based Caernarfon. CofA lapsed 8.2.99. Regd 22.3.00 to Airplan Flight Equipment Ltd, Manchester (based Barton); stored Eggington [8.01]. CofA renewed 21.2.03 (based Eggington) but lapsed 20.2.06. Regn cld by CAA 20.5.09. Regd

10.6.09 to previous owner; stored for spares Egginton [8.10; 7.15]. CofA not renewed. Regn cld by CAA 19.12.12.

BH120-412   Model 130. Regd **G-BHZT** 23.7.80 to British Aerospace Aircraft Group, Scottish Division. Ff 9.9.80. CofA issued 12.9.80 (2 months); ferried via Shoreham 18.9.80 to Botswana. Regn cld 8.10.80 as sold Botswana. To Z1 Unit, Thebephatshwa AB, Botswana Defence Force as **OD-6**. Regd **G-BHZT** 4.3.91 to AW Aviation Ltd, Sandown; ferried ex Botswana to Luqa, Malta & stored. Regd 14.9.92 to Sayf Aviation Ltd, Yarmouth, IoW (still stored Luqa). Ferried to Henstridge [7.95] & regd 2.10.95 to Mrs Jean Mary Bax, Amesbury, nr Salisbury. CofA renewed 30.1.96 & based Old Sarum. Regd 30.5.00 to David Maurice Curties, Malmesbury (based Kemble). Currently regd.

G-BHZT served with the Botswana Defence Force as OD-6. *(PH)*

BH120-413   Model 125A. Ff 5.3.81 as **G-31-34**. Ferried ex Prestwick 28.4.81 to Jordan. To Royal Jordanian AF as **RJAF 1134**; later re-serialled **RJAF 413**. Sold 21.7.03 to Vision Engineering Group, Amman. Sold 5.05 to Barry Pope & regd **N46678** 8.5.06 to William Barry Pope, Farmington, MI (based Grosse Ile). CofA issued 2.8.06. Sold 4.11.06 & regd 22.1.07 to William D Bowen, Tifton, GA. Sold 30.6.11 & regd 3.8.11 to Dewey L Morgan, Sylvania, GA. Currently regd.

BH120-414   Model 125A. Ff 6.3.81 as **G-31-35**. Ferried ex Prestwick 22.4.81 to Jordan. To Royal Jordanian AF as **RJAF 1135**; later re-serialled **RJAF 414**. Noted on Amman/Mafraq dump [6.95; 4.96] presumably after accident.

BH120-415   Model 125A. Ff 16.3.81 as **G-31-36**. Ferried ex Prestwick 8.5.81 to Jordan aboard C-130H 345. To Royal Jordanian AF as **RJAF 1136**; later re-serialled **RJAF 415**. Sold 21.7.03 to Vision Engineering Group, Amman. Sold 28.11.05 to Barry Pope & regd **N8089D** 15.5.06 to William Barry Pope, Farmington, MI (based Grosse Ile. CofA issued 19.7.06. Sold 20.8.07 to Sunpoint Marine Ltd, Sidney, BC. Regn cld 5.9.07 as sold Canada but no regn known (it should be noted that many production aircraft in Canada are registered as 'home-built' types for certification purposes and thus this might be masquerading under another name).

BH120-416   Model 125A. Ff 3.4.81 as **G-31-37**. Export CofA E-2514-1 issued 6.5.81. Ferried ex Prestwick 8.5.81 to Jordan aboard C-130H 345. To Royal Jordanian AF as **RJAF 1137**; later re-serialled **RJAF 416**. Sold 21.7.03 to Vision Engineering Group, Amman. Sold 30.12.04 to Gesoco Industries Inc, Swanton, VT. Sold 20.6.05 to Steve Starakakis, Minden, NV. Sold 13.6.06 & regd **N416JA** 29.8.06 to Kevin J Lyons, Incline Village, NV (based Truckee). CofA issued 31.8.06. Crashed on landing Truckee 19.5.08. Regn cld 7.10.09. Wreck sold 12.8.08 to James Dennis, Pleasant Grove, CA; appln made 27.7.15 to restore to register but not progressed.

BH120-417   Model 125A. Ff 20.5.81 as **G-31-38**. Ferried ex Prestwick 17.8.81 to Jordan. To Royal Jordanian AF as **RJAF 1138**; later re-serialled **RJAF 417**. Gifted by Prince Feisal to British Disabled Flying Club; airfreighted to RAF Wittering 11.03 & stored locally. Regd G-CCZE 25.8.04 to Roger David Dickson, t/a British Disabled Flying Association, Lasham (stored 7.05). No CofA issued. Regn cld 16.11.06 as sold USA. Regd N138P (reserved 26.8.08) 13.9.08 to William Barry Pope, Farmington, MI. CofA issued 6.10.08. Regd 14.2.09 to Midwest Petroquip Inc, Blaine, MN. Regd 5.7.13 to Mark R Reed, Half Moon Bay, CA. Currently regd.

BH120-418   Model 123 Regd **G-BJNR** 27.10.81 to British Aerospace plc. Ff 23.10.81. CofA issued 20.11.81 (2 months); ferried ex Prestwick 29.9.82 to Nigeria. Regn cld 14.10.82 as sold Nigeria. To Nigerian AF as **NAF253**. Wfu 7.87 & stored Kaduna [2.06]; offered for sale 6.12. Open storage at Palmerston North, New Zealand (6.14).

BH120-419   Model 123 Regd **G-BJNS** 27.10.81 to British Aerospace plc. Ff 28.10.81. CofA issued 20.11.81 (2 months); ferried ex Prestwick 29.9.82 to Nigeria. Regn cld 14.10.82 as sold Nigeria. To Nigerian AF as **NAF254**. Wfu 7.87 & stored Kaduna [6.02; 2.06].

BH120-420   Model 123 Regd **G-BJNT** 27.10.81 to British Aerospace plc. Ff 4.12.81. CofA issued 7.2.82; ferried ex Prestwick 29.9.82 to Nigeria. Regn cld 14.10.82 as sold Nigeria. To Nigerian AF as **NAF255**. Fate unknown.

Note: c/n's 421-429 allocated to BAe Jetstreams.

BH120-430   Model 123 Regd **G-BJNU** 27.10.81 to British Aerospace plc. Ff 14.1.82. CofA issued 23.2.82 (2 months); ferried via Biggin Hill 10/11.10.82 to Nigeria. Regn cld 29.10.82 as sold Nigeria. To Nigerian AF as **NAF256**. Fate unknown.

BH120-431   Model 123 Regd **G-BJNV** 27.10.81 to British Aerospace plc. Ff 15.2.82. CofA issued 23.2.82 (2 months); ferried via Biggin Hill 10/11.10.82 to Nigeria. Regn cld 29.10.82 as sold Nigeria. To Nigerian AF as **NAF257**. Fate unknown.

BH120-432   Model 125A. Ff 1.6.82 as **G-31-40**. Ferried ex Prestwick 30.7.82 to Jordan on C-130H 345. To Royal Jordanian AF as RJAF 1139; later re-serialled **RJAF 412**. Written off c1.87.

BH120-433   Model 125A. Ff 21.6.82 as **G-31-41**. Ferried ex Prestwick 30.7.82 to Jordan on C-130H 345. To Royal Jordanian AF as **RJAF 1140**; later re-serialled **RJAF 418**. Gifted by Prince Feisal to British Disabled Flying Club; airfreighted to RAF Wittering 11.03 & stored locally. Regd **G-CCZF** 25.8.04 to Roger David Dickson, t/a British Disabled Flying Association, Lasham (stored 7.05). No CofA issued. Regn cld 16.11.06 as sold USA. Regd **N230JR** 7.8.07 to Robinson Air Crane Inc, Opa Locka, FL. Regd 22.7.17 to Sam Matta, Houston, TX. No CofA issued. Currently regd.

BH120-434   Model 125A. Ff 5.7.82 as **G-31-43**. Ferried ex Prestwick 27.8.82 to Jordan on C-130H 346. To Royal Jordanian AF as **RJAF 1141**; later re-serialled **RJAF 419**. Preserved on pole at King Hussein Air College Collection, Mafraq [5.94; 6.14].

BH120-435   Model 125A. Ff 9.8.82 as **G-31-44**. Ferried ex Prestwick 27.8.82 to Jordan on C-130H 346. To Royal Jordanian AF as **RJAF 1142**; later re-serialled **RJAF 420**. Gifted by Prince Feisal to British Disabled Flying Club; airfreighted to RAF Wittering 11.03 & stored locally. Regd **G-DISA** 25.8.04 to Roger David Dickson, t/a British Disabled Flying Association, Lasham. CofA issued 22.7.05. Regd 13.9.07 to British Disabled Flying Association, Camberley (based Lasham). Regd 27.11.12 to Ian Willis Whiting, Vaud, Switzerland; operated by British Disabled Flying Association, Blackbushe; later by Aerobility, Inverness & Broadford, Skye. Currently regd.

Note: c/n's 436 to 445 were also allocated to Bulldogs but were not built.

The last Bulldog RJAF420 left the factory in August, 1982. *(PH)*

SAL BULLDOG

REGISTRATION CROSS-REFERENCE

Reg'n	c/n	Reg'n	c/n	Reg'n	c/n	Reg'n	c/n	Reg'n	c/n	Reg'n	c/n
G-ASAL	239	G-AZWM	184	G-BDUC	387	G-CBEK	349	HA-TUK	145	N524SB	324
G-AXEH	001	G-AZWN	185	G-BDUE	388	G-CBFP	306	HA-TUL	196	N525UK	211
'G-AXEH'	375	G-AZWO	186	G-BDUF	389	G-CBFU	293	HA-TUM	193	N527BD	213
G-AXIG	002	G-AZWP	187	G-BDUG	390	G-CBGX	287	HA-TUV	190	N540BD	232
G-AYWN	101	G-AZWR	188	G-BDUH	391	G-CBID	242	HA-TUZ	175	N544BD	236
G-AYWO	102	G-BACR	189	G-BFUW	394	G-CBJJ	211	HA-TVA	134	N553X	246
G-AYWP	103	G-BACS	190	G-BFUX	395	G-CBJK	362	HA-TVB	102	N556WH	249
G-AYZL	104	G-BACT	191	G-BFUY	396	G-CCMI	199	HA-TVC	191	N560XX	256
G-AYZM	105	G-BACU	192	G-BFVJ	397	G-CCOA	375	HA-TVD	176	N575KM	298
G-AZAK	106	G-BACV	193	G-BFVK	398	G-CCZE	432	HA-VUK	135	N621BD	285
G-AZAL	107	G-BACX	194	G-BFVL	399	G-CCZF	433	HA-	103	N632BD	297
G-AZAM	108	G-BACY	195	G-BFWO	400	G-CDVV	291	HA-	112	N635XX	305
G-AZAN	109	G-BACZ	196	G-BFWP	401	G-DAWG	208	HA-	113	N640RH	310
G-AZAO	110	G-BADA	197	G-BFWR	402	G-DDOG	210	HA-	133	N661BD	319
G-AZAP	111	G-BADB	198	G-BFWS	403	G-DISA	435	HA-	152	N686XX	332
G-AZAR	112	G-BBHF	239	G-BFWT	404	G-DOGE	126	HA-	154	N689BD	335
G-AZAS	113	G-BBJJ	250	G-BFWU	405	G-DOGG	308	HA-	172	N697BD	346
G-AZAT	114	G-BBJK	251	G-BHXA	407	G-EDAV	220	HA-	174	N701AB	350
G-AZEN	117	G-BBJL	252	G-BHXB	408	G-GGRR	272	HA-	184	N701BD	107
G-AZEO	118	G-BBJM	262	G-BHZP	409	G-GRRR	229	HA-	194	N706BD	353
G-AZEP	119	G-BBJN	263	G-BHZR	410	G-JWCM	408	HA-	195	N706X	355
G-AZES	121	G-BBJO	264	G-BHZS	411	G-KDOG	289	JY-ADW	298	N708BD	357
G-AZET	122	G-BBJP	265	G-BHZT	412	G-KKKK	199	JY-ADX	299	N709AB	331
G-AZHV	124	G-BBJR	266	G-BJNR	418	G-OPOD	148	JY-ADY	300	N713AM	157
G-AZHW	125	G-BBOU	267	G-BJNS	419	G-RAIG	146	JY-ADZ	301	N713Z	362
G-AZHX	126	G-BBOV	268	G-BJNT	420	G-RNRS	132	JY-AEA	302	N747BD	110
G-AZHY	128	G-BBOW	269	G-BJNU	430	G-SIJW	295	JY-AEL	338	N1004N	167
G-AZHZ	129	G-BBOZ	270	G-BJNV	431	G-TDOG	230	JY-AEM	339	N1080V	245
G-AZIS	130	G-BBPA	271	G-BPCL	393	G-UDOG	204	JY-AEN	340	N2077N	107
G-AZIT	132	G-BBPB	278	G-BULL	392	G-ULHI	148	JY-BAH	378	N3014T	212
G-AZIU	133	G-BBPD	280	G-BWIB	227	G-UWAS	235	JY-BAI	377	N3043A	355
G-AZIV	134	G-BBPE	281	G-BXGU	229	G-WINI	238	JY-BAJ	379	N3672	330
G-AZIW	135	G-BBPF	282	G-BZDP	244	G-31-17	239	JY-BAK	380	N4321B	119
G-AZJO	137	G-BBPG	283	G-BZEP	257	G-31-18	392	JY-BAL	382	N7507P	138
G-AZJP	138	G-BBPI	284	G-BZFM	209	G-31-19	393	N19FG	139	N8089D	415
G-AZJR	139	G-BBPR	279	G-BZFN	325	G-31-33	409	N25GA	275	N8267E	171
G-AZJS	141	G-BCAA	298	G-BZLB	331	G-31-34	413	N50UP	328	N8272R	164
G-AZJT	142	G-BCAU	299	G-BZLR	236	G-31-35	414	N51TL	162	N8804P	338
G-AZJU	143	G-BCAV	300	G-BZMD	247	G-31-36	415	N68TL	121	N9043A	302
G-AZMP	145	G-BCAW	301	G-BZME	347	G-31-37	416	N100MY	162	N9151R	378
G-AZMR	146	G-BCAX	302	G-BZMH	341	G-31-38	417	N101MY	166	N9179C	233
G-AZMS	148	G-BCSN	338	G-BZML	342	G-31-40	432	N104MR	165	N9206F	298
G-AZMT	149	G-BCSO	339	G-BZOJ	215	G-31-41	433	N105MR	138	N9875N	379
G-AZMU	151	G-BCSP	340	G-BZON	214	G-31-43	434	N108BD	108	N43219	119
G-AZPI	152	G-BCTL	364	G-BZPS	316	G-31-44	435	N114EC	132	N46678	413
G-AZPJ	154	G-BCTM	365	G-BZXC	260	C-FLBD	241	N118BD	118	N82696	128
G-AZPK	155	G-BCTN	366	G-BZXS	296	C-	145	N123MY	124	N	155
G-AZPL	156	G-BCTO	367	G-BZXZ	294	C-	415	N123SY	158	N	290
G-AZPM	157	G-BCTP	368	G-CBAB	235	F-AZKI	273	N129BD	129	N	432
G-AZPN	158	G-BCTS	369	G-CBAM	272	F-AZKJ	248	N138P	417	OY-	111
G-AZPO	162	G-BCUN	370	G-CBAN	326	F-AZLK	321	N146EC	146	OY-	125
G-AZPP	163	G-BCUO	371	G-CBBC	201	F-AZLZ	217	N178BD	215	SE-FVX	130
G-AZPR	164	G-BCUP	372	G-CBBL	243	F-AZOA	334	N207MR	165	SE-LLB	108
G-AZPS	165	G-BCUS	373	G-CBBR	290	F-AZOB	218	N230JR	433	SE-LLC	107
G-AZTX	166	G-BCUT	374	G-CBBS	343	F-AZOD	255	N321BD	292	SE-LLD	118
G-AZTY	167	G-BCUU	375	G-CBBT	344	F-AZOG	254	N402JA	300	SE-LLE	129
G-AZTZ	171	G-BCUV	376	G-CBBU	360	F-AZOI	340	N415BD	246	SE-LLF	132
G-AZUA	172	G-BDIN	377	G-CBBW	277	F-AZOZ	221	N416JA	416	SE-LLG	110
G-AZUB	173	G-BDIO	378	G-CBCB	223	F-AZRM	274	N427VC	258	SE-LLH	143
G-AZUC	174	G-BDIP	379	G-CBCO	238	F-AZTF	309	N432BD	163	SE-LLI	146
G-AZUD	175	G-BDIR	380	G-CBCR	351	F-AZTV	322	N433VB	222	SE-LLK	148
G-AZUE	176	G-BDIS	382	G-CBCT	322	HA-BUL	122	N457FS	129	SE-LLL	155
G-AZWH	179	G-BDOG	381	G-CBCV	348	HA-IHS	149	N514XX	227	SE-LLM	111
G-AZWI	180	G-BDTY	383	G-CBDK	259	HA-TUG	181	N516BG	202	SE-LNA	119
G-AZWJ	181	G-BDTZ	384	G-CBDS	356	HA-TUH	189	N516XX	202	SE-LNB	124
G-AZWK	182	G-BDUA	385	G-CBEF	286	HA-TUI	219	N518BD	205	SE-LNC	125
G-AZWL	183	G-BDUB	386	G-CBEH	207	HA-TUJ	104	N523BD	209	SE-LND	165

Reg'n	c/n
SE-LNE	171
SE-LNF	121
SE-LNG	128
SE-LNH	157
SE-LNI	163?
SE-LNI	164?
SE-LNM	166
SE-LNN	122
SE-LNO	126
SE-LNP	167
SE-LNR	162
SE-LNS	158
VH-CHU	110
VH-XVE	348
YV-375-CP	406
YV-2037P	406
ZK-WUF	315
9H-ADQ	337
9H-ADR	345
9H-ADS	358
9H-ADT	363
9M-EAO	123
9M-EEE	150
9M-EMM	115
9M-ERR	unkn
9M-EZZ	177

RAF serials

RAF serials	c/n
'CB733'	376
XX513	199
XX514	200
XX515	201
XX516	202
XX517	203
XX518	204
XX519	205
XX520	206
XX521	207
XX522	208
XX523	209
XX524	210
XX525	211
XX526	212
XX527	213
XX528	214
XX529	215
XX530	216
'XX530'	307
XX531	217
XX532	218
XX533	219
XX534	220
XX535	221
XX536	222
XX537	223
XX538	230
XX539	231
XX540	232
XX541	233
XX542	234
XX543	235
XX544	236
XX545	237
XX546	238
XX547	240
XX548	241
XX549	242
XX550	243
XX551	244
XX552	245
XX553	246

RAF serials

RAF serials	c/n
XX554	247
XX555	248
XX556	249
XX557	253
XX558	254
XX559	255
XX560	256
XX561	257
XX562	258
XX611	259
XX612	260
XX613	261
XX614	272
XX615	273
XX616	274
XX617	275
XX618	276
XX619	277
XX620	285
XX621	286
XX622	287
XX623	288
XX624	289
XX625	290
'XX625'	126
XX626	291
XX627	292
XX628	293
XX629	294
XX630	295
XX631	296
XX632	297
XX633	303
XX634	304
XX635	305
XX636	306
XX637	307
XX638	308
XX639	309
XX640	310
XX653	311
XX654	312
XX655	313
XX656	314
XX657	315
XX658	316
XX659	317
XX660	318
XX661	319
XX662	320
XX663	321
XX664	322
XX665	323
XX666	324
XX667	325
XX668	326
XX669	327
XX670	328
XX671	329
XX672	330
XX685	331
XX686	332
XX687	333
XX688	334
XX689	335
XX690	336
XX691	337
XX692	341
XX693	342
XX694	343
XX695	344
XX696	345

RAF serials	c/n
XX697	346
XX698	347
XX699	348
XX700	349
XX701	350
XX702	351
XX703	352
XX704	353
'XX704'	376
XX705	354
XX706	355
XX707	356
XX708	357
XX709	358
XX710	359
XX711	360
XX712	361
XX713	362
XX714	363
8767M	305
8997M	327
9197M	307
9288M	206
9289M	323
9290M	291
9291M	332

Swedish AF/Army

Swedish AF/Army	c/n
61045	157
61046	158
61047	162
61048	163
61049	164
61050	165
61051	166
61052	167
61053	171
61054	172
61055	173
61056	174
61057	175
61058	176
61061	179
61062	180
61063	181
61064	182
61065	183
61066	184
61067	185
61068	186
61069	187
61070	188
61071	189
61072	190
61073	191
61074	192
61075	193
61076	194
61077	195
61078	196
61079	197
61080	198

Botswana DF

Botswana DF	c/n
OD-1	407
OD-2	408
OD-3	409
OD-4	410
OD-5	411
OD-6	412

Royal Jordanian AF

Royal Jordanian AF	c/n
RJAF 400	298
RJAF 401	299
RJAF 402	300
RJAF 403	301
RJAF 404	302
RJAF 405	338
RJAF 406	340
RJAF 407	378
RJAF 408	377
RJAF 409	379
RJAF 410	380
RJAF 411	382
RJAF 412	432
RJAF 413	413
RJAF 414	414
RJAF 415	415
RJAF 416	416
RJAF 417	417
RJAF 418	433
RJAF 419	434
RJAF 420	435
RJAF 1139	432
RJAF 1140	433

Swedish AF/Army

Swedish AF/Army	c/n
61001	101
61002	102
61003	103
61004	104
61005	105
61006	106
61007	107
61008	108
61009	109
61010	110
61011	111
61012	112
61013	113
61014	114
61015	117
61016	118
61017	119
61018	121
61019	122
61020	124
61021	125
61022	126
61023	128
61024	129
61025	130
61026	132
61027	133
61028	134
61029	135
61030	137
61031	138
61032	139
61033	141
61034	142
61035	143
61036	145
61037	146
61038	148
61039	149
61040	151
61041	152
61042	154
61043	155
61044	156

Royal Jordanian AF

Royal Jordanian AF	c/n
RJAF 1141	434
RJAF 1142	435

Lebanese AF

Lebanese AF	c/n
L-141	364
L-142	365
L-143	366
L-144	367
L-145	368
L-146	369

Nigerian AF

Nigerian AF	c/n
NAF221	250
NAF222	251
NAF223	252
NAF224	262
NAF225	263
NAF226	264
NAF227	265
NAF228	266
NAF229	267
NAF230	268
NAF231	269
NAF232	270
NAF233	271
NAF234	278
NAF235	279
NAF236	280
NAF237	281
NAF238	282
NAF239	283
NAF240	284
NAF241	394
NAF242	395
NAF243	396
NAF244	397
NAF245	398
NAF246	399
NAF247	400
NAF248	401
NAF249	402
NAF250	403
NAF251	404
NAF252	405
NAF253	418
NAF254	419
NAF255	420
NAF256	430
NAF257	431

Kenya AF

Kenya AF	c/n
701	144
702	153
703	161
704	170
705	178
706	383
707	384
708	385
709	386
710	387
711	388
712	389
713	390
714	391

Ghana AF

Ghana AF	c/n
G-100	224
G-101	225
G-102	226
G-103	227
G-104	228
G-105	229
G-106	370
G-107	371
G-108	372
G-109	373
G-110	374
G-111	375

Hong Kong DF

Hong Kong DF	c/n
HKG-5	392
HKG-6	393

Malta DF

Malta DF	c/n
AS 0020	337
AS 0021	345
AS 0022	358
AS 0023	363
AS 0124	240

Malaysian AF

Malaysian AF	c/n
FM1220	115
FM1221	116
FM1222	120
FM1223	123
FM1224	127
FM1225	131
FM1226	136
FM1227	140
FM1228	147
FM1229	150
FM1230	159
FM1231	160
FM1232	168
FM1233	169
FM1234	177
M25-01	115
M25-02	120
M25-03	123
M25-04	127
M25-05	136
M25-06	147
M25-07	150
M25-08	159
M25-09	160
M25-10	168
M25-11	169
M25-12	177

APPENDIX ONE
BULLDOG CUSTOMERS

In addition to the two prototypes (c/n B125-001 and -002) and a static test airframe (B125-003) a total of 325 production Bulldogs were built. Also completed was one Bullfinch prototype (c/n 381). They were

allotted constructors numbers BH100-101 to BH100-198 and BH120-199 to BH120-420 and BH120-430 to BH120-435. In addition, one Srs. 124 development and test aircraft was built (G-ASAL,

c/n 239) and one Srs. 129 aircraft was delivered to a private owner in Venezuela (c/n 406, YV-375-CP).

The Bulldog was delivered to the RAF and ten other military operators, as follows:

Customer	Model	No. Delivered
Botswana	Srs.130	6
Ghana	Srs.122	5
Ghana	Srs.122A	8
Hong Kong	Srs.128	2
Jordan	Srs.125/125A	22
Kenya	Srs.103	5
Kenya	Srs.127	9

Customer	Model	No. Delivered
Lebanon	Srs.126	6
Malaysia	Srs.102	15
Malta	Srs.121	(5)
Nigeria	Srs.123	37
Sweden, Air Force	Srs.101	58
Sweden, Army	Srs.101	20
UK, RAF	Srs.121	130
Total		323

Brief details of the military fleets and their deployment are as follows:

ROYAL AIR FORCE

The RAF received 130 Bulldog T.1s (Srs. 121), allocated with serial numbersXX513 to XX562, XX611 to XX640, XX653 to XX672 and XX685 to XX714. They were required to replace the large fleet of Chipmunks in service as basic trainers and with the University Air Squadrons and with Air Experience Flights giving basic flying experience to RAF Air Cadets and members of the CCF (Combined Cadet Force). The first aircraft, XX513, was formally handed over on 12 February, 1973. Initially, they went to the UASs and 17 units used Bulldogs, namely, Aberdeen, Dundee and St. Andrews, Belfast, Birmingham, Bristol, Cambridge, Northumbrian, East Lowlands, East Midlands, Glasgow & Strathclyde, Liverpool, London, Manchester & Salford, Northumbrian, Oxford, Southampton, Wales and Yorkshire. The first unit to re-equip with the Bulldog was the University of London Air Squadron based at Abingdon. From 1996, when the Chipmunks were retired, many of the UAS units also parented the

XX514 is seen here coded 44 whilst serving with CFS at Little Rissington. It ended its RAF career with 1 FTS at Linton-on-Ouse where it suffered a PFL accident but was later sold to the USA as NX516BG. (PH)

AEFs, and Bulldogs served with the UAS/AEF organisation until 2001 when they were replaced by the Grob G.115E Tutor with London UAS again the first to receive the new aircraft. Other Bulldog operations also included Airwork's contract to provide flying grading services for the Royal Navy's Britannia Flight at Plymouth-Roborough and it also used Bulldogs for its contracted operation of No.1 FTS at RAF Linton-on-Ouse.

SWEDISH AIR FORCE

The 58 Bulldogs for the Swedish Air Force were to replace the Saab Safir (Sk.50) training and communications aircraft. They were given the type number BH.100 by Scottish Aviation and designated as the Srs. 101. Delivery commenced in 1972

and aircraft were ferried to the Air Force Flight Academy (F5) at Ljungbyhed where they received Swedish military serials Fv61001 to Fv61058 and Fv61061 to Fv61080. As aircraft could not be ferried abroad carrying Class B registrations they were registered in the UK and the registration cancelled on arrival in Sweden. Only the first aircraft was delivered in a finished paint scheme. The second aircraft was delivered in a primer finish and the remainder were in bare metal. All aircraft were equipped with the minimum avionics for the ferry flight and the full avionics fit was installed by the Air Force. The majority of aircraft were the unarmed variant, designated SK 61A, but six aircraft were equipped to carry the RB 53 wire-controlled Bantam missile and designated SK 61B. The missile was

After serving with the Swedish Air Force FV61033 was acquired by the Ljungbyhed Aeronautiska Sallstap. *(PH)*

The Maltese Armed Forces acquired five former RAF Bulldogs including AS-0022 which had formerly served as XX709 with RNEFTS, CFS and Yorkshire UAS. *(RS)*

positioned on the starboard wingtip and controlled from the starboard seat. SK 61Bs were used occasionally to acquaint AJ 37 Viggen pilots with basic missile use before beginning training on the advanced RB 05 missile. Since all SK 61s were considered as potential combat aircraft, rather than being painted in the yellow training scheme, they wore the Air Force's combat scheme of dark olive green/dark blue camouflage on the upper surfaces and blue-grey on under surfaces. When the Army transferred its Bulldogs to the Air Force they were repainted with olive green upper surfaces and silver grey under surfaces. Aircraft were allocated to the Air Force Academy (F5) at Ljungbyhed as basic trainers and students flew 40 hours in the SK 61 before moving onto the SK 60 jet trainer.

SWEDISH ARMY

The 20 Swedish Army aircraft were ordered to replace Super Cubs (Fpl.51) and were designated FpL61C. These aircraft (Fv61061 to Fv61080) were fitted with a third rear seat and an opening rear window for photography and were used for artillery spotting and liaison duties. While the Army Bulldogs had a training role they were also required as AOP aircraft

in the event of war. In 1989 they were handed over to the Air Force as Sk61Cs when the Army re-equipped with helicopters.

BOTSWANA DEFENCE FORCE

Botswana received six Bulldog Srs. 130s (c/n 407 to 412) serialled OD-1 to OD-6 which were delivered between July and September 1980. One aircraft (OD-3, c/n 409) was written off in service in November 1982. In 1991 the remaining Bulldogs were withdrawn from use and sold to AW Aviation in the UK. Following a period of storage they were sold to UK private owners.

GHANA AIR FORCE

13 Bulldogs were delivered to Ghana (Srs. 122 c/n 224 to 229 and Srs. 122A 370 to 376) serialled G-100 to G-112. The first batch was delivered by sea in July 1973 and the second batch was ferried by air to Ghana between December, 1975 and June, 1976. During service with the Ghanaian Air Force at least three were written off in accidents. The Bulldogs were retired from service in the mid-1990s and eight were sold to the UK, ending up with private owners, and one was retained as an instructional airframe at Accra.

MALTA ARMED FORCES

Malta was not an original customer for the Bulldog but the Air Wing acquired five ex-RAF Srs. 121 aircraft in 1999, these being XX547, XX691, XX696, XX709 and XX714 which received Maltese serials AS0020 to AS0023 and AS0124. They were mainly used for coastal patrol around the island of Malta and AS0124 was written off on just such a sortie when it crashed at Santa Pietru on 5 August, 2007.

ROYAL HONG KONG AUXILIARY AIR FORCE

The RHKAF received two Bulldog Srs. 128s (c/n 392 and 393) which were serialled HKG-5 and HKG-6. They were shipped to Hong Kong in late 1977 and were used for training and for coastal patrol and search and rescue support. They continued in service until 1988 when they were declared surplus and sold to a private owner in the UK.

ROYAL JORDANIAN AIR FORCE

22 Bulldog Srs. 125s were sold to the Royal Jordanian Air Force and were initially allocated to the Royal Jordanian Academy of Aeronautics in Amman with civil registrations

The Bulldog FV61074 is now an instructional airframe at Flygteknik Centrum, Hasslo airfield. *(PH)*

Seen prior to delivery in B-Conditions markings, G-31-33 became OD-3 of the Botswana Defence Force. It was written off in an accident in 1982. *(RS)*

The first batch of Bulldogs for the Royal Jordanian Academy of Aeronautics was ferried to Jordan in March and April, 1976, one being RJAF 407. *(PH)*

Bulldog G-BBPE is seen here at Shoreham en route for Nigeria in October, 1974. It became NAF237 on arrival at Kaduna. *(KB)*

in the range JY-ADJ to JY-AEA, JY-AEL to JY-AEN and JY-BAH to JY-BAL. They were employed on basic training and aerobatics. The final batch of nine aircraft was delivered directly to the Royal Jordanian Air Force (RJAF) with military serials 1134 to 1142. All the earlier Bulldogs were subsequently transferred to the RJAF and received new serial numbers in the range 400 to 420 (one aircraft, JY-AEM had already been written off so did not get a serial number). They were operated by No.4 Sqn. based at Mafraq until retired from service in 2004. Two aircraft were retained as museum exhibits at the King Hussain Air College at Mafraq, two were sold to the UK for private owners and 12 ended up in the USA being sold on the civil market.

KENYA AIR FORCE

The Kenya Air Force received 14 Bulldogs in two batches. The first batch of five Srs. 103 aircraft, which received Kenyan serials 701 to 705, were airfreighted to Nairobi in July, 1972. The second batch of nine Srs.127s (706 to 714) were air ferried to Kenya between July and November, 1976. The Bulldogs were acquired in order to replace the ageing fleet of DH Chipmunks and DHC Beavers with the Kenya

Flying Training School. By 2013 it was reported that approximately ten Bulldogs remained in service but that they would be replaced by new Grob G.120s, the first six of which were delivered in November of that year (with another six on option).

LEBANESE AIR FORCE

Six Bulldog Srs. 126s were delivered to the Lebanese Air Force (c/n 364 to 369) and ferried to Beirut in September and October, 1975, becoming L-141 to L-146 in Lebanese Air Force service. By 2008 just three of these remained in service, having been refurbished that year, and the other three had been handed over to the Lebanese Air Force Museum.

ROYAL MALAYSIAN AIR FORCE

The RMAF had 15 Bulldog 102s which were delivered by sea between December, 1971 and September, 1972 and assembled at Kuala Lumpur with Malaysian serials FM1220 to FM1234. They were operated by the RMAF Air Force Academy at No 2 Air Base Alor Setar, Kedah, replacing the survivors of a fleet of 24 Hunting Provosts. They remained in service till the late 1980s with all surviving examples finally withdrawn in 1990 and being replaced by the

locally-manufactured SME MD.3-160 Aero Tigas, all of which have also been withdrawn. They were replaced with the Pilatus PC-7.

NIGERIAN AIR FORCE

37 Bulldog Srs. 123s were delivered to Kaduna in Nigeria in three batches with the first of 20 (c/n 250-252, 262-271 and 278-284) being ferried out starting in January, 1974, the second 12-aircraft batch (c/n 394 to 405) in mid-1978 and the last five (c/n 418 to 431) leaving Prestwick in September and October, 1982. They were serialled NAF221 to NAF257. In June, 2012 the Nigerian Air Force put the surviving Bulldogs up for sale in scrap condition and six fuselages and 20 sets of wings were sold to Milsom Aerospace at Palmerston North in New Zealand for possible refurbishment and civil sale.

Part of the first batch of five Bulldogs for the Kenya Air Force, 702 was air freighted from Prestwick in July, 1972. *(PH)*

Bulldog M25-08, which is now in the Royal Malaysian Air Force Museum in Kuala Lumpur, is thought to be the former FM1227 which was written off in March, 1973. *(RS)*

APPENDIX TWO

BULLDOGS IN RAF SERVICE

The majority of the Bulldogs spent much of their RAF careers with the UASs, replacing DH Chipmunks. The UAS concept goes back to 1925 when, firstly, Cambridge UAS was formed, soon followed by Oxford UAS. Early in World War II they were followed by further units including Bristol, Glasgow, Southampton and Yorkshire giving basic induction and pilot training to university students. Many of the UAS units were closed after the war but were later revived flying, firstly, DH Tiger Moths and then DH Chipmunks. The Scottish Aviation Bulldogs started taking over from the Chipmunk in 1973 with Cambridge UAS and were also allocated to the CFS and to the RNEFTS and later to 3FTS and 6FTS. They also operated with the

XX528 was one of the three Bulldogs comprising the Bulldog Aerobatic Team. It is seen here coded 10 with 2FTS at Church Fenton. *(PH)*

AEFs, serving the Air Training Corps (ATC) and Combined Cadet Force (CCF), mainly using UAS aircraft. Starting in 1999, the Bulldogs were retired and disposed of on the civil market, being replaced by the Grob G.115E Tutor.

The listings shown below, which relate to the period of operation of the Bulldog by the RAF, detail the various units operating the aircraft, identifying any changes in names and designations and the bases involved and including (in brackets) the individual code numbers worn. It should be noted that many Bulldogs were loaned out for a few weeks at a time to fellow units but such short term loans have been ignored since the aircraft soon returned back to their original unit.

THE UNIVERSITY AIR SQUADRONS

Unit Name	Base	Codes	Bulldogs used
Aberdeen UAS (Note A)	Dyce, to Leuchars 12.80	A to E 01 to 08	XX522 (06), XX525 (03), XX527 (D & 05), XX537 (02), XX561 (A), XX662 (A), XX663 (B & 01), XX664 (04), XX665 (E), XX666 (C & 08), XX667 (D), XX693 (07), XX709 (C) XX885 (C)
Birmingham UAS	Shawbury, to Cosford 3.78	A to H	XX521 (G), XX534 (B), XX558 (A), XX621 (H), XX668 (A), XX669 (B), XX670 (C), XX671 (D), XX672 (E), XX699 (F) XX705 (A),
Bristol UAS	Filton, to Hullavington 3.92, to Colerne 11.92	A to K	XX516 (A), XX541 (F), XX624 (E), XX628 (J), XX632 (D), XX640 (K), XX653 (E), XX654 (A), XX655 (B), XX656 (C), XX689 (D), XX692 (A), XX697 (H), XX713 (G),
Cambridge UAS	Teversham, to Wyton 9.99	Note B	XX516 (C), XX518 (Z), XX529 (F), XX532 (E), XX615 (U), XX624 (D), XX634 (C), XX657 (U), XX658 (A), XX659 (S),
East Lowlands UAS	Turnhouse, to Leuchars 2.96	01 to 08 Note C	XX521 (01), XX522 (06), XX525 (03), XX534 (04), XX537 (02), XX629 (08), XX664 (05), XX665 (06), XX693 (07), XX703 (02),
East Midlands UAS	Newton	Note D	XX520 (A), XX535 (S), XX538 (E), XX556 (M & S), XX623 (M), XX630 (α), XX634 (A), XX635 (β & S), XX638 (Υ), XX639 (δ), XX640 (ε), XX687 (A), XX694 (E), XX702 (S), XX704 (U)
Glasgow & Strathclyde UAS	Perth, to Abbotsinch 1.93	Note E	XX525, XX557 (03), XX559 (01), XX560 (02), XX611 (04), XX665, XX686, XX693, XX702 (03)
Liverpool UAS	Woodvale	Note F	XX515 (4), XX523 (X), XX539 (L), XX555 (U), XX629 (V), XX630 (A), XX656 (C), XX685 (L), XX686 (U), XX687 (A), XX688 (S), XX690 (A), XX696 (S), XX711 (X)
London UAS	Abingdon, to Benson 7.92	01 to 10 Note G	XX524 (04), XX535 (10), XX544 (01), XX545 (02), XX546 (03), XX547 (05), XX548 (06), XX550 (08), XX552 (08), XX553 (07), XX554 (09), XX556 (10), XX639 (02), XX691 (10), XX695 (10), XX701 (08),
Manchester & Salford UAS	Woodvale	I to 6 Note F	XX515 (4), XX536 (6), XX549 (5), XX614 (1), XX615 (2), XX616 (3), XX617 (4), XX668 (1), XX695 (3), XX710 (5), XX712 (1),

Unit Name	Base	Codes	Bulldogs used
Northumbrian UAS	Leeming	T to Z	XX515 (U), XX533 (U), XX550 (Z), XX562 (18), XX614 (V), XX619 (T), XX624 (T), XX629 (V), XX631 (W), XX633 (X), XX636 (Y), XX637 (U & Z), XX664 (04)
Oxford UAS	Bicester, to Abingdon 9.75 and Benson 7.92	A to F Note G	XX523, XX526 (C), XX528 (D), XX551 (E), XX614 (B), XX660 (A), XX661 (B), XX695 (A), XX711 (F)
Queen's UAS (Belfast)	Sydenham, to Aldergrove by 1.92	Note H	XX561 (Q), XX562 (S & E), XX612 (U), XX613 (A), XX619 (U), XX640 (B, Q & U), XX666 (A), XX697 (Q & C), XX704 (U), XX711 (S & D),
RAF College AS	Cranwell, to 3FTS, 6.95	A1 to A2 B1 to B2 C1 to C2	XX515 (A2), XX519 (A1), XX522 (B2), XX540 (C2), XX667 (C1), XX700 (B1),
Southampton UAS	Hamble, to Hurn 12.78, to Lee-on- Solent 4.88 and Boscombe Down 4.93	01 to 07	XX513 (01), XX549 (06), XX551 (03), XX552 (02), XX555 (04), XX556 (05), XX558 (06), XX612 (05), XX627 (07), XX701 (02), XX705 (05 & 06), XX706 (01), XX707 (04), XX708 (03),
Wales UAS	St. Athan	45 to 48 01 to 06	XX525, XX531 (06, 04), XX612 (05, 03), XX625 (45, 01), XX626 (46, 02), XX627 (47, 03), XX628 (48, 04),
Yorkshire UAS	Church Fenton, to Finngley 8.75, Church Fenton 10.95, to Linton- on-Ouse 4.96	A to J V to Z Note I	XX532 (J, D), XX537 (C), XX543 (F), XX547 (A), XX618 (A), XX619 (B), XX620 (C), XX621 (D, G), XX622 (E, B), XX623 (F), XX624 (G), XX632 (A), XX637 (U), XX638 (H), XX639 (D), XX659 (E), XX690 (A), XX691 (H, G), XX692 (A), XX709 (E, H), XX714 (D),

Note A Aberdeen UAS was renamed Aberdeen, Dundee & St.Andrews UAS, 12.10.81. It used codes A to E but when it absorbed East Lowlands UAS in March, 1996 it adopted their codes 01 to 08

Note B Cambridge UAS initially used codes C, U, A and S but added Z in 1987 and D, E and F in 1996.

Note C East Lowlands UAS was absorbed into Aberdeen, Dundee & St.Andrews UAS, 3.96. Bulldog XX539 is also reported as in use 5.79 to 1.80 wearing code 46 from its previous unit.

Note D East Midlands UAS initially used the Greek letters Alpha, Beta, Gamma, Delta, Epsilon. Following a 1977 fleet change the letters EMAUS were used. In 1995 it jointly used a Bulldog coded Pi (π) with 7 AEF.

Note E Glasgow & Strathclyde initially used codes 01 to 04 but all codes were removed from around 1989

Note F Liverpool UAS initially used codes L, U, A & S, later extended to include X. The unit shared Woodvale with Manchester & Salford UAS and fleets were on occasion shared or exchanged. Additionally, it seems that for later acquisitions, Liverpool sometimes simply retained codes from previous units.

Note G London UAS used codes 01 to 10 but it also operated from airfields with Oxford UAS (which had letter codes) and fleets were occasionally shared or exchanged.

Note H Queen's UAS Initially used codes Q, U, A & S but shared airfields with 13 AEF and operated their Bulldog XX711 coded E. Later briefly adopted codes B to D, but these reverted to the initial coding system.

Note I Yorkshire UAS initially used codes A to G, later extended to J. In 1992 five of the fleet transferred to locally-based 6 FTS and were recoded V to Z.

AIR EXPERIENCE FLIGHTS

The following Air Experience flights operated Bulldogs, "parenting" with University Air Squadrons and using their aircraft.

Air Exp Flt	Model	Base	Air Exp Flt	Model	Base
1 AEF	Wales	St.Athan	8 AEF	Birmingham	Shawbury, Cosford
2 AEF	Southampton	Hurn, Boscombe	9 AEF	Yorkshire	Finningley, Ch.Fenton
3 AEF	Bristol	Colerne	10 AEF	Manchester & Salford	Woodvale
4 AEF	Glasgow & Strath	Abbotsinch	11 AEF	Northumbrian	Leeming
5 AEF	Cambridge	Teversham	12 AEF	East Lothian	Leuchars
6 AEF	London	Benson	13 AEF	Queen's	Sydenham
7 AEF	East Midlands	Newton			

XX515 of CFS, Little Rissington is shown here coded 7 and named "Winston". *(PH)*

Glasgow and Strathclyde UAS had Bulldog XX559 in their fleet. *(RSh)*

*Notes: **5AEF** initially operated XX529 (F) from Sept. 1995 but it was then absorbed into CUAS in Jan. 1996. **7AEF** initially operated XX556 (76), XX702 (77) and XX520 (78) from Jan. 1995. **9AEF** initially operated XX621 (87), XX622 (88) and XX631 (89) from Feb.1995. **13AEF** initially operated XX711 (E) from Oct. 1978, replaced by XX562 (77) in Oct. 1986. Also used XX695 from Sept. 1982 to Jan. 1983.*

THE RAF CENTRAL FLYING SCHOOL

CFS was initially based at RAF Little Rissington but moved to RAF Leeming in April, 1976 (when its fleet was integrated with the RNEFTS). It was reformed as a separate unit again in April ,1984, moved to Scampton in September, 1984 to Cranwell in March, 1995 and was then absorbed into 3 FTS. A considerable number of the early Bulldogs were initially delivered to the CFS and then issued to various units and these have been ignored in the following listing. Codes used by CFS were 40 to 49 but on re-formation in 1984 new codes 1 to 10 were used and were later extended to 14. Aircraft concerned were as follows: XX513 (10), XX514 (44), XX515 (7 & 40), XX516 (41 & 1), XX517 (42 & 8), XX518 (43), XX520 (2), XX531 (4), XX532 (5 & 7), XX536 (9), XX538 (45), XX539 (1 & 46), XX540 (47), XX541 (48), XX542 (49), XX549 (14), XX555 (10), XX614 (6 & 11), XX634 (1), XX638 (12), XX668 (45), XX689 (3), XX690 (5), XX692 (5), XX693 (11 & 4), XX696 (8), XX698 (9), XX709 (12), XX711 (40), XX713 (41 & 6), XX714 (7 & 12).

THE ROYAL NAVY EFTS

The RNEFTS was formed in April, 1973 within 2 FTS at RAF Church Fenton. It moved to RAF Leeming in November, 1974 (within 3 FTS), then to RAF Linton-on-Ouse (within 1 FTS) in April, 1984 although it actually operated from RAF Topcliffe. The Bulldogs were replaced by Slingsby T67s in July, 1993. Individual aircraft codes were initially allocated as 1 to 20 and then, later, codes 21 to 34 were used, mainly for those Bulldogs absorbed from CFS. Aircraft concerned were as follows: XX513 (31 & A), XX514 (7, 25 & B), XX515 (10), XX516 (C), XX517 (23 & S), XX518 (24), XX519 (1), XX520 (2), XX521 (3), XX524 (4 & E), XX523 (5 & F), XX525 (7), XX526 (8), XX527 (9 & G), XX528 (10), XX529 (11 & H), XX530 (12), XX531 (14 & B), XX532 (15), XX533 (16 & J), XX534 (17), XX535 (18), XX536 (19 & D), XX537 (6), XX538 (P), XX539 (12), XX540 (28 & K), XX541 (29 & L), XX542 (13), XX543 (20), XX549 (T), XX550 (8), XX551 (32 & M), XX555 (20), XX556 (17), XX612 (17), XX638 (21 & N), XX666 (V), XX668 (26 & P), XX689 (3), XX690 (6), XX698 (D), XX699 (30 & Q), XX700 (27 & R), XX707 (20), XX709 (33), XX710 (34), XX712 (6 & D), XX713 (22).

NO. 3 FLYING TRAINING SCHOOL

In March, 1995, 3 FTS took over the CFS Bulldogs (using their existing codes in the range 3 to 12). In June, 1995, it also took over the fleet operated by the RAF College Air Squadron and these extended the codes up to 19. Aircraft concerned were as follows: XX513 (10), XX515 (2), XX519 (14), XX522 (11), XX532 (1), XX538 (18), XX540 (15), XX561 (7), XX562 (19), XX614 (6), XX617 (2), XX630 (5), XX638 (12), XX654 (3), XX661 (6), XX667 (16), XX685 (11), XX686 (4), XX687 (13), XX688 (8), XX689 (3), XX690 (5), XX693 (4), XX696 (8), XX698 (9), XX700 (17).

NO. 6 FLYING TRAINING SCHOOL

This unit had a small number of Bulldogs on strength in 1976/77 at RAF Finningley, with codes representing the last two of the serial (with one aberration). Five were transferred from locally based Yorkshire UAS in 1992/93 and given codes V to Z. The aircraft were as follows: XX513 (06), XX529 (W), XX538 (V & X), XX551 (51), XX621 (X), XX624 (Y), XX706 (06), XX708 (08), XX713 (Z).

INDEX

PEOPLE

References to Bulldog, Scottish Aviation and Prestwick are too numerous to include in the index.